Afghanistan Declassified

Afghanistan Declassified

A Guide to America's Longest War

Brian Glyn Williams

PENN

UNIVERSITY OF PENNSYLVANIA PRESS

PHILADELPHIA

Published by
University of Pennsylvania Press
Philadelphia, Pennsylvania 19104-4112

Printed in the United States of America on acid-free paper
10 9 8 7 6 5 4 3 2 1

Library of Congress Cataloging-in-Publication Data

Williams, Brian Glyn.
  Afghanistan declassified : a guide to America's longest war / Brian Glyn
Williams. — 1st ed.
      p. cm.
  Includes index.
  ISBN 978-0-8122-4403-8 (hardcover : alk. paper)
  1. Afghan war, 2001—Personal narratives, American.   2. Williams, Brian
Glyn—Travel—Afghanistan.   3. Afghanistan—Description and travel.
I. Title.
  DS371.413.W55 2012
  958.104'7—dc23

                                                        2011025251

Photographs on pages 14, 50, 57, 75, 93, 113, and 191 by Brian Glyn Williams;
photographs on pages 96, 135, and 167 from the author's private collection.

For my parents, Gareth and Donna Williams

Contents

Preface

Throughout the 2000s, I traveled across Afghanistan, living with warlords, interviewing Taliban who had been taken prisoner, meeting gray-bearded elders, talking to women newly liberated from Taliban strictures, and working with U.S. and Coalition troops serving in the country. My adventures ranged from the mundane—eating rice pilaf and flat naan bread in the Hindu Kush Mountains with Hazara-Mongol villagers—to the exciting—tracking suicide bombers for the CIA's Counterterrorist Center. These experiences, combined with years in graduate school earning a PhD in Central Asian history, have given me insight into a country that has seemed to many to belong as much to the Middle Ages as to the twenty-first century.

For me there is no country on earth as primeval, exciting, and beautiful as Afghanistan. Although many people who have not been there define it in abstract terms as a grim land of opium barons, warlords, Taliban fanatics, and oppressed women, I know Afghanistan as a land of castles, incredibly hospitable villagers, stunning landscapes, and epic tales of empires and conquest. I have long wanted to share the story of this Afghanistan with Westerners.

In 2008 I had the opportunity to do so as an advisor to the U.S. military's Joint Information Operations Warfare Command (JIOWC). There I met a group of thinking man's soldiers who were focused on saving Coalition lives in Afghanistan by understanding the country's history, society, politics, and terrain. They were desperately trying to provide the missing background context to ongoing military activities in the Afghan theater of operations, and I admired their desire for knowledge.

With the Taliban sweeping out of their sanctuaries in Pakistan's tribal zones and conquering much of Afghanistan's southeast by 2007, a palpable sense of urgency fueled their mission. Coalition troops were dying in larger numbers in Afghanistan than Iraq. Afghanistan, "the Forgotten War," was, according to some pundits, in danger of being lost, and everyone understood that this might have catastrophic results for both the Afghans and the American-led NATO alliance. As the Taliban carved out an autonomous territory in the tribal hill provinces of neighboring Pakistan, Osama bin Laden and Al Qaeda plotted further attacks on the West from their sanctuary on the Pakistani-Afghan border. Losing Afghanistan to the Taliban and Al Qaeda alliance might mean destabilizing nuclear Pakistan and granting victory to the terrorist network that had killed three thousand people on 9/11. It would also be a setback in human terms for the millions of Afghans, especially the women and non-Pashtun-Taliban ethnic groups, who suffered under the Taliban's misrule.

As the above events unfolded, the U.S. military and millions of Americans and their Western allies began to remember Afghanistan, the original theater of operations for the war on terror. Since then tens of thousands of American troops have begun a surge to Afghanistan to try to save the situation. NATO members—including Britain, Canada, and Australia at various times over the last ten years—have also dispatched troops to help wage war against the emboldened Taliban in the mountains and deserts of Afghanistan. In December 2009 President Barack Obama, after much agonizing, announced the surge of thirty thousand troops to a war he labeled a conflict of "necessity."

By the summer of 2010, Afghanistan had become the longest war in American history. U.S. Central Command appeared to be dedicated to sticking out the war for many years to come, regardless of the mounting cost in men and materiel. The Obama administration has committed to keeping troops (currently numbered at roughly one hundred thousand) in Afghanistan until at least 2014 and perhaps longer in a training and support role. The long anticipated death of Osama bin Laden in May 2011 did not mean an end to the U.S. and NATO mission designed to prevent Al Qaeda from creating a terrorist base in the Pakistani-Afghan tribal lands.

It was in this context that I was originally asked to write a field manual for the JIOWC that might provide the U.S. military with an introduction to the history, culture, tribes, and the ongoing war in Afghanistan. As one of my JIOWC colleagues put it, "If someone was fighting a war in the U.S. they'd need to know the difference between Maine and the Mississippi River, between Abraham Lincoln and Mohammad Ali, and between Catholics, Protestants, Hispanics, Blacks, Asians, Indians, and Whites. We need the same thing for Afghanistan if we're going to win this war."

I took these words to heart in writing this book and felt this was something from which civilians could also benefit. This book is a declassified civilian version of the manual I wrote for the JIOWC. It aims to bring Afghanistan's diversity to life for the average reader who might have a family member serving in that theater of operations, or for those who simply have an interest in knowing more about a land where American troops are fighting and dying. It is a book aimed at helping the reader understand the country as it is, and not as the much-romanticized place that appears in movies and books, from *Rambo III* to *The Kite Runner.*

On one level the book provides the crucial geographic, political, historic, and cultural context to the ongoing war in Afghanistan and summarizes major developments in that conflict in nonacademic terms. On another level it is also an effort to bring the real beauty of this country to life for Westerners who might see this land only through the lens of the war on terror. In this respect I hope it both paints the Afghans and their culture in a three-dimensional light and helps readers understand what is happening in a war that for far too long was defined not as the original epicenter of the war on terror but as "the Forgotten War."

Original Military Manual Introduction

It is a well-proven maxim of war that those who have a deep understanding of their theater of operations have a tactical advantage over their enemies. This rule was proven at our cost on 9/11 when nineteen Arab hijackers infiltrated the U.S. mainland and used their knowledge of our society against us. The terrorists' intimate familiarity with U.S. geography, English language, security measures, idioms, and culture gave them an advantage that they exploited to kill almost three thousand innocents on 9/11. Such knowledge was not gained overnight—it was the result of patient background studies, painstaking research, and cultural immersion.

This manual is written with the understanding that the U.S. military similarly needs to enhance its knowledge of the enemy, friends, terrain, history, ethnic groups, politics, and culture in Afghanistan to empower itself. It is only by carefully understanding these factors in their totality that the United States can match its enemies in a conflict fought not on our soil, but on theirs. Such "theater awareness" is an asset from the top down for members of the U.S. military operating in this relatively unknown land. Every Coalition soldier serving in this country should have a basic awareness of the *context* in which his or her actions are taking place.

Although there have been many general books written on Afghanistan that discuss topics ranging from the struggle of women to historic architecture, this work is written with an eye to providing information that is broadly applicable to the war in Afghanistan. Although not all the information here is directly related to military operations, the underlying principle is that all the cultural, political, historical, and geographic information selected for this volume will enhance the U.S. military's overall operating knowledge of the Afghan people and their homeland. This background knowledge can empower even the most mission-focused soldier by making a relatively unknown land and people familiar.

Introduction

In April 2007 I boarded a plane in Baku, the capital of Azerbaijan—a former Soviet Muslim country located in the Caucasus Mountains south of Russia—and flew over the Caspian Sea, crossed Iran, and descended through the snowcapped Hindu Kush Mountains to Kabul. Azerbaijan had been fascinating. Baku, formerly the fifth-largest city in the USSR, was a wonderful port on the Caspian Sea made up of fifteenth-century Muslim palaces, nineteenth-century Tsarist-era buildings, Stalin-era drab apartment housing for the proletariat, and gleaming post-Soviet skyscrapers—the latter built with new money coming into the country from local oil.

It was great to be able to use both my Russian and my Turkish among the Russified Azerbaijani Turks, who seemed more inclined to drink the local beer than attend the rare mosque I saw in the country. But as my plane made its final approach over the Afghan capital, I put Azerbaijan behind me and stared out the cabin windows with a mixture of expectation and excitement. After months of planning for this occasion, it was finally here. I was now descending into a land that was defined in most Americans' imagination simply as a theater of action for the "war on terror."

But as my plane touched down, I realized that I was seeing Kabul, the capital of Afghanistan, in a way that few Americans ever do: as a sprawling city located at the foot of the Hindu Kush that seems to rise out of the brown earth from which it is made. I was seeing it not as a backdrop for a thirty-second CNN sound bite on a suicide bombing or part of a disjointed series of images related to the war against the Taliban, but as a living, breathing city.

Suicide Bombers, Traffic Jams, and Poverty: Kabul in Three Dimensions

The first sight that greets you when you deplane at Kabul International Airport's crumbling concrete terminal is the large military transport aircraft from various NATO countries involved in the struggle against the Taliban. Their looming presence serves to remind that you are entering a country that is in the throes of war and is home to enemies that many in America prematurely wrote off as "dead-enders" back in 2002.

But most travelers are not immediately concerned with such larger issues. The traveler's initial "war" involves navigating the chaos of Kabul Airport. When I arrived, the airport terminal lacked electricity, foreign women from various NGOs (nongovernmental organizations) were scrambling to put on their modest head scarves, and Afghan customs officials sought in vain to channel incoming passengers through a series of ad hoc customs checkpoints.

Having made my way through this controlled chaos relatively unscathed, I walked out into the 80-degree sunlight to find that my host, a member of the Karzai clan who ran a small think tank, had not arrived. A friendly Afghan porter promptly offered his cell phone and contacted my host who said the driver was on his way. My driver apologetically explained that he had been delayed by traffic jams in Kabul.

This fact in and of itself was important, since Kabul was not always packed with the hordes of exhaust-spewing cars that fill it today. Under the Taliban, the population of Kabul was considerably smaller, the local economy was in tatters, and many luxury products, such as televisions, radios, VCRs, cell phones, and Western clothing (and even Western "infidel" haircuts) were both unaffordable and forbidden. But things had changed since the city was liberated in December 2001 and hundreds of thousands of Afghans have come back to the city.

As we made our way through the city in our Japanese SUV, I even sensed tremendous transformations in Kabul since my last visit in the summer of 2005. Several modern steel and glass buildings had gone up downtown, every street corner seemed to have a Roshan brand cell phone shop, and many young men were wearing trendy Western fashions (some even sported fashionable goatees) that would have gotten them beaten with iron cables during the Taliban period.

Most important, among the ghostlike forms of women clad in blue *burqas*, I saw hordes of young women out and about with their heads covered only with head scarves. Amazingly, many of these women were wearing makeup and fashionable clothing. Many were frankly stunning.

This had certainly not been the case two years earlier and was of course cause for beatings and imprisonment during the Taliban's rule. But here these young Afghan women were confidently navigating the crowds of turbaned men and burqa-clad women. From my perspective, the multitude of new cars, liberated young men and women, and Western-style billboards were cause for optimism.

But despite such outward signs of progress, I could not help but notice that a great deal of Kabul operated much as it had in the Taliban period, seemingly unaffected by the sweeping changes that had transformed Afghanistan's comparatively moderate, urbane capital. The hordes of barefoot street urchins hawking items on the streets, beggars with outstretched hands, and simple folk desperately trying to eke out an existence reminded us that this was the poorest country in the world outside of sub-Saharan Africa.

As we made our way through the throngs of Kabulis, my driver continued to point out evidence that the outward signs of progress did not mean that the days of the Taliban were gone forever. He disconcertingly slowed down to show me places where suicide bombings had taken place in the past year. Here a gaping hole blown into the road, there a building pockmarked by shrapnel. Each spot spoke of a tragedy that had been inflicted on innocent bystanders. Every blast mark sent us a clear message: the grim Taliban masters who had transformed this vibrant capital into a religious prison camp were down, but they were far from out. They had made a comeback.

For all of the outward signs of progress and security, there was little the pro-American Karzai government could do to keep fanatical Taliban suicide bombers from infiltrating the city and wreaking havoc. Ironically, since my last visit, Operation Iraqi Freedom had spawned a virulent form of suicide bombing in Iraq that appeared to have inspired the fanatical Taliban guerrillas. What had begun as a trickle of bombings had become a full-fledged campaign, and Afghanistan's fragile progress appeared to have been jeopardized.

Reflecting on the hatred that would drive a suicide bomber to transform his own body into so many pieces of bone-shrapnel, I was grateful to arrive safely at our compound in a Kabul suburb. I was also ready to begin exploring the city, but my eagerness was accompanied by the shadow of lurking suicide bombers hanging over me.

A Taliban Beheading

The next day I decided to visit central Kabul. My journey began on a hilltop in the center of the city that was topped by a shell-blasted concrete mausoleum belonging to the former king of Afghanistan. As I arrived on the hilltop plateau, a group of Afghan soccer players came over to say hello and welcome me to their country.

They were thrilled when I offered to take their photograph and show it to Americans back home. I invariably found this to be the case as I strolled through the city below. Although the burqa-less girls were often shy when I took their picture, everyone from bread sellers to wandering Sufi fortune-tellers and bicyclists seemed to have an almost childlike delight in having a foreigner take their photograph. Many said, "Hello welcome," and this English catchphrase seemed to be widespread in the city.

But as I made my way to the town center, I encountered a sad sight that reminded me that this was still a country threatened by those who were less than welcoming to outsiders. On a small knoll I noticed a gathering of Afghans dressed in Western clothing. There I found a group of local journalists commemorating the death of one of their own. In the middle of the crowd I found pictures of an Afghan freelance journalist and translator who had recently been beheaded by the Taliban.

The journalist's name was Ajmal Naqshbandi. His name is not as widely known as that of his former compatriot, an Italian correspondent named Daniele Mastrogiacomo. Mastrogiacomo made headlines around the world when he was kidnapped in the south by the Taliban. He was eventually released in exchange for the return of five Taliban commanders held captive by the Karzai government. Mastrogiacomo's five-to-one release came about as a result of Italian government pressure.

But Afghanistan's Karzai government refused to release further Taliban prisoners to obtain Naqshbandi's release. The government feared that it would set a bad precedent and set off a cycle of Taliban kidnappings. As a result, Naqshbandi was brutally beheaded on film, another practice traceable to Iraq. The Afghans with whom I spoke resented the implication that a foreigner's life was worth more than that of an Afghan. They also bemoaned the fact that the news of Naqshbandi's beheading had not been as widely reported abroad as the story of Mastrogiacomo's release.

Although I was reflexively inclined to argue against the Afghan journalists' belief that the life of a Westerner was worth more than that of an Afghan, I knew better. A burnt-out war correspondent I met in Kosovo back in 2001 had told me of a racist "mathematical equation" that appalled me at the time but helped explain the lack of Western journalists at Naqshbandi's memorial. The correspondent's bitter equation for American reporting priorities went something like this: One dead American was equal to two dead Englishman, who were equal to five French, who were in turn equal to ten Arabs, and so forth until you finally reached China.

"Americans aren't interested in the tragedies of the world," my cynical war correspondent informed me after having one too many whiskeys in a Kosovar bar. "They are less interested in hearing about the ten thousand dead Bangladeshis than they are about who Britney Spears is dating in any given week."

Although this might be the unavoidable truth, I hated it then and I hate it now. For this reason alone, I wanted to share the name of Ajmal Naqshbandi, whose mourning friend I photographed as she signed a condolence book at the site of his memorial. I later saw her wandering the streets of Kabul with tears still in her eyes, and my heart went out to her. Having appreciated the hospitality Afghans gave me every time I visited their country, I felt as if I owed it to her and her people to share her friend's tragic story with my countrymen—even if he was, in one war correspondent's terms, unworthy of a higher ranking in the "mathematical equation."

The Secret Life of Foreigners in Kabul

The next day I decided to see how foreigners live in Kabul, a capital under siege. On my previous trips I had used Kabul as a springboard for launching myself into the less-stable provinces to do research. For this reason I was not as familiar with Afghanistan's relatively safe capital. Nor was I familiar with that strange breed of foreigners who leave their safe homes to live and work in Kabul.

It is from the Afghan capital that the world is directing the reconstruction of this war-torn country, and for this reason it has a considerable foreign presence. Although the only foreigners I saw in the northern deserts and mountains through which I tended to travel were the occasional heavily armed International Security and Assistance Force (ISAF) patrol, in Kabul one finds UN representatives, war correspondents, NGO aid workers, diplomats, and foreigners tied to a wide variety of international groups, all involved in the rebuilding of Eurasia's most shattered country.

One night I met with some French members of the UN who were assisting me in gaining access to captured Taliban prisoners of war. In the process I was introduced to the foreign expatriate life that I had missed during my previous expeditions. Expatriate stories rarely get told but are nonetheless fascinating.

Foreigners involved in helping the Afghan people recover from over twenty-five years of war live in a place that is both alien and, on occasion, dangerous (foreign workers have been kidnapped, blown up by suicide bombers, beheaded, and gunned down by the Taliban). The stress of working in such an environment, often for stints that last years, takes its toll on even the strongest individuals. Many have been shaken by incidents that have left them traumatized.

One woman I flew out with a few years ago had to leave the country after a Taliban terrorist threw a live hand grenade into her van's half-open window. Luckily, the grenade landed on the lap of a fast-thinking coworker, who reflexively tossed it back out the half-open window seconds before it exploded, covering her in shards of glass.

To survive in such a world, the foreigners in Kabul have created safe havens that aim to bring them many of the amenities of home and provide momentary reprieve from the troubles they encounter. One such place is the Mustafa Hotel. The Mustafa Hotel was opened within days of the Taliban's fall by a colorful Afghan exile who had been living in New Jersey since the Soviet invasion of the 1980s. As the ultimate "fixer," and the only person in Kabul driving a Camaro with a Jersey accent, Wais Faisi quickly became a legend. He became known as "the Fonz of Kabul" after he was described as a wheeler-dealer in a novel by Christina Lamb titled *The Sewing Circles of Herat,* and he ran the first functioning bar in post-Taliban Afghanistan. He could also solve any problem you brought to him and get you a fine Scotch or a pint of beer.

When I went to him in 2003, he asked me what he could do for me. Although I was initially taken aback by his *Sopranos*-style accent and appearance, I began to negotiate the price for one gunman and a driver to take me over the Hindu Kush Mountains to meet the larger-than-life Uzbek warlord General Rashid Dostum. Dostum had led his horsemen in attacking the Taliban in 2001's Operation Enduring Freedom and was said to resemble his Mongol ancestors.

"Are you with CIA?" was Faisi's first response. I promptly replied, "Nope, UMD [University of Massachusetts Dartmouth]."

"Never heard of 'em before," was his reply. "Whatever outfit you're with it'll cost you two thousand dollars, take it or leave it. But either way, you're coming to my barbecue Friday night. You have balls to go try hanging with Dostum."

Although I never attended one of Faisi's legendary rooftop barbecues (and ultimately I found some local Uzbek tribal militiamen to take me to Dostum with the help of the Turkish embassy), I had the chance to meet many interesting characters in Faisi's bar. They ranged from Dyn-Corp contract soldiers (DynCorp is a competitor to the more infamous Black Water military contractor and I was told to never call them mercenaries) to war correspondents who had returned from "embeds" with U.S. troops fighting the Taliban in the south and east.

Recalling Faisi's well-known skills as a "fixer," I decided to pop in to the Mustafa Hotel to look him up again soon after I arrived in 2007. But my host broke the bad news to me. Faisi had been killed in the past year under mysterious circumstances. My host on this trip (an organization run by a nephew of President Hamid Karzai) claimed that he was killed by the Taliban teetotalers as punishment for his creation of a "den of iniquity." Another source claimed it was because the Mustafa Hotel had actually been a "spy den," which would not surprise me.

Regardless of what sort of "den" his hotel actually was, Faisi's fate served as a cautionary tale. In the Taliban period one could be killed for drinking alcohol. Even today many traditional Afghans frown on drinking and the socializing of unmarried men and women in restaurants. Alcohol has the same connotation in Afghanistan that drugs do in the United States. Taliban terrorists and fighters routinely rail against the recent import of "alcohol, drugs, prostitutes, and sex" into Islamic Afghanistan. At least one Taliban suicide bomber targeted an Internet café with foreigners in it.

For this reason the few bars and restaurants that are available for home-sick foreigners to "come down" from the hard realities of Afghan daily life tend to be rather low-key, if not hidden, and Afghans are forbidden from drinking in them. Take, for instance, the French venue my hosts took me to one night called L'Atmosphere. "L'Atmo," as it is known among expats, is located on a dark, unpaved, pothole-filled back alley in a rather nondescript Kabul neighborhood. The only indication that you have ar-rived at L'Atmosphere is the presence of machine-gun-toting guards who suddenly materialize out of the gloom to inspect your car.

Assured that we were harmless foreigners, not Taliban suicide bomb-ers, the guards waved us through to a sandbagged entrance and a metal detector to a faceless walled compound. Although it initially felt as though we were entering a bunker, when we walked out of the checkpoint entrance we found ourselves in a beautiful courtyard garden with a swimming pool, tiki torches, tables with candles on them, and a fully functioning French restaurant complete with two bars and cuisine I could not pronounce.

As my hosts ordered a bottle of wine, everybody unwound from the day's events (one of my hosts had been calculating war deaths in the vari-ous provinces that week), and for a few minutes we forgot we were in Kabul, Afghanistan. My hosts were an eclectic crowd and were wonder-ful: a French-Canadian who had married a Kirghiz woman and spoke fluent Dari; a Pakistani-English woman who specialized in counterter-rorism. As our food arrived, I relished the chance to eat something be-sides rice pilaf, soup, and flat naan bread (all of which I actually love, but not every day) and immersed myself in the momentary *bon vivre*.

It was not until a UH-60 Black Hawk military helicopter clattered over us in the star-filled night and shook us out of our reverie that we were reminded we were not in Paris but Kabul. As if shaken from a trance, everyone decided to return to their various homes and compounds to prepare for another day in the outer world known as Afghanistan.

PART I

The Basics

Chapter 1

The Ethnic Landscape

> Many outsiders think we are one race. But we are not, we are many peoples.
> —Afghan Uzbek parliament member Faizullah Zeki, Mazar i Sharif, 2005

Centuries of history contributed to the political and cultural landscape of Afghanistan today. The legend of the Kalash people of Pakistan is a good place to begin to understand that history.

High in the snowcapped Hindu Kush Mountains on the Afghan-Pakistani border lived a Dardic-Vedic people who claimed to be the direct descendants of Alexander the Great's troops, who had once occupied the land as a distance outpost of empire, only to be erased by succeeding waves of invaders. While the neighboring Pakistanis in the Punjab and Sindh were darker-skinned Muslims, these isolated mountain people had light skin and blue eyes. Although the Pakistanis proper converted to Islam over the centuries, the Kalash people retained their pagan traditions and worshipped their ancient gods in outdoor temples. Most important, they produced wine much like the Greeks in antiquity (although this is no proof of a link to the Greeks)—this, in a Muslim country that forbade alcohol.

In the nineteenth century most of the Kalash—or Kafirs (Infidels) as they were formerly known—were brutally conquered by the "Iron Amir of Afghanistan," Abdur Rahman. Their ancient temples and wooden idols were destroyed, their women were forced to burn their folk costumes and wear the burqa or veil, and the entire people were converted at sword-point to Islam. Their land was then renamed Nuristan, the Land of Light. Only a small pocket of this vanishing pagan race survived across the border in three isolated valleys in the mountains of what would become Pakistan in 1947.

I had never visited the pagan Kalash tribe but had always hoped to. After we discussed the Kalash in one of my history classes, a student challenged me to follow the advice I gave my classes, which was to get out and see the world. In June 2010 my colleague Adam and I set out to travel into the Hindu Kush on the Afghan-Pakistani border to see this ancient race for ourselves. But when we arrived at our Pakistani host's house in Lahore after flying through Abu Dhabi, he cautioned us regarding our goal of visiting the lost descendants of Alexander the Great: "It's a dangerous two-day journey off-road into the mountains," Rafay warned us. "But that's not the most important obstacle you'll have to overcome. To get to the remote homeland of the Kalash you need to cut through the Swat Valley."

Rafay then pointed to our intended route on a map, and Adam and I groaned. Our dream was falling apart. We both knew that the Swat Valley was a stronghold of the Pakistani Taliban. In 2007 the Taliban brutally conquered this beautiful valley and forced a puritanical version of Islam on the local people. The Taliban also used it as a springboard for sending suicide bombers through Pakistan.

"But all hope is not lost," Rafay continued. "The Pakistani army just reconquered most of the valley this winter and have opened the main road through it. If you don't stray from the road and there is no fighting, you just might be able to pull it off."

Nervous about the prospect of adding a journey through a war zone to our trip to the Kalash, Adam and I then traveled to the capital, Islamabad. There, after much searching, we found an ethnic Pashtun driver who claimed to have once traveled to the remote homeland of the Kalash. He not only knew the route but had a tough SUV to get us there.

After haggling over the price of the trip, we set out driving across the plains of Pakistan, where the heat soared to 120 degrees. Finally, after traversing the country from the Indian border to the Afghan border, we arrived at the mountains. And what mountains they were. The Hindu Kush are an extension of the Himalayas and soar to twenty-five thousand feet. As we drove into the tree-covered mountains, the temperatures blissfully began to drop. And although we found respite from the heat, everyone grew tense. Saki, our driver, warned us that we were now in Taliban territory. We had entered the Swat Valley.

We did not travel far before we were stopped at the first of many Pakistani army checkpoints we would encounter. When the soldiers manning it discovered that there were two Americans in the truck, they strongly warned us to avoid leaving the road. One of them asked us to sign our names in a registration book and proclaimed that we were the first foreigners to enter the Swat since the Taliban had taken it in 2007.

That night we stayed in Dir, a Swat Valley village that locals claimed had briefly served as a hiding place for Osama bin Laden when he fled

Afghanistan during 2001's Operation Enduring Freedom. Kidding or not, that night we slept fitfully. As a precaution, Adam piled chairs against our inn room's door to keep out any Taliban or Al Qaeda intruders. In the back of our minds we always had the story of *Wall Street Journal* reporter Daniel Pearl, who was captured by Al Qaeda in Pakistan and beheaded.

The next day we made it safely out of the Swat Valley after crossing a mountain pass at ten thousand feet and a nearby glacier. We were now in the scenic Chitral Valley. We drove up this valley for several hours before our driver grew excited. Gesturing to the dark mountains on our left along the Afghan border, he said one word with a grin—"Kalash."

With mounting excitement we left the main "road," crossed a large river, and began to drive up a mountain trail straight into the mountains. This continued for a couple of hours before the narrow valley opened up and our exhausted driver announced that we had finally arrived in Rumbur, the most isolated of the Kalash valleys. Having made our way from Boston to Abu Dhabi to Lahore to Islamabad to Swat to Chitral, we had finally reached our destination in the high mountains on the Afghan border. It was now time to meet the Kalash.

It did not take us long to find them. Adam was the first one to spot a Kalash shepherdess in the trees wearing a stunningly bright peasant costume. After seeing the faceless burqas of the women of the Swat, the juxtaposition between Muslim women and this Kalash woman could not have been greater. As we drove along we saw several more brightly clad Kalash women. But when we tried to take their pictures they ran off and hid behind trees. Worried that we might break some local taboo on photography, we continued on our way.

Soon we entered the Kalash village of Rumbur. The wooden houses were built in steps above one another up the valley's walls, and the village square filled with Kalash curious to see us. Among them was Kazi, the village holy man. Everyone stood back as he approached us and heard our request to stay with the Kalash for a few days to learn about their culture. Kazi heard us out and thought about it for a while. After some thought, he finally smiled and gave us his blessing. He proclaimed that as blue-eyed "pagans" (the Kalash believe Christians worship three gods, that is, the Trinity) we were like the Kalash and welcome to stay with them.

With that, everyone's shyness was forgotten and the village men and women proudly posed for photographs and allowed us into their homes. Once again the contrast to the Muslims in Swat and greater Pakistan was startling. The conservative Muslims of Swat had women's quarters in their houses where no outsiders were allowed. The Kalash women were free and dressed in beautiful costumes that seemed to belong to a different era.

Members of the Kalash in traditional dress.

During our stay we hiked up into the mountains overlooking the Afghan border and were taken to the Kalash people's outdoor temples. There they made sacrifices of goats to their mountain gods. Sadly, most of their ancient wooden idols had been stolen or defaced by neighboring Muslim iconoclasts who considered them heathen abominations. We were also told that one of the local leaders who fought in the courts to protect the Kalash from such problems had recently been assassinated. On many levels we sympathized with the Kalash—who were losing numbers to conversion to Islam—as a race facing an existential threat. And I must say that after the heat, pollution, and crowds of Pakistan proper, we found this pristine mountain enclave filled with incredibly hospitable farmers and shepherds to be a veritable Shangri-la. Time and again we were invited by smiling Kalash into their simple wooden houses for meals where we talked about life beyond their remote valley. Most Kalash had only left their valley a few times in their lives, usually to go to a neighboring Kalash valley for a marriage or to celebrate a great festival.

On our final evening in Rumbur, the villagers held a feast for us. We celebrated with the famous Kalash red wine. My most endearing memory of the mystical night was of Adam doing a snake dance with a local elder, snapping his fingers in rhythm and dancing lower and lower to the ground in the center of the clapping audience.

The next morning we were awoken by the sound of cows being led by children through the misty village. We said our good-byes to everyone and drove out of Rumbur. As I looked back I saw several Kalash girls standing on a terraced hill above us in their bright costumes, waving to us. With our driver recovering from the previous night's festivities, we took leave of our hosts. It was now time to reenter Pakistan proper, a land that seemed far removed in space and time from the ancient rhythms of the Kalash villages.

* * *

As our journey to the vanishing Kalash people of the Afghan-Pakistani border revealed, the region is home to many different ethnic groups. One of the most difficult concepts for outsiders to grasp is the variation between the groups that make up Afghanistan's ethnic mosaic. And no subject is more complex than that of the competing allegiances of Afghanistan's people to clan, village, valley, tribe, or ethnic group. Depending on the situation, all of the above groups can be defined by the Afghan word *qawm* (pronounced "kawum"), which is usually translated in a rather simplistic fashion to mean "tribe" or "ethnic group."

There is also the question of the various Afghan tribes' identification with an overarching sense of Afghan citizenship. Depending on the context, Afghans will identify themselves by their clan, ethnic group, or national identity. There is no better testament to the importance of understanding this thorny issue than the battered remains of Kabul, which was until recently a blasted ruin. Its destruction was caused not by Soviet aerial bombardments but by intraethnic fighting in the 1990s Afghan civil war. The destruction of Kabul is vivid testimony to the importance of ethnicity in Afghanistan today. Although ethnic issues have been tempered since 2001, an understanding of the various ethnic groups can empower outsiders operating in this alien environment. Military leaders have long understood that knowledge of the adversary is critical to operational success. Cultural awareness is an increasingly important component of this knowledge. Indeed, the more unconventional the adversary, the more important it is for the U.S. military to understand the adversary's society and underlying ethnic-cultural dynamics as a means of waging counterinsurgency.

The Pashtuns: Afghanistan's Dominant Ethnic Group

Perhaps the biggest mistake Americans make in dealing with Afghanistan is in referring to the Afghans (or even worse, the "Afghanis," a term that actually denotes Afghanistan's currency) as a unified or homogeneous people like the Japanese. Afghanistan is more like Switzerland, a multiethnic European country that is home to Germans, French, Italians, and Romansh (there is no "Swiss" language, of course).

But a comparison to the British may be more apt. Historically, multiethnic Afghanistan was formed in much the same way as Great Britain, through the conquest and subjugation of neighboring peoples. At one time or another in their history, the English, Britain's ruling race, ruled over the French in Normandy, the Celtic-speaking Scottish Highlanders, the Celtic-speaking Welsh, and the Gaelic-speaking Irish Catholics. This does not mean that the French, Scots, Welsh, or Irish Catholics were, or are, English. And one must never make the mistake of calling a Welshman, a Scot, or an Irishman "English" even though he might have a British passport.

Similarly, Afghanistan's ruling race, the Afghans or Pashtuns (often called Pathans in Pakistan), expanded from their core lands and conquered a kingdom they named for themselves. But this does not make everyone whose lands were forcefully included in the Afghan Kingdom an Afghan in the strictest sense of the term, even though he or she might carry an Afghan passport. However, it should be stated that there is a vague, supraethnic sense of being an Afghan citizen that is perhaps comparable to the British identity of Northern Irish, Scots, and Welsh who are not actually English.

Afghan citizens of Uzbek (Turkic-Mongol), Tajik (Persian-Iranian), and Hazara (Shiite Mongol) extract all share common Afghan cuisine, irrigation techniques, basic clothing, housing structures, fighting tactics, patriarchal traditions, and language of interethnic communication (Farsi-Dari), not to mention an identification with Afghanistan as their broader national homeland. But many non-Pashtun ethnic minorities have a chip on their shoulder stemming from their original conquest by the Afghan-Pashtuns in the nineteenth century. To understand their sense of victimhood, one must understand their conquerors, the Pashtuns.

The origins of the Afghans or Pashtuns are murky and lost in the mist of time. They are, however, seen as being descendants of the Indo-Iranians, an ancient people who are also known as the Aryans. The Aryans settled in Iran (which is a cognate of the word *Aryan*) and subsequently moved in a southeasterly direction through Afghanistan into India sometime between 2000 and 1000 B.C. Although many people think of Aryans as being Germans, the wave of Aryans that settled in what would one day become Afghanistan and Iran were no less Aryan in their Western complexions. For this reason it should be no surprise that Indo-Iranian is also a member of the same linguistic group as Indo-European, a family of languages that includes Greek, Latin, Slavic, and Germanic languages such as Anglo-Saxon English. Incidentally, the Aryans who passed southward to India established a caste system there based on their lighter skin that allowed them to discriminate against the darker peoples of the south.

The Afghan-Pashtuns are proud of their Aryan heritage and named their national airline Ariana; they have had symbols, such as the wheat with which the mythical Aryan king Yama was crowned, emblazoned on their national flag. Although Afghans are often black-haired or dark-skinned, their features are frequently European-looking and many have light blue or green eyes. The Afghan girl with haunting green eyes on the famous 1984 cover of *National Geographic* was, for example, an Afghan-Pashtun.

The "real" Afghans, or the Pashtuns, are a disunited conglomeration of peoples made up of two large tribal confederations (the Ghilzais and Durranis), which are broken down into sixty major tribes and more than four hundred sub-clans. Among the most important of the Pashtun sub-tribes are the Wazirs, Afridis, Mahsuds, Mohmands, Shinwaris, and Yusufzais, many of which straddle the artificial border that cuts through the heart of their tribal lands known as the Durrand Line (that is, the post-1893 "frontier" between Pakistan and Afghanistan that was actually imposed on the Afghans by their nineteenth-century British colonial rulers).

The Pashtuns, who make up 40 percent of Afghanistan and 15 percent of Pakistan, speak an Indo-European (Aryan) language known as Pastho that is distantly related to Persian-Tajik, although it is not mutually understood. There are two major Pashtun dialects: that of Peshawar, Pakistan, in the northeast and Kandahar in the southwest.

The Pashtuns are perhaps the world's largest tribal group, and they have tended to reject state dominance (even by a Pashtun state). For this reason they are defined more by their shared culture, language, and traditions than by a modern sense of nationality. Among the Pashtuns' most famous traditions is their ancient code of Pashtunwali, which serves them well in lieu of a central state authority. In his book *Afghanistan* (1973), Louis Dupree describes Pashtunwali as "a stringent code, a tough code for tough men who of necessity live tough lives. Honor and hospitality, hostility and ambush are pared in the Afghan mind." Many aspects of Pashtun society are shaped by this code, which is a mixture of Islamic law and local traditions.

The Pashtunwali code is not seen by Pashtuns as a defining text like the Declaration of Independence or the Bushido Code of the Samurais. Rather, it is a vague set of cultural values that are instilled in children from birth. Simplistic efforts to capture the real nature of this complex societal code often end up glamorizing the Pashtuns as a heroic race of primeval clan warriors. Other accounts depict the Pashtuns as barbarian fanatics who live only to carry out blood feuds and stone women to death.

Such Western interpretations do not offer a balanced view of a culture that dominates the lives of millions of Pashtuns on either side of the border. Perhaps the most controversial practice of the Pashtuns involves *purdah*, the confinement, protection, or veiling of women. This tradition is ancient and probably predates Islam. Although the Prophet Muhammad had his later wives veiled to keep the hordes of visitors from seeing them, it should be recalled that the Prophet Muhammad's first wife, Khadija, and daughter, Fatima, were powerful, independent women. These strong, outspoken women led the early Islamic community and influenced the decision making of men and society around the Prophet. They were active in ways that most Pashtun women are forbidden from today (although Pashtun women often have tremendous influence in their homes).

The conquering Arabs probably picked up veiling from the pagan Persian rulers who had a tradition of veiling the women in their harems to keep them from the eyes of commoners. Regardless of the practice's origins, in the tribal society inhabited by the Pashtuns, where bloody skirmishes and raids were the order of the day, keeping women from the eyes of other men made good sense. It was the women who were seen as carrying the virtue or honor of the family or clan. For this reason their purity had to be safeguarded from those who would rape or dishonor them and thereby dishonor the clan.

In this culture that mixed tribal beliefs with Islam, a woman who dishonored her clan by having an extramarital tryst or relation with another man brought a stain on her kinfolk. Sadly, a woman who was raped was equally seen as a stain (*tor*) on her community. In such a case it was often the women of the clan as much as the men who called for the woman to be ostracized or killed. It was only by means of such killing that the clan's honor could be restored. It should be stated that, as vessels of the clan's honor, Pashtun women take these rules seriously and go to extraordinary lengths to protect their honor. Men must also be careful, for if they are caught having illicit sex with a woman, they too can be killed without fear of *badal* (revenge).

For all of these reasons, the Pashtun men work hard to protect their women. I will share two stories that capture this tradition, as told to me by a Pashtun friend from Kandahar who works for the Karzai government. My friend was a rather Westernized pro-Karzai Pashtun who nonetheless was strongly shaped by his people's culture. He told me stories that captured the Pashtuns' tradition of *namuz*, the protecting of their womenfolk (and often their faith and homeland, which are defined in similar protective terms).

On the first occasion, my source went to the hospital in the city of Kandahar with his mother and aunts when he was a young boy. While waiting in the emergency room, he noticed another man in the lobby who he believed was secretively glancing in the direction of his mother and aunts. Although he was only ten years old at the time, my friend threatened the older man for insulting his sense of *namuz*.

On another occasion, while crossing a checkpoint into Pakistan, border guards opened his family's suitcases looking for weapons or contraband. When they opened one of his sister's bags and found women's underwear, he and his brothers began screaming at the soldiers in fury even though they themselves were unarmed. The armed guards quickly closed the suitcase because they were aware of how important the issue was to these Pashtun men.

Such issues are of course compounded when non-Muslim outsiders intrude on these trigger-point issues. Nothing will infuriate a conservative Pashtun clan or village like an intrusion into the world of their women. This was best demonstrated when the Afghan Communist government tried banning dowries and child marriages for girls in 1978. It was this act more than anything else that drove the people to rise in rebellion and declare a jihad on the Communists.

Pashtun men try to keep their women from such exposure to outsiders' eyes, and one finds far fewer women out on the streets in the Pashtun villages of southern Afghanistan than in Kabul, Tajik-dominated Herat, or the Hazara or Uzbek lands of the north. Those Pashtun women who are out and about are covered from head to toe in *burqas*. The only Pashtun women who do not cover in this fashion are the Kuchis, nomadic Pashtuns who wander around Afghanistan like Gypsies and live in tents. The Kuchi women often wear bright scarves and dresses similar to those worn by the Hazara women.

When the Pashtun-Taliban conquered the comparatively liberal, cosmopolitan city of Kabul in 1996, they were horrified by the sight of women independently interacting with men. These women were seen as weak and prone to sex. For this reason the Taliban quickly threw women out of their workplaces, including schools where they played a vital educational role, and hospitals where they tended to women's issues.

Although the Taliban were not enforcing the Pashtunwali code per se, their Deobandi school of Islam mixed with Pashtun traditions to create a hyper-strict version of *purdah*-style veiling enforcement that was not entirely alien to the Pashtuns. However, the excesses that the Taliban carried out in the name of returning women to their "proper place" exceeded those of even the Pashtun traditionalists. But many Pashtuns nonetheless welcomed the Taliban and their strict treatment of women. These conservatives saw the Taliban as a force that protected the Pashtun version of "family values" and ended the "infidel" experiment in women's liberation begun by the Communists in the late 1970s.

Another component of the Pashtunwali code that is often romanticized or demonized by outsiders is the code of *melmastiia*, hospitality. This code is a point of honor for Pashtuns. I myself have been treated with extraordinary hospitality by Pashtuns who welcomed me into their home. Even poor families who cannot usually afford to eat meat will kill a prized lamb or goat and serve it to an honored guest. Should anything happen to a guest, it is a disgrace on the honor of the entire family and clan.

In the 1980s, passing mujahideen were fed and given shelter by Pashtun villagers who considered offering them hospitality to be a matter of honor. The same certainly holds true today for Taliban in areas that have turned against the government, they too are given hospitality. The Arabs who fought and shed their blood fighting alongside the mujahideen in the 1980s have also been offered the protection of *melmastiia*.

A famous example of *melmastiia* took place in Kunar Province in 2005 when a group of elite Navy SEALs was attacked by more than 150 Taliban. One of the wounded SEALs escaped and was found by a local shepherd who took him back to his village. When the Taliban discovered this, they went to the village to demand that the American be turned over to them. But the villagers, who had no ties to the Americans, resisted on the grounds that the SEAL was their guest. In the end the Taliban withdrew for fear of causing a blood feud, and the SEAL was turned over to American authorities.

The code is not carved in stone, however. There are examples of guests being betrayed or of Pashtuns offering hospitality for a price, but this is rare, especially when it comes to turning a guest over to outsiders. This helps explain why it is so hard to convince Pashtun clans in the Pakistani tribal region to turn over their Al Qaeda or Taliban guests, even though there are millions of dollars in bounty money offered for them. To betray a guest would be both un-Islamic and disgraceful in a society where honor is held at a premium. To turn over a guest such as bin Laden to American infidels or to the Pakistani government would be a sin that would stain the souls and reputation of an entire family. Keeping out intrusive outsiders and protecting those who are on the "inside" is ingrained in this culture that does not respect any government, much less an "infidel" or "apostate" regime.

The concept of *melmastiia* is especially strong among members of the same tribe. Many Taliban leaders from Afghanistan who fled to Pakistan in 2001 to avoid U.S. bombs found sanctuary with fellow tribesmen on the Pakistani side of the border. Recently, however, local Pashtuns in the Pakistani provinces of Waziristan have made a business out of offering *melmastiia* to wealthy Arabs. In effect, the Arabs have to buy their hosts' protection.

There are also limits on *melmastiia*, as demonstrated in the case of the Pakistani Taliban leader Mullah Nazir. In 2007 Mullah Nazir led his tribe in attacking militants from the Islamic Movement of Uzbekistan, a jihadi group tied to Al Qaeda, who had been involved in killing local *malik* elders. Nazir's tribesmen drove the Uzbeks from their mountain positions killing over a hundred of them despite the fact that they were previously considered guests.

This brings us to the much-discussed Pashtun concept of *badal*, revenge. Although *badal* sanctions the killing of those who have killed a clan member, such revenge killing can only be carried out under certain conditions. More often in a case requiring *badal*, village elders meet in a *jirga* (tribal council) to iron things out in much the same way that the U.S. legal system does in the United States. But instead of having a distant government enforce such arbitrary laws as "Three strikes and you're out" (that is, three crimes and you go to jail for life), in the Pashtun case a culprit is judged by local elders who not only know him but know his case intimately. Death is, however, rarely the outcome; when it is, it is often administered by a member of the grieved party's clan.

Political map of Afghanistan.

In the West, the judiciary focuses on incarceration, fines, and punishment (up to and including the death penalty in the United States). In the Pashtun code, revenge is mediated in most instances, and compensation—not another death—is sought. If a man has been killed, his family has lost a worker who was capable of providing income. To compensate for his death, the *jirga* may award a daughter of the offending clan to the victim's family to provide them with another work hand. In some cases a *nake* or "blood price" is paid to the victim's family. In such cases *nanawatay* (reconciliation or forgiveness) is ordered, not revenge killing. The overarching aim of this sort of reconciliation effort is of course to maintain peace and order in a tumultuous tribal land where there is little or no state or civil authority.

But reconciliation does not always work, in which case a member of the victim's clan can kill a member of the enemy clan (it does not have to be the actual perpetrator, who is often hidden for his own protection). The concept of collective guilt or punishment is strong, and Pashtuns who declare *badal* can take their entire clan down the path to a full-blown blood feud.

Not surprisingly, a society made up of hundreds of egalitarian tribes and clans who are armed and eager to defend their honor has had its share of tribal conflict. For this reason the Pashtun lands are filled with mud-walled compounds or fortresses that protect their inhabitants from other tribes who might have vendettas against them. Other laws in the Pashtunwali "Code of the Hills" include *meranah*, a type of chivalry; *ghayrat*, the defense of property and honor; and *tureh*, the code of the sword.

A couple of Pashtun *landays*, or poems, capture the fighting spirit of the Pashtuns and help shed light on the various tribal codes. Louis Dupree cites the following *landay* in his book *Afghanistan*:

My beloved returned from battle unsuccessful,
I regret the kiss I gave him last night.

If you don't wield a sword, what else do you do?
You who have been suckled at the breast of an Afghan mother!

My sword I gird upon my thigh,
To guard our nation's ancient fame.
Its champion in this age am I
The Khatak Khan, Kushel is my name.

No one captured this world of jostling tribes better than Winston Churchill, then an English journalist who served with British forces suppressing a Pashtun rebellion in the Swat Valley in 1897. In his book *The Story of the Malakand Field Force: An Episode in the Frontier War*, Churchill provided an insightful account of the Pashtuns and their culture that is, for all of its colonial-era attitudes, still applicable to today:

The inhabitants of these wild but wealthy valleys are of many tribes, but of similar character and condition. The abundant crops which a warm sun and copious rains raise from a fertile soil, support a numerous population in a state of warlike leisure. Except at the times of sowing and of harvest, a continual state of feud and strife prevails throughout the land. Tribe wars with tribe. The people of one valley fight with those of the next. To the quarrels of communities are added the combats of individuals. Khan assails khan, each supported by his retainers. Every tribesman has a blood feud with his neighbor. Every man's hand is against the other, and all against the stranger.

Nor are these struggles conducted with the weapons which usually belong to the races of such development. To the ferocity of the Zulu are added the craft of the Redskin and the marksmanship of the Boer. The world is presented with that grim spectacle, "the strength of civilization without its mercy." At a thousand yards the traveler falls wounded by the well-aimed bullet of a breech-loading rifle. His assailant, approaching, hacks him to death with the ferocity of a South-Sea Islander. The weapons of the nineteenth century are in the hands of the savages of the Stone Age.

Every influence, every motive, that provokes the spirit of murder among men, impels these mountaineers to deeds of treachery and violence. The strong aboriginal propensity to kill, inherent in all human beings, has in these valleys been preserved in unexampled strength and vigor. That religion, which above all others was founded and propagated by the sword—the tenets and principles of which are instinct with incentives to slaughter and which in three continents has produced fighting breeds of men—stimulates a wild and merciless fanaticism. The love of plunder, always a characteristic of hill tribes, is fostered by the spectacle of opulence and luxury which, to their eyes, the cities and plains of the south display. A code of honor not less punctilious than that of old Spain, is supported by vendettas as implacable as those of Corsica. . . .

In such a state of society, all property is held directly by main force. Every man is a soldier. Either he is the retainer of some khan—the man-at-arms of some feudal baron as it were—or he is a unit in the armed force of his village—the burgher of mediaeval history. In such surroundings we may without difficulty trace the rise and fall of an ambitious Pathan. At first he toils with zeal and thrift as an agriculturist on that plot of ground which his family have held since they expelled some former owner. He accumulates in secret a sum of money. With this he buys a rifle from some daring thief, who has risked his life to snatch it from a frontier guardhouse. He becomes a man to be feared. Then he builds a tower to his house and overawes those around him in the village. Gradually they submit to his authority. He might now rule the village; but he aspires still higher. He persuades or compels his neighbors to join him in an attack on the castle of a local khan. The attack succeeds. The khan flies or is killed; the castle captured. The retainers make terms with the conqueror. The land tenure is feudal. In return for their acres they follow their new chief to war. Were he to treat them worse than the other khans treated their servants, they would sell their strong arms elsewhere. He treats them well. Others resort to him. He buys more rifles. He conquers two or three neighboring khans. He has now become a power.

Many, perhaps all, states have been founded in a similar way, and it is by such steps that civilization painfully stumbles through her earlier stages. But in these valleys the warlike nature of the people and their hatred of control, arrest the further progress of development. We have watched a man, able, thrifty, brave, fighting his way to power, absorbing, amalgamating, laying the foundations of a more complex and interdependent state of society. He has so far succeeded. But his success is now his ruin. A combination is formed against him. The surrounding chiefs and their adherents are assisted by the village populations. The ambitious Pathan, oppressed by numbers, is destroyed. The victors quarrel over the spoil, and the story closes, as it began, in bloodshed and strife.

The conditions of existence, that have been thus indicated, have naturally led to the dwelling-places of these tribes being fortified. If they are in the valley, they are protected by towers and walls loopholed for musketry. If in the hollows of the hills, they are strong by their natural position. In either case they are guarded by a hardy and martial people, well armed, brave, and trained by constant war.

This state of continual tumult has produced a habit of mind which wrecks little of injuries, holds life cheap and embarks on war with careless levity, and the tribesmen of the Afghan border afford the spectacle of a people, who fight without passion, and kill one another without loss of temper. Such a disposition, combined with an absolute lack of reverence for all forms of law and authority, and a complete assurance of equality, is the cause of their frequent quarrels with the British power. A trifle rouses their animosity. They make a sudden attack on some frontier post. They are repulsed. From their point of view the incident is closed. There has been a fair fight in which they have had the worst fortune. What puzzles them is that "the Sirkar" should regard so small an affair in a serious light. Thus the Mohmands cross the frontier and the action of Shabkadr is fought. They are surprised and aggrieved that the Government are not content with the victory, but must needs invade their territories, and impose punishment. Or again, the Mamunds, because a village has been burnt, assail the camp of the Second Brigade by night. It is a drawn game. They are astounded that the troops do not take it in good part.

They, when they fight among themselves, bear little malice, and the combatants not infrequently make friends over the corpses of their comrades or suspend operations for a festival or a horse race. At the end of the contest cordial relations are at once re-established. And yet so full of contradictions is their character, that all this is without prejudice to what has been written of their family vendettas and private blood feuds. Their system of ethics, which regards treachery and violence as virtues rather than vices, has produced a code of honour so strange and inconsistent, that it is incomprehensible to a logical mind. I have been told that if a white man could grasp it fully, and were to understand their mental impulses—if he knew, when it was their honour to stand by him, and when it was their honour to betray him; when they were bound to protect and when to kill him—he might, by judging his times and opportunities, pass safely from one end of the mountains to the other. But a civilised European is as little able to accomplish this, as to appreciate the feelings of those strange creatures, which, when a drop of water is examined under a microscope, are revealed amiably gobbling each other up, and being themselves complacently devoured.

All are held in the grip of miserable superstition. The power of the ziarat, or sacred tomb, is wonderful. Sick children are carried on the backs of buffaloes, sometimes sixty or seventy miles, to be deposited in front of such a shrine, after which they are carried back—if they survive the journey—in the same way. It is painful even to think of what the wretched child suffers in being thus jolted over the cattle tracks. But the tribesmen consider the treatment much more efficacious than any infidel prescription. To go to a ziarat and put a stick in the ground is sufficient to ensure the fulfillment of a wish. To sit swinging a stone or coloured glass ball, suspended by a string from a tree, and tied there by some fakir, is a sure method of securing a fine male heir. To make a cow give good milk, a little should be plastered on some favorite stone near the tomb of a holy man. These are but a few instances; but they may suffice to reveal a state of mental development at which civilisation hardly knows whether to laugh or weep.

Their superstition exposes them to the rapacity and tyranny of a numerous priesthood—"Mullahs," "Sahibzadas," "Akhundzadas," "Fakirs,"—and a host of wandering Talib-ul-ilms, who correspond with the theological students in Turkey, and live free at the expense of the people. More than this, they enjoy a sort of "droit du seigneur," and no man's wife or daughter is safe from them. Of some of their manners and morals it is impossible to write. As Macaulay has said of Wycherley's plays, "they are protected against the critics as a skunk is protected against the hunters." They are "safe, because they are too filthy to handle, and too noisome even to approach."

Yet the life even of these barbarous people is not without moments when the lover of the picturesque might sympathise with their hopes and fears. In the cool of the evening, when the sun has sunk behind the mountains of Afghanistan, and the valleys are filled with a delicious twilight, the elders of the village lead the way to the chenar trees by the water's side, and there, while the men are cleaning their rifles, or smoking their hookas, and the women are making rude ornaments from beads, and cloves, and nuts, the Mullah drones the evening prayer. Few white men have seen, and returned to tell the tale. But we may imagine the conversation passing from the prices of arms and cattle, the prospects of the harvest, or the village gossip, to the great Power, that lies to the southward, and comes nearer year by year. Perhaps some former Sepoy, of Beluchis or Pathans, will recount his adventures in the bazaars of Peshawar, or tell of the white officers he has followed and fought for in the past. He will speak of their careless bravery and their strange sports; of the far-reaching power of the Government, that never forgets to send his pension regularly as the months pass by; and he may even predict to the listening circle the day when their valleys will be involved in the comprehensive grasp of that great machine, and judges, collectors and commissioners shall ride to sessions at Ambeyla, or value the land tax on the soil of Nawagai. Then the Mullah will raise his voice and remind them of other days when the sons of the prophet drove the infidel from the plains of India, and ruled at Delhi, as wide an Empire as the Kafir holds to-day: when the true religion strode proudly through the earth and scorned to lie hidden and neglected among the hills: when mighty princes ruled in Bagdad, and all men knew that there was one God, and Mahomet was His prophet. And the young men hearing these things will grip their Martinis, and pray to Allah, that one day He will bring some Sahib—best prize of all—across their line of sight at seven hundred yards so that, at least, they may strike a blow for insulted and threatened Islam.

Churchill's observation that the Pashtuns' "superstition exposes them to the rapacity and tyranny of a numerous priesthood—'Mullahs,' 'Sahibzadas,' 'Akhundzadas,' 'Fakirs,'—and a host of wandering Talib-ul-ilms [Taliban]" certainly holds true today. Such adventurers and extremists as the fanatical Taliban leader Mullah Dadullah Akhund (*Akhund* is a title meaning "scholar"), Nek Muhammad (a former car thief turned Pakistani Taliban commander), Jalaluddin Haqqani (a tribal warrior who became a powerful mujahideen commander and Taliban leader), and Mullah Omar (the Taliban "Commander of the Faithful") would have been quite at home in the wars against the nineteenth-century British. The clay-walled *qalas* (castle compounds), with underground communication tunnels and battlements with slats for shooting (which the Taliban still use today), were also used against the British in previous wars.

Churchill commented that the Afghans used modern weapons to engage in tribal warfare, and today's "Taliban-ul-ilms" also fight with modern weapons, including IEDs, suicide bombers, mortars, and Kalashnikovs. And although the Coalition troops fighting in Afghanistan might think that their struggles with local insurgents are unique, their role as meddling outsiders means that their war is anything but unique. Thus the timeless struggle that pits invaders against prickly Pashtun tribesmen who have their own codes and faith continues as it has for centuries.

The Tajiks: Afghanistan's Second Race

The Tajiks are, like the Pashtuns to whom they are distantly related, descendants of the Aryans or Indo-Europeans. They are proud of the fact that they are descended from the Bactrians and Sogdians who fought Alexander the Great to a standstill until he married one of their princesses (Roxanne) and declared "victory." The Tajiks also have Persian blood in their veins, and it was from their land that the great Prophet Zoroaster, the founder of a faith known as Zoroastrianism, came. Although their ancient language was Persianized in succeeding centuries, the scattered Tajiks of Central Asia continued to speak an archaic version of Persian-Farsi known as Dari.

The name *Tajik* was applied to this people only after the advent of Islam when Turkic nomadic tribes came to the area. These horse-mounted tribes used the pejorative "Tat," "Taj," or "Tajik" to describe the settled people living in the villages, mountains, and oases of the region. In this sense *Tajik* simply meant "non-nomadic Persian speakers."

Over the centuries the Tajiks, who were largely farmers, merchants, and craftsmen, came to be dominated by Turkic-Mongol tribes. In the 1500s they were conquered by Shaybani Khan's Uzbek tribes, who then ruled over them until the nineteenth century. The Tajiks living north of the Amu Darya in what is today Tajikistan were ruled directly by the powerful Uzbek khans of the legendary Silk Road city of Bukhara, while those living south of the Amu Darya in the Afghan province of Badakshan were ruled by the Uzbek khans of Kunduz.

During this period the Tajiks often served in the governments of their nomadic Uzbek masters as scribes, poets, tax collectors, and officials. In the process, there was a gradual blurring of Tajik and Uzbek cultures, and the Uzbek elite gradually came to speak Tajik-Dari, just as medieval English rulers spoke both French and English. To the south of the Hindu Kush, the expansionist Pashtuns similarly came to speak Tajik-Farsi (which became known as Dari or "Court Persian" in the twentieth century).

Also during this period, there was no overarching sense of modern Tajik national unity or identity. In fact, many groups that are labeled Tajiks today did not identify themselves as such until they were told they were Tajiks during the 1990s civil war. Prior to this, they did what most groups did in the region—they defined themselves by their locale. Thus Panjsheris, Heratis, Badakshanis, Kabulis, Mazaris, and Samarkandis constituted *qawms* with their own sub-dialects, leaders, and ties to non-Tajiks (especially Uzbeks) with whom they often intermarried.

When the Tajiks living south of the Amu Darya were conquered and included in the Afghan state in the nineteenth century, they played a unique role considering they were non-Pashtuns. As men of trade, governance, and literature they helped forge the Pashtun state and were generally treated better than their Uzbek or Hazara counterparts. Tajik-Dari became the court language of the Pashtun rulers.

Tajiks subsequently played a key role in the Afghan Communist government as well. Conversely, under Massoud the Lion of Panjsher, the Panjsheri Tajiks played a major role in the Afghan mujahideen resistance to Communism. The Tajiks were the most effective members of the mujahideen resistance. When the jihad came to an end, diverse Tajik subgroups, including the Heratis who lived close to Iran and Mazaris in the north, began to call themselves "Tajiks" as a catchall ethnic term. During the 1990s the Tajiks dominated the Afghan government led by President Burhanuddin Rabbani and his powerful defense minister Ahmad Shah Massoud. To this very day, Tajiks, who make up the second-largest ethnic group in Afghanistan (25 to 30 percent of the population, or between seven and eight million people), place images of Massoud on their stores, cars, and homes as a sign of ethnic solidarity with their *Milli Kahraman* (National Hero).

The rule of Tajiks in Kabul during the 1990s was, however, seen by many Pashtuns as a return to the days of Bacha i Saqao, an early twentieth-century Tajik usurper who overthrew the Pashtun king Amanullah. One of the Taliban's promises was to return Pashtun rule to Kabul and expel Massoud and his Tajiks. Today the Taliban still exploit this issue and claim to be fighting against the Tajiks' behind-the-scenes manipulation of the Karzai government.

Although Tajiks living in Herat, Mazar i Sharif, Kabul, and other regions were conquered by the Taliban from 1995 to 1998, those living in the high mountains of the northeast remained free under Massoud's protection. There they fought a tenacious battle with the Taliban and kept them out of the northern Shomali Plain, Panjsher, Takhar, Badakshan, and neighboring lands. The Tajiks received help from the Shiite government of Iran based on their shared Farsi language (although the Tajiks are of course Sunnis) as well as from their former enemies, the Russians, who feared having the Taliban spread fundamentalism into post-Soviet Central Asia.

During 2001's Operation Enduring Freedom, the new leader of the post-Massoud Tajik component of the Northern Alliance anti-Taliban opposition, Mohammad Qasim Fahim (also known as Fahim Khan, the successor to the recently slain Massoud), led the Tajiks in liberating Kabul, a Tajik-dominated city, from the Taliban. Pakistan, which played a key role in supporting the Pashtun Taliban and the U.S.-led war on terror under Musharraf, was unhappy to see the Northern Alliance Tajiks take Kabul. The United States was also distrustful of Fahim Khan and his followers, in part because of fears of their ties to Shiite Iran and Khan's forced seizure of land in Kabul. For this reason they moved quickly to appoint a Pashtun president of Afghanistan (Hamid Karzai) at the Bonn Conference, which chose a new government in the winter of 2001. The Tajiks realized they could not rule the Pashtun-dominated country and gave up control to the Westernized Pashtun leader, Hamid Karzai.

Fahim Khan nonetheless kept his troops in the city and used his position as defense minister to seize whole districts in the capital. When reports of land confiscation and expulsion of tenants reached President Karzai, he decided to move against Khan. Fahim Khan, Afghanistan's most powerful warlord, was subsequently removed and was confined to his power base in his native Panjsher. In 2009 he was, however, rehabilitated by President Karzai and chosen as his running mate in the August elections held that year.

The Tajiks still play a major role in the new government and in police and army forces. Their numbers in the military and perceived dominance over the Karzai administration have led many Pashtuns to distrust the government. The Taliban have also exploited this issue and tried to portray Karzai as a puppet of the warlords of the Tajik-dominated Northern Alliance. The Pakistanis also distrust the Tajiks in the government and in 2010 pushed Karzai to fire Amrullah Saleh, the Tajik head of the Afghan National Directorate of Security.

In response to their gradual loss of key positions, in 2007 such key Tajik leaders as Ismail Khan, Fahim Khan, Yunnus Qannuni, and Zia Massoud (Massoud's brother) reorganized the Northern Alliance as the "United National Front" to pressure the Karzai government. This powerful political bloc (which also included such leaders as Abdul Rashid Dostum and Sayid Mansur of the Ismaili Hazaras) represented a potent third force in an Afghanistan that was already divided between the Taliban and the Karzai government.

Having gained unprecedented influence in the government, police, and military, the Tajiks aim to maintain their power at all costs. Clearly, the Pandora's box of ethnicity that was opened during the 1990s civil war remains wide open today. Should the U.S.-led Coalition or the Karzai government control weaken, the Tajiks are poised to reenter the struggle for control of the country that began with the fall of the Communist Najibullah government in 1992. Thus the demons of the unfinished wars of Afghanistan's past lurk beneath the surface.

The Uzbeks: The *Buzkashi* Players of the North

Although many outsiders operate under the misconception that Turks come from the Middle East (after all, Turkey is in the Middle East), their origins are actually deep in the heart of Central Asia in the vicinity of Mongolia. Like their neighbors and distant kin, the Mongols, the shamanistic-pagan Turks have lived since the fourth century on the vast open plains of Eurasia in what is today northern Afghanistan, Kazakhstan, Kyrgyzstan, Uzbekistan, Turkmenistan, Mongolia, Inner China, and Ukraine. There they traveled on horseback in seasonal migrations with herds of horses, sheep, Bactrian camels, and goats. Their homes were yurts—round, dome-shaped, portable tents made of felt. Life was harsh and unforgiving in the vast plains of Eurasia. As tribes jostled one another for control of pastures, the weaker tribes tended to migrate westward or southward to try their luck.

The West knows these migrating horsemen, who were superior riders and archers, by various names, including the Huns of Attila who helped destroy Rome; the Seljuk Turks who converted to Islam and settled in Anatolia (a land they called Turkey); the Seljuks' heirs, the Ottoman Turks, who spread Islam into Eastern Europe from Istanbul; and the Moghuls, who conquered Hindu India and built the Taj Mahal. These Turkic-Mongol tribes brought new blood into the Muslim world when they converted from shamanism to a watered-down, mystic version of Islam known as Sufism. Turkish *akincis* (raiders) made it as far west as Vienna in 1529, swept across northern Africa to Morocco, spread Islam to Kosovo, Bosnia, and Albania, and became the third people of Islam after the Arabs and the Persians (Iranians).

But not all Turks were defenders of Islam. A subsequent wave of pagan Turkic tribes made up the majority of Genghis Khan's Mongol army, which devastated the Islamic world in the thirteenth century. These pagan Turks rode alongside Genghis Khan's grandson Hulegu when he sacked Baghdad, the seat of the Arabic Muslim caliphate, in 1258.

But for all the damage they inflicted on the Muslim world, this second wave of pagan Turkic-Mongol tribes eventually converted to Sufi Islam as well. When the Mongol empire subsequently broke up in the mid-1300s, one group of these Muslim Turkic-Mongols created a powerful state in what is today Ukraine and Russia known as the Golden Horde. This state eventually fractured and a group of Turkic-Mongol tribesmen migrated into the flat steppes (plains) of what is now Kazakhstan. There they became known as the Uzbeks—meaning "self-masters" (Uz=self, Bek=master)—a name that captures their propensity for infighting and resistance to outsiders.

Not content to remain on the cold northern steppe, in the early 1500s the restless Uzbek tribes migrated southward and conquered the great trading cities of the Silk Road (a transcontinental series of trade routes that link China to the West on which Marco Polo traveled), namely Bukhara and Samarkand. The area around these great centers of Central Asian Islam gradually ceased to be known as Turkistan and was given the name Uzbekistan.

From Bukhara, the Uzbeks rounded out their conquests of the flat plains of southern Turkistan (Central Asia) by capturing the southern city of Balkh (in the Mazar i Sharif area) and migrating southward into the foothills of the Hindu Kush Mountains. For hundreds of years the Uzbek horsemen dominated the flat northern lands of what would one day become known as Afghanistan.

In the nineteenth century the Uzbeks were definitively conquered from the north by the Russians and from the south by the Afghans. Making use of superior weapons, the Russians conquered Bukhara and Samarkand and other lands of Uzbekistan while the Afghans used British cannons and rifles to fully conquer those Uzbeks living in the south. It was this southern section of the Uzbek realm (lying *south* of the Amu Darya River) that was eventually conquered by the Afghan ruler Abdur Rahman, known as the Iron Amir, and incorporated into centralizing Afghanistan in the nineteenth century. The southern Uzbeks, like the southern Tajiks, thus found themselves cut off from their ethnic kin in the north who were subsequently incorporated into the atheist USSR in the twentieth century. The Uzbeks were then divided into Uzbekistan in the north and Afghanistan in the south.

Prior to their conquest by the Afghans, the southern section of Uzbeks dominated the plains around Mazar i Sharif through a series of small states ruled by horse-mounted *khans* (commanders). Strict Sunni Muslims, the Uzbeks also regularly attacked Shiite Iran for slaves, raided the

Shiite Hazaras of the Hindu Kush, and dominated the settled Tajiks who lived to the east of them in the province of Badakhshan. The Uzbeks often intermarried with Tajiks, and most Uzbeks today speak the Tajik language of Dari in addition to Uzbek.

As previously noted, the Uzbeks fought a long battle to repulse the Russians from the north and the Afghan-Pashtuns from the south, but in the nineteenth century their lands were divided between Russia and Afghanistan. Both the Russians and the Pashtuns had superior weapons and numbers, and they ultimately crushed the Uzbeks, who were better horsemen. Today, despite past defeats, the Uzbeks are numerically the largest people in post-Soviet Central Asia and make up somewhere between 8 and 10 percent of Afghanistan's total population (between two and three million people). They are often identifiable by their Turkic-Mongol complexions (often with Tajik admixtures) and their long, quilted riding jackets (*chapans*) and tight-woven turbans.

The Uzbeks gradually began to settle down in clay-walled villages known as *kishlaks* by the late eighteenth and nineteenth centuries. But they never lost their love of horses. To this very day local *khans* gain respect by sponsoring the Uzbeks' favorite pastime, *buzkashi* (goat grabbing). This rough-and-tumble sport was made famous in *Rambo III* and is part polo, part rugby scrum. It revolves around scoring a goal with the carcass of a dead calf or goat. First developed by Genghis Khan's troops to help them train for warfare, *buzkashi* involves dozens of riders clad in *chapans* whipping one another as they fight to drag a decapitated *buz* (goat) to a goal. It was rumored that Uzbek mujahideen (anti-Soviet rebels) also played the game with the bodies of slain Soviet soldiers in the 1980s, and the term *buzkashi* has often been used to describe the Uzbeks' form of rough politics.

Consigned to being a subject people in a state run by Afghan-Pashtuns following their nineteenth-century conquest, the Uzbeks remembered their people's past in *destans* (epics) of the Golden Horde. From 1880 to the 1980s, Afghan Uzbeks were reduced to a second-class race of farmers, shepherds, wool merchants, and village traders. Like the Hazara Mongol "flat noses," they were denied access to anything but the lowest ranks of the government and military. But as fellow Sunnis, they were not proactively victimized by the Afghans as the Shiite Hazaras were.

When the Soviets invaded Afghanistan in 1979, Afghan Uzbeks whose parents (known as *muhajirs* or "religious emigrants") had fled collectivization and other unpopular Communist policies in the Soviet republic of Uzbekistan led the way in creating Uzbek mujahideen resistance groups. However the Uzbeks were too far from the Pakistani border to use it as a safe haven and the efforts on the part of an Uzbek nationalist named Azad Beg to create a jihad party for Uzbeks and their fellow

Turks, the Turkmen, failed. Uzbek mujahideen claimed that the Pashtuns and the Tajik mujahideen groups did not support the formation of a separate Uzbek mujahideen party.

Instead, the Communist government reached out to the disenfranchised Uzbeks and gave them an Uzbek-language newspaper known as *Yulduz* (The Star), the right to use their own language in schools and politics, and the right to establish their own pro-Communist government militias. General Abdul Rashid Dostum's Jowzjani Militia subsequently became the most important of these pro-Communist militias. Although they were not devoted Communists, the Uzbek commanders tended to be a comparatively secular lot known for drinking, visits to Uzbekistan, and distrust of militant Islam and Pashtuns.

When the Communist government of President Mohammad Najibullah was overthrown in 1992 and the various jihad parties of the Tajiks and Pashtuns became more ethnocentric, Uzbek mujahideen defected from the legendary Tajik leader Massoud and the fanatic Pashtun leader Gulbuddin Hekmatyar and joined up with the secularist Uzbek leader Rashid Dostum. This union of Uzbek mujahideen and Uzbek Communist militias eventually became the dominant force in Dostum's Jumbesh Party. The Jumbesh Party helped nationalize the Uzbeks, who had never really been ethnically aware prior to the party's rise to power.

The Uzbeks' heyday was from 1992 to 1998, when they dominated the great northern city of Mazar i Sharif and the rest of the north. This halcyon period came to an end when the Taliban conquered the plains of Afghan Turkistan from 1997 to 1998 and forced out the Uzbeks' secular protector, General Dostum. As Dostum's Massachusetts-size mini-state fell to the Taliban in 1998, the Uzbeks were put back in their place and horribly oppressed by Mullah Omar's Pashtun Taliban forces. The Uzbeks waited until April 2001 for the *Pasha* (General Dostum) to return, then rode to the high mountains to fight the Taliban under his command. In November 2001 Dostum led them out of the mountains and down to Mazar i Sharif, which they conquered alongside Northern Alliance commanders Ustad Atta and Karim Khalili and U.S. special forces.

Today the Uzbeks have, despite their distrust of the Pashtuns, accepted the rule of the Karzai administration. The stability and reconstruction that the current government brings has won their support. Many Uzbeks I met in Afghanistan asked me to tell the Americans and other Coalition members not to leave Afghanistan. The Republic of Turkey, which led the NATO Coalition in 2003, has supported the building of schools, hospitals, and roads in the Uzbek lands in the name of reaching out to their Turkic *irkdashlar* (kin). These ties go back to the Turkish MIT (National Intelligence Organization) service's support for the exiled Dostum following his overthrow by the Taliban in 1997 and 1998.

Although many in the Karzai government would like to remove Dostum from his seat of power, he still has many Uzbek supporters in Afghanistan who respect him for protecting their interests vis-à-vis the Pashtuns. Others see Dostum as a warlord who has no role in today's Afghanistan. Regardless, in August 2009 Karzai called upon Dostum, who was living in exile in Turkey, to come back to the country and rally Uzbek votes for his presidential candidacy run. Dostum fulfilled his end of the bargain and was reinstated as chief of staff of the Afghan army by Karzai. Many Western voices criticized this bargain, but it won Dostum tremendous support from among the Uzbeks who were happy to see one of their own given this symbolically important position. And as Taliban infiltrators continue to make inroads into the Uzbek-dominated provinces of Kunduz, Baghlan, Badghis, and Faryab, even Dostum's critics understand that he and his Uzbeks could one day serve as a bulwark against their enemies' re-infiltration.

The Hazaras: Afghanistan's Oppressed Shiite Minority

The Hazaras, who make up between 10 and 12 percent of Afghanistan's population, have long been one of Afghanistan's most isolated ethnic groups. Their homeland is found in the windswept Hazarajat mountain plateau of the central Hindu Kush. Although there is considerable debate on the ethnic origins of the Hazaras (whose name means "One Thousand" in Persian, from the term for a Mongol fighting unit), most anthropologists see them as being descended from Genghis Khan's Mongol hordes. These Mongols mixed with the earlier Persian-speaking Indo-Europeans who had long lived in the Hindu Kush and previously built the ancient Buddhas of Bamiyan. In the process of settling, they gradually began to speak a Persian (Farsi) dialect known as Hazaragi, which is filled with Mongol words.

This mixed origin is plainly visible in the physiognomy of many Hazaras. Although most Hazaras have Turkic-Mongol features, some have an admixture of Indo-European characteristics, including green or blue eyes and lighter complexions. Some Hazara nationalists have tried to link their people to the Kushan or Tokharian creators of the Buddhas at Bamiyan. Although the blood of these ancient Indo-Europeans may flow in the Hazaras, who are, like all of Afghanistan's races, mixed, the Hazaras' Mongol features would indicate stronger Mongol bloodlines.

In the centuries following their conquests of the Hindu Kush Mountains, the Hazaras' pagan Mongol ancestors converted to Islam, but they eventually made the fateful decision to convert to Shiite (minority) Islam in the sixteenth century. They may have done so under the influence of

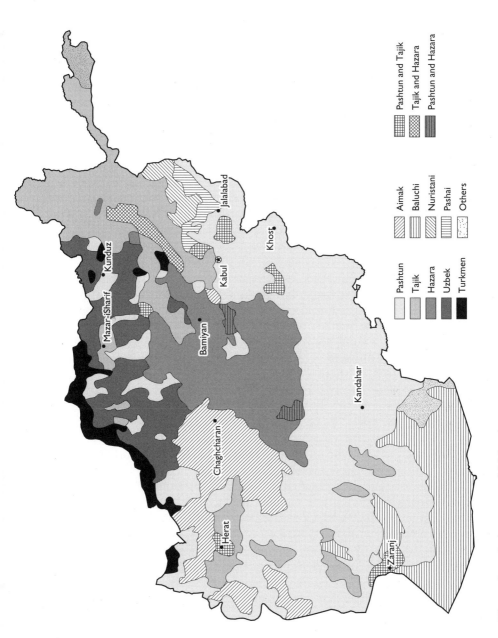

The major ethnic groups of Afghanistan.

Legend:
Pashtun
Tajik
Hazara
Uzbek
Turkmen

Aimak
Baluchi
Nuristani
Pashai
Others

Pashtun and Tajik
Tajik and Hazara
Pashtun and Hazara

Mazar-i-Sharif · Kunduz · Bamiyan · Chaghcharan · Herat · Zaranj · Kandahar · Kabul · Jalalabad · Khost

Shiite states, such as the Safavid empire, in neighboring Iran. Their decision made the Hazaras the victims of the neighboring Sunni Muslim tribes and states, all of whom preyed on the Hazaras as "heretics." For centuries the Uzbeks, Turkmen, and Pashtuns raided the Hazara lands for slaves. All of the region's great Sunni rulers made military forays into the Hazara lands of the Hindu Kush, from Tamerlane and Babur to Shaybani Khan and Ahmed Shah Durrani. However, the fiercely independent Hazara tribesmen seem to have been quite skilled in repulsing these efforts to conquer them.

The Iron Amir Abdur Rahman finally conquered the Hazaras with British assistance in the 1890s. The final conquest of their homeland was a catastrophe for the Hazaras, who had for so long fought to keep their Sunni enemies out. They were persecuted by the Sunni Pashtuns, who despised them for their liberal treatment of women, their Shiite Islam, and their efforts to prevent Pashtun Kuchi nomads from taking their lands in the south. Nineteenth-century sources speak of Hazara villagers being led from their burning villages in chains to Kabul and of rebellious Hazara chieftains being tortured to death by the Pashtun conquerors.

Although the Hazaras revolted on several occasions, their uprisings were put down with great ferocity by the Afghan-Pashtuns. In the process, the Hazaras were displaced from their ancestral lands to the north of Helmand and Kandahar, and this area has been a zone of contention between Pashtun settlers and Hazaras ever since. The Hazaras have never forgiven the Pashtuns for conquering them, enslaving many of their people, and making them a despised caste of Shiites.

Culturally the Hazaras have had a more relaxed interpretation of Islam than their Sunni neighbors but have been ruled by a strict tribal hierarchy. The elites known as *shaikhs*, *mirs*, or *arbabs* had more authority than their Pashtun counterparts.

Hazaras who left their impoverished homeland to seek work in the Afghan cities were treated terribly. They were forced to carry out the most menial of jobs and could be found working as trashmen, street sweepers, *chowkidars* (gate guards), and maids, as well as in other positions that paid them a pittance. In American terms, Hazaras were considered to be somewhere between newly freed African American slaves and today's illegal Mexican workers. To this very day they are discriminated against when it comes to access to cherished slots at universities or government jobs.

Hazaras were also taxed at a higher rate than the Pashtuns, a perennial complaint that led to revolts right up to the time of King Zahir Shah. The Pashtun mistreatment of Hazaras was masterfully captured in Khaled Hosseini's best seller *The Kite Runner*. Hosseini's work tells the tale of a lowly Hazara whose loyalty to his Pashtun master is not repaid. The

Hazara servant is eventually left to the mercy of the Taliban, who kill him just as they did many of his people in the 1990s.

In the 1970s tens of thousands of impoverished Hazaras migrated to Mazar i Sharif and Kabul. By the late 1970s west Kabul was predominantly made up of Hazara slums. In the 1978 Saur Revolution, which saw the Afghan Communists overthrow President Mohammad Daoud and seize power, the Hazaras' position improved somewhat as the new Communist regime sought to reach out to disaffected minorities like the Uzbeks and Hazaras with Soviet-style positive discrimination programs. For the first time in history, a Hazara, Sultan Ali Kishtmand, was made Afghan prime minister by the Communists.

Not surprisingly, the Hazaras welcomed such developments, and many Hazaras in the cities joined the Communist Party. This was facilitated by the fact that the Hazaras' society proved to be more susceptible to secularism and the redistribution of land to the poor than were the religiously conservative Pashtuns who had more land. One group of Ismaili Hazaras (a Shiite minority) residing in the northern province of Baghlan even provided a militia led by their *pir* (holy man), Sayid Jaffer Naderi, to support the Communists.

But not all Hazaras supported the Communist regime. When the mujahideen rose up against the Communists, the main body of Hazaras living in the central Hazarajat Mountains became cut off from other parts of the country. Like all of Afghanistan's peoples, these Hazaras established mujahideen groups to fight the infidel Communists. But the Afghan Communists and their Soviet allies did not attempt to crush the Hazaras. Instead, they essentially let this marginal mountainous area go, and it became de facto autonomous during the 1980s. The only Communist government presence was in the town of Bamiyan. For this reason there was no major fighting between the Soviets and the Hazara mujahideen in the mountains of the Hazarajat during the war.

But that does not mean there was no fighting in the Hazara lands. At this time what amounted to a civil war broke out among the Hazara mujahideen. This war pitted Hazara revolutionary groups sponsored by Ayatollah Khomeini's Iran against the traditional elite made up of *shaykhs* (religious leaders) and *mirs* (the equivalent of tribal khans). The Iranian-backed revolutionary parties eventually defeated the more traditionalist parties but later reunited with them to increase their strength vis-à-vis other ethnic groups when the struggle for post-Communist Afghanistan began in 1992. At this time the Hazaras ceased their internal struggles and created a unifying umbrella organization known as the Hezb i Wahdat (Party of Unity), which was headed by Abdul Ali Mazari.

There was also fighting in the south of the Hazarajat as the Hazaras took advantage of the weakness of the central government to push Pashtun interlopers out of traditional Hazara lands in the province of Ghazni. This fighting presaged the general devolution of the anti-Communist jihad into an ethnic war for power in the 1990s. As the Communist Najibullah government collapsed in 1992, the powerful Pashtun-dominated mujahideen parties staked their claim to Kabul. The alliance between Dostum's Uzbeks and Massoud's Tajiks, and Mazari's Hazaras, however, denied Hekmatyar's Pashtun mujahideen the ability to take the capital.

With this victory came a newfound Hazara assertiveness that resembled the empowerment of Dostum's Uzbeks. When the Communist government collapsed in 1992, the Hazaras established their positions in the western neighborhoods of Kabul where their people predominated. Tragically, this eventually led to war with the Tajik-dominated Rabbani Government in 1993. This war stemmed largely from the fact that the mujahideen government was made up of Sunni Tajik and Pashtun parties. These factions refused to let the Shiite Hazaras or the Uzbek Communists into the government. Rabbani's government also resented the fact that the Hazaras controlled parts of its capital and sought to displace the Hazaras from the districts they controlled.

In the ensuing war, as many as seven hundred Hazaras of the Afshar District of western Kabul were slaughtered by Massoud and Rasul Sayyaf's victorious troops. In the process, much of western Kabul was also flattened or turned into a minefield.

As the Hazaras reeled from Rabbani Government attacks, the Taliban appeared on the outskirts of Kabul in 1995. The Shiite Hazaras expected little but trouble from the Sunni Taliban as a militant Pashtun-Sunni fundamentalist movement, and their expectations were soon fulfilled. After establishing a truce with the Taliban, the Hazara Hezb i Wahdat leader Abdul Ali Mazari went to meet with them. But the Taliban broke the truce and killed Mazari by throwing him from a helicopter. Mazari's body was subsequently discovered by Hazaras who took it on a long funeral procession to Mazar i Sharif where he is buried.

Thus began a war with the Taliban that saw the Hazaras gradually pushed deeper and deeper into the Hazarajat. Thousands of Hazaras living in Mazar i Sharif had their throats slit by the Taliban when they reconquered the city in 1998 (in retaliation for an earlier massacre of the Taliban's followers by Hazaras). By the end of that year the Taliban had also conquered Bamiyan and the Hazarajat plateau. The Taliban subsequently carried out several massacres of Hazaras in the mountains, including one documented in the BBC documentary *Behind the Veil* in which Hazara civilians were skinned alive.

Free Hazara opposition pockets nonetheless survived in the high mountains north of Bamiyan and in the Dar y Suf Valley. After 9/11, the United States liaised with the leaders of the Hazara Northern Alliance opposition fighters, Karim Khalili (Mazari's heir) and Mohammad Mohaqeq. These fighters then helped the U.S. Special Forces liberate Mazar i Sharif, Bamiyan, and the central Hazarajat highlands in November 2001.

Today Hazaras are officially protected by the Karzai government, which recognizes Shiite as well as Sunni Islam. Several of their representatives, including Karim Khalili, who served as vice president, have held government portfolios. Strangely enough, the Hazarajat also seems to have been spared the sort of anti-Shiite terrorism that had defined the Sunni insurgency in Iraq. There have been almost no acts of suicide bombing or other terrorism in this isolated zone. Hazaras have also served reliably against Taliban insurgents in the south in the Afghan army.

The Hazaras are currently trying to bring tourism back to the scenic mountain valley of Bamiyan that was previously home to Afghanistan's greatest historical landmarks, the massive stone carvings of Buddha erected in the fifth century A.D. Tragically these Buddha megaliths were blown up by fanatical Taliban iconoclasts as heathen idols in 2001. There are claims that the shattered Buddhas will be rebuilt, although this seems highly unlikely considering their fragmented condition. Interestingly enough, the governor of Bamiyan who has encouraged this tourism, Hababi Sarabi, is also a woman (Afghanistan's first female governor). But for all of the progress they've made, the Hazaras still face widespread discrimination in Afghanistan and find it difficult to get into universities or gain access to government jobs in Kabul. Their region has also received much less development funding than the Pashtun south or the plains of Turkistan.

Smaller Ethnic Groups

In addition to the Big Four ethnic groups—the Pashtuns, Tajiks, Uzbeks, and Hazaras—Afghanistan has several smaller ethnic groups made up of fewer than a million people (some are micro nations of just a few thousand). Altogether they make up 10 to 15 percent of Afghanistan. They include the following groups.

Turkmen

The Turkmen speak a language that is very close to the Turkish of the Republic of Turkey. This is no coincidence since the two people are related and stem from the same medieval Turkish invasion. In the mid-eleventh century a group of newly Islamized Turkish nomadic tribes called the Seljuks migrated from what is today the former Soviet republic of Turkmenistan and conquered Iran. Groups of Seljuk Turkish raiders then conquered neighboring Anatolia, which gradually became known as Turkia or Turkey. However, not all of the Turks settled in Iran and Turkey. Some remained in their original homeland in the Kara Kum Desert of what later became known as Turkmenistan. These disunited Turks, known as Turkmen, were notorious slavers and raided Shiite Iran for generations to steal hundreds of thousands of slaves for sale in the Uzbek Silk Road cities of Khiva, Samarkand, and Bukhara.

In the late 1800s the Russians conquered the fiercely independent Turkmen tribes of Turkmenistan in a series of brutal battles. The skilled Turkmen horsemen who had once been considered invincible were beaten by superior Russian military technology. But not all of the Turkmen were forcefully included in the Russian Empire. Small groups of Turkmen were found scattered in northern Iran and northern Afghanistan. These Turkmen in Afghanistan belonged primarily to the Yomut and Esari tribes and remained more nomadic than their Turkic kin and neighbors, the Uzbeks. The Turkmen, who number just over half a million, live primarily in the areas along the south side of the Amu Darya (Oxus) River, which separates Afghanistan from Uzbekistan in the provinces of Balkh, Jowzjan, Faryab, and Kunduz. Their main town is Akche, which lies between Mazar i Sharif and Sheberghan.

Many Turkmen in Afghanistan are also the descendants of refugees who fled Soviet Turkmenistan during the period of forced collectivization and a revolt against the Soviet state in the 1920s. These later emigrants are called *muhajirs* (emigrants) and were led by a Turkmen holy man known as the Kizil Ayak (Red Foot) Sheikh. This religious leader became the head of the Turkmen community in Afghanistan. Abdul Kerim Mahdum, the Kizil Ayak Sheikh in the early 1980s, and many other devout Muslim Turkmen fled to Attock and Peshawar, Pakistan, to wage jihad against the Soviets. However, they and their Turkic Uzbek kin received no help from the larger Pashtun and Tajik mujahideen parties and were unable to create a Turkmen-Uzbek mujahideen front. The Kizil Ayak Sheikh then emigrated to eastern Turkey, where he still lives among a large Turkmen emigrant community settled by the Turkish government.

When the Taliban later entered the plains of Afghan Turkistan, the Turkmen joined Uzbek commander General Dostum in fighting them. Several of these Turkmen, including Commander Tila of Kunduz, became great Northern Alliance leaders. Today the Turkmen are still aligned with Dostum's Jumbesh Party, although many resent being "little brothers" to their more powerful Uzbek kin.

In addition, Turkmen have traditionally been involved in the export of beautiful red carpets made from Karakul sheep. Their carpets are famous throughout the Middle East and are prized for their quality.

Aimaqs

The Aimaqs are nomadic or semi-nomadic people who live to the northwest of the Hindu Kush Mountains in an area extending from Herat to Bamiyan to Mazar i Sharif. They number between half a million and a million people and are found mainly in Herat, Badghis, and Ghor provinces (as well as in the neighboring Iranian province of Khorasan). The word *Aimaq* means "tribe" in Mongol and hints at their Turkic-Mongol origin, as do the names of some of their tribes: Qipchak (a Turkic confederation), Chengiz (that is, Genghis), Chagatai (a son of Genghis Khan), and Timuri (that is, Tamerlane, a Turkic-Mongol warlord). Some of the Aimaqs also live in Mongol-style yurt tents.

The Aimaqs also have a strong Persian admixture, and their language is Dari or Farsi. The Aimaqs are often known as the Chahar Aimaqs (Persian for "Four Aimaqs") owing to the name of an earlier tribal confederation of four of their major tribes. The Aimaqs formed as a people sometime in the 1500s and were an independent tribal confederation that fought with neighboring tribes until they were conquered by the Pashtuns between the eighteenth and early nineteenth centuries. Due to the fact that Aimaqs speak Persian-Dari, they were often labeled Tajiks, but they tend to be more nomadic and Turkic-Mongol than the Tajiks. The Aimaqs have never mobilized on an ethnic-political basis, but many did fight for the mujahideen and against the Taliban. The Aimaqs of Ghor, however, joined the Taliban when they conquered their province from 1995 to 1997.

Nuristanis

The Nuristanis number perhaps one hundred thousand and live in the forested mountains along the Pakistani border to the northeast of Kabul. They speak six mutually unintelligible, mainly Dardic (Indo-Aryan), languages and are known for their light-skinned Mediterranean-style complexions. They are probably the descendants of ancient Indian Aryans, although they claim to be the descendants of Alexander the Great's troops. This fiercely independent pagan-polytheistic people defied such conquerors as Genghis Khan and Tamerlane and maintained their worship of wooden idols and mountain gods as the surrounding areas converted to Islam. For this reason they were originally known as Kafirs (Infidels) by the neighboring Muslim peoples who clashed with them. In 1895, however, the Iron Amir Abdur Rahman dragged his cannons into their mountain and declared a jihad on them. After fighting back fiercely, the Kafirs were brutally conquered and their pagan temples were destroyed. Only a small pocket of Kafirs, known as the Kalash, who lived across the border in British India (later Pakistan) were able to maintain their ancient pagan ways.

Having forcefully spread the light (*nur*) of Islam to the region, Abdur Rahman renamed it Nuristan and its inhabitants Nuristanis. As is often the case with new converts, the Nuristanis became very devout in their new religious beliefs. Many even joined Abdur Rahman's army. Almost a century later they were the first to revolt against the Afghan Communists' "infidel" policies in the 1980s and fought ferociously to keep the Soviets out of their territory. During this period their region remained autonomous under a Wahhabi fundamentalist government known as the Dawlat (State). The Taliban later overthrew this state. After 2001 a governor was appointed to this province by the new Karzai government. Although many Nuristanis support the new Coalition-backed government, others who are more Wahhabi have followed in the previous jihad tradition and are waging war against Americans who are operating from several forward operating posts in the region. Since 2001 there have also been clashes between the two major Nuristani tribes, the Kushtaz and the Kamozi.

Kizil Bashis

The Kizil Bashis are the Dari-speaking descendants of Persian Turkmen soldiers who settled in Kabul during the time of an early eighteenth-century Persian conqueror named Nadir Shah. They are also the descendants of Turkmen who later came from Persia to assist the founder of Afghanistan, Ahmed Shah Durrani, as his elite fighting units. The term *Kizil Bash* in Turkmen means "Red Head" and refers to the Kizil Bashis' red turbans. Although the Kizil Bashis were Shiites, they were nonetheless used as an elite bureaucratic military class by the Sunni Afghan rulers of Kabul who came after the founding father of Afghanistan, Ahmed Shah Durrani. During the reign of the Iron Amir Abdur Rahman, however, they were persecuted for their Shiite beliefs and moral support for the Shiite Hazaras who were being conquered at the time. Many subsequently fled to British India and still live today in what is now Pakistan. The Kizil Bashis number perhaps one hundred thousand and form an urban elite in Kabul and to a lesser extent in other Afghan cities. It is hard to know the exact number of Kizil Bashis because it is rumored that they practice *taqiya* (that is, they pretend to be Sunnis to protect themselves from persecution).

Baluchis

The Baluchis or Baluch are a slightly dark-skinned semi-nomadic people who live scattered across the Dasht i Margo and Rigestan deserts of southern Afghanistan (Nimruz, Farah, Helmand, and Kandahar provinces). Their language, Baluchi, has elements of Indian-Aryan Dravidian and a larger Farsi-Persian component. Some Baluchis also speak Brahui, which is a Persian language. They spread across the border into Pakistan where they inhabit that country's largest province of Baluchistan. They also live in southwest Iran and, like their counterparts in Pakistan, find themselves at war with the local government. As Sunnis, the Iranian Baluchis resent Shiite discrimination in Iran and feel excluded from development in their own province in Pakistan.

Throughout history the Baluchis served as caravan drivers and often slave raiders. The fiercely independent Baluchis were first conquered by Ahmed Shah Durrani in the eighteenth century but rebelled on several occasions and broke away before they were definitively conquered by Abdur Rahman, Iran, and the British in the nineteenth century. Today the Baluch in Afghanistan number from one hundred thousand to two hundred thousand and are dwarfed by the number of Baluchis in Pakistan and Iran. The Baluchis were mainly engaged in herding and trading before their lands were divided by the Durand Line (which separates Pakistan from Afghanistan) in the late nineteenth century. They do not recognize this border and continue to migrate across it. In the 1980s the Baluch assisted the mujahideen in exchange for money even though the Communists recognized their language as one of the country's official languages for the first time. They are also accused of smuggling weapons to the Taliban today.

The Baluchis are led by tribal Serdars, or Khans, to whom they have considerable loyalty. They also have a code that is similar to the Pashtun code of Pashtunwali, called Baluchmayar. The Baluchis have settled down to a degree in the last half century but still engage in seasonal migrations and herding. Due to their nomadic traditions, their women tend to be freer than the neighboring Pashtuns. Like the Kuchi Pashtun nomads and other semi-nomadic peoples in Afghanistan, the Baluchis are not completely integrated into the urban social system of the country.

Kirghiz

The Kirghiz are an ancient Kipchak Turkic people related to the Uzbeks who live high in the Pamir Mountains of the Wakkhan Corridor, a "peninsula" of land that juts out of northeastern Afghanistan toward China and Pakistan. This high mountainous plateau used to be the summer pasture for the Kirghiz nomads who wandered into these mountains from neighboring China to graze their sheep when the snow melted. But when the borders were sealed and Communists forced other nomads to settle in China, they chose not to return to their summer pastures in China. Instead, this small Kirghiz community kept its original nomadic traditions and continued to live in yurts and graze their animals in the high mountains of the Wakkhan. Although the rest of their kin were Sovietized in the USSR or settled in China and thus lost their ancient traditions, this small Kirghiz community living high in the snow-covered Pamir Mountains retained them. The Kirghiz continued to wear felt-fringed fur hats called *kalpaks* and long woolen jackets and boots, and their women were comparatively free.

In the late twentieth century, the three to five thousand Kirghiz living in Afghanistan were led by a *khan* or *tekin* named Rahman Kul, who lent sheep from his vast flocks to his people to help them survive in their precarious mountain environment. Tragically, the new Afghan Communist government that came to power in 1978 saw Rahman Kul as an enemy and attacked his tribe. Fleeing for their lives, the Kirghiz migrated over the Pakistani border into the neighboring province of Gilgit. There they and their flocks began to die from the heat and unsanitary conditions. Their women, who had never worn veils as nomads, were also forced into seclusion of *purdah*. As their community suffered, the Kirghiz asked for visas to migrate to Alaska, which they thought might resemble their original mountain homeland, but they were denied. Fortunately, in 1982 the republic of Turkey saw them as Turkic *irkdashlar* (kin) and helped just over a thousand of them migrate to a mountainous area in eastern Turkey near the Iranian border (Van area).

Today only a small community of about two thousand Kirghiz remains in the Wakkhan area of Afghanistan. There they continue to lead a nomadic lifestyle under the rule of their native khans. They received international attention when Greg Mortenson, author of the best-selling book *Three Cups of Tea*, described building a school in one of their villages in his second book *Stones into Schools*. Today most Kirghiz live in the former Soviet republic of Kirghizstan (Kyrgyzstan) where they have been settled and Sovietized, or they live in western China where their ancient culture was similarly disrupted by Communism.

Pashai

The Pashai live to the northeast of Kabul and are considered a Dardic (related to the early Aryan-Indian migrations) people, although many speak Pashto. The Pashai are an ancient people who were mentioned by such sources as Marco Polo and the Moghul ruler Babur. They number roughly half a million and are found in the provinces of Kunar, Nuristan, Laghman, Nangarhar, and parts of Kapisa. In the past they were often called Kohistanis (Mountaineers) along with some of the neighboring peoples. They have traditionally been engaged in farming, herding, and timber farming. Many of them fought against the Soviets in the 1980s, including the famous Pashai commander Hazrat Ali. Hazrat Ali played a key role in the Northern Alliance, and his Pashai fighters from the so-called Eastern Alliance joined U.S. Special Forces in attacking Al Qaeda in the mountains of Tora Bora in December 2001's Operation Enduring Freedom. Since then, Hazrat Ali, who has widespread support among his people, was elected to the Wolesi Jirga (Parliament). However, not all Pashai have sided with the government. Those Salafite/Wahhabi-inspired Pashai living in Kunar's remote Korengal Valley are actively involved in the insurgency against the U.S. forces in the region.

Arabs

The Arabs (not to be confused with Arab jihadi volunteers who came to Afghanistan starting in the 1980s to fight the Soviets) are the descendants of the original medieval Arab armies that conquered Afghanistan in the 700s A.D. There is also a large group of Arabs who fled to northern Afghanistan from the Soviet Union in the 1920s to avoid Communism. The Arabs are primarily nomadic pastoralists who live in the mountains and deserts of Afghan Turkistan, with concentrations found around Kunduz and in neighboring Takhar and Baghlan provinces. They lost their Arabic language as early as the time of Babur, who mentioned that they spoke Uzbek and Dari languages, which they continue to speak to this day. There are no estimates on their size, but they probably number under one hundred thousand.

Jats

The Jats are a Pashto- and Dari-speaking Indian-Aryan race that previously ruled Kandahar prior to the Moghul invasions. They later converted to Islam. Like the Kuchis they roam the countryside and cities selling goods. *Jat* is a derogatory term in Afghanistan today (much as *Gypsy* is in parts of Europe) and implies a wandering beggar living on the fringes of society who provides services. Like Gypsies, the Jats engage in fortune-telling, magic tricks, leather working, selling small household items, and the like. Their numbers are unknown. They are also known as Jugis, Gujis, or Gujurs.

Pamiris

The Pamiris are a mixed Ismaili (Shiite) ethnic group living in the Wakkhan Corridor as well as across the Panj and Amu Darya Rivers in neighboring Tajikistan, Pakistan, and China. They are followers of the Agha Khan, a religious head of the Ismaili Shiite sect. Every valley in the region has its own ancient language such as Wakhi, Sanglechi, Munji, Shughni, and Roshani. Their languages are classified as East Iranian and are close to Dari. The Pamiris were ruled for hundreds of years by the Uzbek khans and emirs of Bukhara, and most of them were annexed into the USSR in the 1920s, leaving only a small group in Afghanistan. They are primarily herders and farmers and have played no major role in the recent Afghan conflicts because of their isolation.

Chapter 2

Extreme Geography

The Afghans are extraordinary fighters, tough and resourceful and cruel, and they know their business inside out. On their own territory they are unbeatable. They love fighting and dealing with invaders. It is almost a game to them. The country is Death Valley 10 times over.
—George MacDonald Fraser, *New York Times,* January 20, 2007

This expedition was to be one of my most ambitious in Afghanistan, a ten-hour journey into the Hindu Kush, the majestic mountain chain linked to the nearby Himalayas. This traditionally lawless area—*Hindu Kush* usually translates as "Hindu Killers"—has always fascinated me, in part due to its inaccessible nature and the mysterious race living there. Known as the Hazaras, the Hindu Kush highlanders are Shiites descended from Genghis Khan's Mongol hordes. The Persian-speaking Hazaras were long feared and still live in relative isolation in their snow-capped peaks.

My journey took me out of the bustling city of Kabul, across the Shomali Plain, and up into a valley carved by a fast-flowing mountain river. As we (my driver and I, along with an English colleague) ascended the Ghor-band Valley, the air began to clear and the nature of the terrain changed. No longer in the hot plains, we were enveloped by barren brown mountains that resembled those of the Sinai Desert or Death Valley. Looming high above the brown mountains, snowcaps melted on distant peaks in the warm spring sun. Their snowmelt flowed down the mountainsides in countless rivulets that cooled the air and brought life to this arid valley.

Along the riverbanks the local Hazaras had carefully cultivated fields and built terraced houses out of clay that resembled the pueblos of the Navajos. As our four-wheel-drive SUV drove along the bumpy excuse for a "road," I noticed that the terrain was not the only thing that was changing. Women working in the fields no longer wore blue *burqas.* Instead, they wore brightly colored dresses and head scarves. When our truck passed them on the road, they pulled their head scarves over their lower faces but continued to stare at us with undisguised curiosity. Clearly the Hazaras had more relaxed notions of veiling than other Afghan peoples.

The men—farmers working in the fields or shepherds leading sheep up the mountainsides or along the road in front of us (thus creating the only "traffic jams" we encountered during our absence from Kabul's busy streets)—were friendly and waved at us as we bounced by. Among the most beautiful sights we encountered were men performing their *maghrib* (evening) prayers in the fields, families eating in meadows in the shadow of ruined medieval castles, and boys with trained hunting hawks on their arms.

But all of this bucolic scenery had its dangers too. At one point, on a mountain pass, our driver had to swerve around rocks on the road and I held my breath as I stared straight down at a frothy river hundreds of feet below. On another turn, we saw a truck that had recently rolled off the side of a mountain road and been crushed on the rocks jutting up from the river.

It was this river that ultimately proved to be our nemesis. After five hours of bone-jarring driving that never allowed us to exceed fifteen miles per hour, we arrived in an open valley and found that the road before us had been washed away for over a mile by the river. In the middle of the river we saw two half-submerged trucks that demonstrated the perils of trying to drive through the fast-flowing water. Although our truck tried to plow forward, it had to return to the bank.

Smiling apologetically, our driver explained that we would have to turn back to Kabul. But having made it this far, I was not inclined to go back. Truth be told, I had a second purpose for this journey—to see the famed Buddhist shrine of Bamiyan located high in the mountains. The Taliban had blown up the world-famous stone carvings of Buddha in 2001, but the isolated Bamiyan enclave was said to be among the most beautiful spots in all Central Asia.

"Bale" (OK), I told my driver. "You head back. As for me, I'm going forward." I turned to my travel companion Marcus, an English colleague working on counterterrorism, and he agreed. Although our driver fretted about security and talked of kidnappings and Taliban, we unloaded our bags and headed up the side of a mountain on a local goat path. The last sight our driver had of us was of us foreigners disappearing into the mountains on a quest to see the ruins of the legendary mountain Buddhas of Bamiyan. Having no cell-phone contact with the outside world, we were now truly on our own.

But far from being nervous, I felt liberated. As I looked up at the valley disappearing in the afternoon haze ahead of us and filled my lungs with the cool mountain air, I finally felt free. Free from the confining protection of my Karzai hosts, the pollution of Kabul, and the war that raged in the lowlands. It was now time to explore one of the most isolated regions of Afghanistan, and I could not have been happier.

Unwilling to be stopped in our quest to see the ancient Buddhist shrine of Bamiyan, we abandoned our vehicle at the flooded road and trekked along the side of the river on a mountain path. Fortunately, when we came back down on the other side of the washed-out road, we were able to find two trustworthy-looking villagers to take us the remainder of our trip. Our expedition was back on track after a quintessentially Afghan "detour." For the next five hours we wound our way up the increasingly narrow valley, and finally, when the river gorge dwindled to a mere stream, our straining truck heaved us up a sheer mountainside. As we crested the mountains, the view below us was spectacular, and it felt as if we had reached the top of the fifteen-thousand-foot Hindu Kush range. We had at long last arrived on the mountain plateau known as the Hazarajat. I had been told by many Afghans—including General Dostum, who had visited this spot in his youth—that this was a must-see site, and I was not disappointed.

For two more hours we drove through an almost lunar landscape that was barren but starkly beautiful. The only humans we encountered were the occasional sun-blackened shepherd armed with a hunting rifle.

And then, just as the sun began to set behind the snow-covered mountains, we entered a dark ravine that took us down into the sacred city of Bamiyan. By now it was, however, too dark to see anything, and we considered ourselves lucky to find an open inn (of sorts) and a warm meal of rice pilaf and greasy lamb.

That night we all fell into an exhausted sleep, but the next morning we rushed out to see the full beauty of the vale of Bamiyan below us. As the sun warmed the cool morning air, we gazed down from our hilltop inn on a rather Tibetan-looking landscape. Below us was a world that seemed to be forgotten by time.

Brightly clad local women walked down dirt roads carrying loads on their heads, men ploughed their fields with teams of oxen, and the sounds of the gurgling river made their way up to our vantage point. Behind this scenery, in the background, loomed the massive, sunlit rock face of the mountain of Bamiyan. Carved into the two-thousand-foot mountain "wall" that dominated the village below were hundreds of caves. On the far extremities we could make out the giant carved niches where the world's largest standing statues of Buddha had guarded the valley for fifteen centuries before being blown to smithereens by the Taliban.

Unable to contain our excitement, we drove down across the valley and met a local Hazara named Rami who agreed to act as our guide.

The scenic vale of Bamiyan. The empty space carved into the mountains in the background marks where the Buddhas stood before they were blown up by the Taliban.

For the next two hours we clambered in the dark, centuries-old caverns carved into the sheer cliffs from which the Buddhas had been cut. As we climbed up, I grew dizzy from the height. When we finally stared out over the valley from a narrow passageway carved behind the largest Buddha, I could not bring myself to look down.

Falling hundreds of feet to the rocks below was not the only potential danger we encountered. As we scrambled up the cliffs around the former

Buddha, our guide repeatedly pointed out rocks daubed with red paint, which warned of buried land mines. But the most interesting part of the climb was our descent to the feet of the larger of the crumbled megaliths. Our guide pointed to two blackened holes in the Buddha's feet that were filled with pieces of twisted metal. He explained that these were the remnants of the actual bombs that had been used to bring down the giant stone sentinel. Handing me a piece of the bomb, our guide told me to take it home with me as a testimonial to the tragedy that had occurred there. Saddened by the tragic destruction of the majestic Buddhas, we thanked our guide and continued our exploration of the valley.

Our next climb took us to the top of a ruined castle built on a conical hill dominating the other side of the Bamiyan Valley. This ruin had not been created by the iconoclastic Taliban fanatics but by a far older destroyer, Genghis Khan. Our guide told us that the city had withstood a Mongol siege for months. But then the local sultan's spoiled daughter secretly let the Mongols in through a hidden well to spite her father.

The Mongols subsequently slaughtered everyone in the city, including the traitorous princess, who had expected to receive wealth and power from Genghis Khan. For this reason, the superstitious Hazaras avoided the haunted place and referred to it as Shehar i Gologola, the "Village of the Screams."

* * *

Foreign conquest, revolution, civil war, and oppressive rule have all been imposed upon the people of Afghanistan over time. They have fought back by making use of the country's rugged landscape. The secret to the Hazaras' isolation from waves of conquering armies for example was their skillful use of their area's unique geography to wage war against lowlanders who sought to conquer their mountainous homeland. The Hazaras were skilled marksmen who ambushed invading forces in deadly defiles and fought from hundreds of hilltop forts. Today's Taliban insurgents fighting in the south and east similarly know the country intimately and use this knowledge to wage a deadly guerrilla war against U.S. and Coalition troops. Despite such obvious facts, it is surprising how little most Americans know about the terrain in Afghanistan. Understanding this landscape is key to understanding the war being fought on it.

Although most Americans have a mental image of Afghanistan as a desert wasteland, this image is wrong. Most of Afghanistan is actually made up of hills and mountains, although these tend to be quite dry and resemble the mountains of the American Southwest. Afghanistan's mountains have traditionally defined its politics, religion, military tactics, and ethnic groups more than its deserts. For this reason, it is crucial that outsiders have at least a basic understanding of the Afghan mountain chains and how they shape conflict in this land.

The Hindu Kush

Afghanistan's primary mountain chain is the Hindu Kush. This range has an average height of 4,500 meters (15,000 feet), but it surpasses 6,000 meters (20,000 feet) in some parts. By contrast, the Rockies are considerably smaller, with their highest peak at 4,399 meters (14,000 feet). The Hindu Kush Mountains form the spine of Afghanistan and separate the hot lowlands of the Indian subcontinent from the vast, windswept plains and open deserts of Inner Asia (the modern-day countries of Uzbekistan, Turkmenistan, Kyrgyzstan, and Kazakhstan).

The water runoff from this snowcapped mountain chain pours down to the surrounding drylands and forms the life-giving rivers of Afghanistan and the nearby regions. Afghan rivers typically start as small rivulets in the mountains, then gradually go on to become raging torrents, especially in April and May, when the snowcaps melt. It is not unusual for roads to be washed away by the spring river torrents and for fields in the low-lying plains to be flooded at this time of year. By summer, when Afghanistan is scorched by months of heat and sunshine, many of the mountain streams begin to dry up.

Among the rivers that have their origins in the Hindu Kush are the Helmand and Argahandab, which flow southward through the Pashtun provinces of Kandahar and Helmand and into the Dasht i Margo Desert. In the west, the Hari Rud and Murgab Rivers flow down toward Iran and Turkmenistan. In the north, the Balkhab, Kokcha, and Kunduz Rivers flow northward out of the mountains toward Uzbekistan. And in the east, the Kabul River flows toward Pakistan, where it joins the Indus River and flows out to the Indian Ocean.

Although there is some debate as to the origin of the meaning of *Hindu Kush*, it probably derives from an ancient Indian-Sanskrit word meaning either "Seat of the Hindus" or "Hindu Killers." According to local legend, thousands of Hindu slaves who were used to the heat of India died in these cold mountains—hence the name. This may reflect the fact that the Hindu Kush has traditionally served as a barrier between the cultures of the Indian subcontinent and those of nomadic, Turkic-Mongol Inner Asia.

Technically, *Hindu Kush* actually refers to the easternmost portion of the mountains of Afghanistan. The high peaks found in the northeast of Afghanistan, the so-called true or eastern Hindu Kush, are an extension of the mighty Himalayas and the Pamir Mountains, the so-called Roof of the World. But the term *Hindu Kush* has come to include all of the smaller

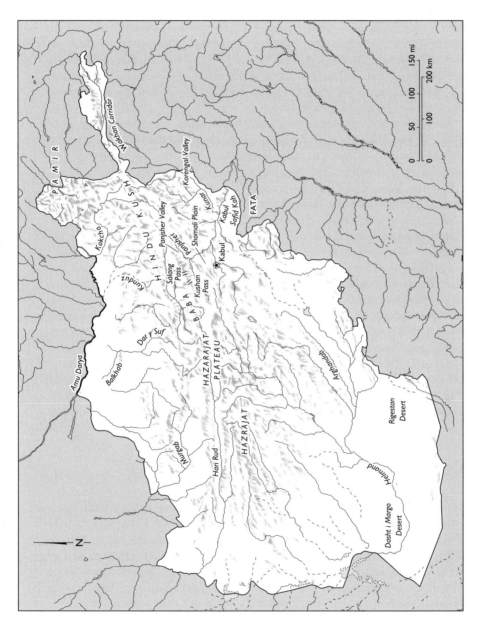

Physical map of Afghanistan.

mountain spurs that radiate off of the Hindu Kush proper in a westward direction toward Iran. These were known in history as the Paropamisus.

As a general rule, the Hindu Kush Mountains begin to lose their height the farther west they extend. The western Hindu Kush spurs include such sub-ranges as the Band e Turkestan, Koh e Baba, Suleiman, Koh e Paghman, Spin Ghar, and Siah Koh. The Hindu Kush and its western sub-chains stretch almost a thousand kilometers (six hundred miles) across the center of Afghanistan and effectively divide the north part of the country from the south.

For this reason the northern plains of Afghan Turkistan have until recently been isolated from the Afghan lands to the south. Until the 1960s, travel from Kabul to the open plains of the north was a dangerous endeavor that involved crossing mountain passes known as *kotals*, which were only open in the warm months. This created communication problems that weakened the Afghan government's control over the northern territories until the Soviets solved the problem for them by building the world's highest mountain car tunnel, the Salang Pass. The pass allows year-round travel between Kabul and the northern provinces. Ironically, in 1979 this "gift to the fraternal people of Afghanistan" also gave the Soviet invaders the means to attack Kabul and resupply their troops during their occupation.

The Salang Pass cuts its way through the mountains from Jabal Saraj (north of Kabul) and winds its way into the snowcaps and crosses the mountains at 3,400 meters (11,000 feet). Travelers who make the spectacular northward journey over the mountains leave the Tajik-dominated Shomali Plain north of Kabul, go through the Salang Tunnel, then descend down a pass into the Uzbek-dominated plains of Afghan Turkistan. The journey from Jabal Saraj to Pul i Kumri, the first noticeable town in the plains, takes six to eight hours.

The Hazarajat

If you turn west at the base of the Salang Pass in the city of Jabal Saraj instead of going straight over the mountains to the north, you can take the scenic Shibar Pass deep into the Hazarajat, the heart of the Hindu Kush Mountains. The Shibar Pass follows a beautiful mountain stream with terraced villages on its banks up to a vast, rugged plateau that forms 30 percent of Afghanistan's land mass. This isolated, rugged heartland is known as the Hazarajat, the land of the Hazaras, and is made up of four provinces: Ghor, Uruzgan, Bamiyan, and Dai Khundi (formerly the northern part of Uruzgan Province). As its name implies, this area is largely inhabited by the Shiite Hazaras.

The Hazarajat was not included in the Sunni Kingdom of Afghanistan until the 1890s when the Afghan ruler Abdur Rahman, the "Iron Amir," used British cannons and guns to conquer it. Prior to their subjugation, the Hazaras lived in comparative isolation from the rest of the Sunni peoples of Afghanistan, secure in their mountain fastness. On occasion their Pashtun (and later Taliban) enemies blockaded the Hazarajat, causing famine and starvation. This rugged area is still isolated from the rest of Afghanistan and is reached only by easily monitored mountain passes. Such inaccessibility might help explain why there has been no Sunni Taliban terrorism against the Shiite Hazaras (a marked contrast to Iraq, where Shiites have taken the brunt of Sunni insurgent attacks on civilians).

The Hazarajat has no cities of any size and is poor in resources (Bamiyan and Yakaolang are its only towns, and they are small). Because of the soil's rocky composition, it also has poor crop yields. But what the windswept Hazarajat plateau lacks in resources it more than makes up for in rugged beauty. As mentioned earlier, among its most noticeable historic sites were the massive stone Buddha statues carved into the sandstone mountains overlooking the scenic village of Bamiyan. These giant megaliths were cut into mountain niches by the long-forgotten Kushans, an ancient Buddhist people whose temples and cave complexes are found dotted throughout the region. Visitors to this peaceful mountain vale have long compared it to the mountain villages of Tibet. Sadly, the massive Buddhas that serenely looked down on the beautiful river-fed valley of Bamiyan for fifteen hundred years were blown up in 2001 by Taliban iconoclasts who considered them "heathen idols."

Traveling westward from Bamiyan, one encounters one of Afghanistan's greatest natural treasures, the magnificent Band e Amir mountain lakes. These turquoise blue lakes are set in a magnificent setting that resembles Yosemite with its natural formations of calcium carbonate.

Traveling farther westward, the main road winds its way out of the mountains and passes a strange minaret standing by itself in the Hindu Kush foothills, the famous Minaret of Jam. Like the Buddhas of Bamiyan and the lakes of Band e Amir, the eleventh-century Minaret of Jam appears on the Afghan currency (the Afghani) and is considered a national treasure.

Moving northward from the Hindu Kush Mountains, one encounters a bleak lunar landscape (the Hindu Kush is largely devoid of trees) that is dissected by the occasional north-flowing river. The most important of these northward-flowing rivers is the Balkhab River, which flows down from the Band e Amir lakes into a widening valley before reaching Mazar i Sharif.

Running parallel to the Balkhab Valley is the Dar y Suf Valley (the Valley of Caves). This valley is a mixed Hazara, Tajik, and Uzbek region known for its coal mines and grazing pastures. Most recently the Dar y Suf Valley was the scene of one of the most successful special forces operations of modern times. In November 2001, two U.S. ODAs (Operational Detachment Alphas—that is, Special Forces A-Teams) saddled up local Uzbek horses and joined Northern Alliance warlords General Rashid Dostum and Ustad Atta in riding down the Dar y Suf Valley toward the northern plains. On November 9, the U.S. Special Forces and their local allies burst out of the valley and destroyed the largest Taliban army in Afghanistan.

The Panjsher Valley

Turning right and going east at Jabal Saraj instead of heading north over the Salang, one enters the narrow entrance to the famous Panjsher, a stunning mountain valley carved by the fast-flowing Panjsher River. This valley, which translates to "Five Lions" Valley, is a natural mountain fortress and was the lair of the famous Afghan mujahideen commander Massoud the Lion of Panjsher.

Soviet forces occupying Afghanistan launched nine major invasions of the Panjsher in the early 1980s and used everything from strategic bombers to heliborne troops to destroy the Tajik mujahideen operating from the valley. Their aim was to eradicate Massoud's supply base and prevent his fighters from sallying forth from the valley to attack their supply convoys on the Doroga Zhizn (Russian for "Road of Life"), the highway stretching from the Soviet border in Uzbekistan over the Salang Pass and down to Kabul.

But on every occasion the hardy Tajik mujahideen retreated up side valleys, mined the Panjsher's main road, launched ambushes, and used the harsh mountain terrain against the Soviets. All of the Soviets' operations failed to destroy Massoud's elusive rebel force. To this very day the scenic valley is littered with the rusting hulks of Soviet tanks and armored personnel carriers.

The Panjsher is an alpine-like world seemingly removed from the rest of Afghanistan. It is almost 100 kilometers (62 miles) in length and has a narrow road cut into its northern bank that runs along the side of the fast-flowing Panjsher River. The locals have built terraced villages and fields on the sides of the narrow valley, and these verdant oases stand in contrast to the bleak, snowcapped mountains towering above them.

Where space allows, the local people have also built small hilltop villages on the banks of the river, including the beautiful village of Jangalak where Massoud's tomb is located. The Panjsher is also known for

Entrance to the Panjsher Valley overseen by a billboard commemorating Ahmad Shah Massoud.

the large quantity of emeralds found in the surrounding mountains. Massoud and his troops used this export commodity to buy arms to fight against the Soviets and later their Taliban enemies from the south. Today the Panjsheris complain that their mountain valley has not been developed like other regions and is accessible only by a tortuous dirt road. Despite its inaccessibility, Kabulis and foreigners living in the capital have begun to travel here on the weekends to get away from the crowds and pollution in the city. Due to its narrow, easily guarded entrance, this valley is very safe for travelers and has seen none of the Taliban terrorism found in other parts of the country.

Badakshan

For all of the Panjsher's legendary appeal, the real heartlands of the Tajiks is found in the neighboring mountain province of Badakshan. Badakhshan and the Panjsher were the only Afghan provinces to totally resist the Taliban, who conquered more than 90 percent of the country by 2001. Massoud kept the Taliban out of Badakshan by building a series of World War I–style trench defenses that stretched their way southward through the neighboring Takhar Province in the west. From there, they cut eastward across the Shomali Plain, which guards the entrance to the Panjsher and over toward Pakistan.

The capital of Massoud's Northern Alliance opposition was in the Badakshani provincial capital of Faizabad, a market town located on the Kochka River that acts as a portal to the mountains of Badakshan. Faizabad is also the main distribution center for Badakshan's bountiful crop of opium. Badakshan ranks second only to Helmand Province in opium production. Badakshan's proximity to Tajikistan facilitates the shipment of opium into post-Soviet Central Asia (the Amu Darya or Penj River separates Badakshani Tajiks from their fellow Tajiks in Tajikistan). Communication between Badakshan and the Panjsher is made possible by the Andjoman Pass, a dangerous foot pass that Alexander the Great crossed in search of the Persian leader Bessus during his conquest of the region in the fourth century B.C.

Badakshan made headlines in August 2010 when a team of ten medical volunteers, including six from the United States, were ambushed and killed there by the Taliban. The Taliban accused members of the team, which included optometrists and dentists who had been administering aid to poor villagers, of trying to spread Christianity.

The Mountains of Nuristan

If you go southward from Badakshan and the Panjsher, you enter the forested mountain provinces of Nuristan. Nuristan, along with Kunar, Logar, and Paktia, is one of Afghanistan's rare forested regions. Unlike neighboring Badakshan, Nuristan's high elevation prevents the cultivation of poppy. Instead, illegal lumbering, mountain sheep herding, and grain growing prevails. The mountain terrain here more closely resembles that of the forested Rockies than the dry desert mountains of the American Southwest that predominate in the rest of Afghanistan. But the comparison ends there. This isolated, cloud-covered region with mountains that soar to six thousand meters (twenty thousand feet) is virtually cut off from the rest of Afghanistan during the winter months. In fact, it was this isolation that kept the ancient proto–Indo European Kafir (later Nuristani) inhabitants of this region free from Muslim rule up until the 1890s.

Fighting ferociously to keep the Muslims out, the Nuristanis built unique terraced houses out of wood, worshipped ancient mountain spirits and gods, and built unique wooden statues of their deceased over their graves. Such statues were considered heathen idols by the Muslims who tried to destroy them. This mountainous realm was also the setting for the movie *The Man Who Would be King* (based on the book of the same name by Rudyard Kipling) and is an extension of the pagan mountain zones in neighboring Pakistan such as the Kalash region of Chitral.

The Afghan ruler Abdur Rahman was, however, able to conquer the various pagan peoples of this land known as Kafiristan (the Land of the Unbelievers) with the help of the British. He then forcefully spread the "light" of Islam to the pagan mountain people and renamed it Nuristan (the Land of Light).

The forested mountains of the Nuristanis form the southern face of the Hindu Kush and look down upon the valley of Jalalabad. They also border the neighboring Pakistani province of Chitral, which was used as a rear-area supply base by the mujahideen in the 1980s. In fact, the jihad uprising against the Communists began in Nuristan and neighboring Kunar (both of which formed a single province at the time) and spread from there throughout the country. During the subsequent war, this area eventually became a "no-go zone" for the Soviets and was organized into an autonomous Wahhabi-fundamentalist *dawlat* (state) by a local mujahideen commander named Maulvi Afzal. The Wahhabis are still influential in the region.

Today it is this proximity to the lawless Pakistani tribal provinces and distance from Kabul that make the "Nuristan-Kunar corridor" such an important hideout and transit route for the Taliban, Al Qaeda, and Gulbuddin Hekmatyar's insurgent group. There have been rumors that Osama bin Laden himself may have also found sanctuary with the Wahhabi-fundamentalists in Nuristan Province, but these rumors have never been substantiated. By 2004, an Arab fighter named Abu Ikhlas al Masri had also established an Afghan-Arab jihadi insurgent group in Nuristan, and his fighters helped the Taliban launch a deadly assault on a U.S. fire base there.

In response to these developments, Regional Command East belatedly enacted Operation Mountain Lion in the summer of 2006, deploying the 10th Mountain Brigade and later the 173rd Airborne to the region to deny the enemy sanctuary in the region. The U.S. forces built command outposts (C.O.P.s) throughout the area at that time. They are currently engaged in surveillance efforts designed to interdict Taliban and Al Qaeda fighters attempting to infiltrate the region from the Pashtun regions of neighboring Pakistan.

The two dozen command outposts in this northeastern area are among the most exposed in all of Afghanistan and are regularly attacked by local insurgents. The U.S. objective in establishing these bases is to maintain a Coalition/government presence and to build roads. This objective is in keeping with former Combined Forces commander General Karl Eikenberry's maxim that "the Taliban begin where the roads end."

The U.S. military also hopes to gain control of such key valleys as the Landay and Nichingal and to displace the Taliban-Hekmatyar insurgents who operate with the support of the local population. A secondary aim is to cut off supply routes from Pakistan, including the Patkyun Pass and Kalash Valley.

Kunar Province

Although most observers see the southern provinces of Helmand and Kandahar as being the heart of the Taliban insurgency, the northeastern border province of Kunar has been described in mythic proportions as one of the most dangerous terrains for U.S. troops anywhere in Afghanistan. U.S. soldiers, who fight a bold enemy in Kunar's rugged mountains, have dubbed it Afghanistan's "Heart of Darkness." In 2007 the province saw 973 insurgent attacks, making it the second most active Afghan province after Kandahar. In 2005 almost one in three U.S. casualties in Afghanistan took place in this small province. In 2010 the movie *Restrepo*, based on Sebastian Junger's harrowing book *War*, brought to life for Western audiences the violent battle to control the Korengal Valley in Kunar. The book and movie chronicle the most dangerous outpost in Afghanistan, named Restrepo for one of the men killed there in combat. This exposed outpost was attacked on a weekly basis and was described as the tip of the spear of U.S. forces in Afghanistan. Sadly, as many as fifty soldiers were killed while fighting in the Korengal before General Stanley McChrystal decided to withdraw troops from the valley in the spring of 2010. In February 2011 U.S. troops were also withdrawn from the nearby Pech Valley after it was determined that their presence there only antagonized the locals and led them to carry out ambushes on U.S. patrols and to attack U.S. combat outposts. By this time the U.S. military had given up on its plans to fight the enemy in the Pech and Korengal Valleys to keep them away from more populated areas. Through trial and error such COIN (Counter Insurgency) tactics were being reconsidered and the cost for holding the Korengal and Pech was deemed too high.

In this region the insurgents wear round *pakols* (felt "berets" of the sort made famous by Massoud), not the black turbans of the southern Taliban. Their battlefield is not the flat open plains or the scrub-covered desert mountains of the south, but rather the forested mountains similar to those found in Colorado's Rockies. What Kunar does share with the southern provinces of Helmand and Kandahar is a "bleed-over" of tribes and loyalties between Pashtuns living in Afghanistan and those found in the Federally Administered Tribal Agencies inside Pakistan (primarily the Bajaur Agency, which shares a border with Kunar).

The combination of lush tree cover, rugged mountains, cross-border sanctuaries, and prickly mountain tribes that resent outside rule is a volatile mixture that has made this prime insurgent territory. This province has been a "no-go zone" since it rose up against the Communists in 1978, and in many ways it remains one today. Kunar made headlines across the world as the location of two of the Coalition's deadliest actions in Afghanistan to date—namely, the June 28, 2005, ambush of a U.S. Navy SEAL team and the shootdown of the Chinook helicopter sent to rescue them (nineteen deaths in all), as well as the summer 2008 swarm attack on a newly built U.S. outpost that almost succeeded in overwhelming the base and led to nine deaths, twenty-one wounded. Both attacks revealed the existence of a bold enemy that had seemingly found the way to use the local terrain and the enemy's unfamiliarity with Kunar's history, tribal politics, culture, and tactics.

Like neighboring Nuristan, Kunar is a rare forested valley carved by the Kunar River, which flows 480 kilometers (300 miles) southward along the Pakistani-Afghan border from Chitral down to the Kabul River near Jalalabad (Kunar Province itself is smaller and has a 175-kilometer [108 mile] border with Pakistan). Along the way, the Kunar is joined by numerous tributaries, such as the Pech Dara, which add to its flow, especially in springtime when the snowpack in the mountains to the north melt. The provincial capital of Asadabad (population 30,000) is found at the confluence of the Pech and Kunar Rivers, one of the province's rare semi-flat areas. Kunar's population is roughly 380,000. Most of the province's inhabitants live in stone-and-timber houses built on the edge of terraced fields on the side of dry, forested mountains. There is very little poppy production in this mountainous region (except in the Pech Valley), and the UN recently declared it poppy-free.

The north-south Kunar Valley parallels the Pakistani border and for centuries has been used as a corridor of communication between the uplands of Badakshan (Tajik territories to the north) and the Pashtun lands of the south. Insurgents have long used the Kunar-Nuristan corridor for attacking Kabul and other parts of Afghanistan. Alexander the Great himself saw the strategic importance of Kunar and invaded the valley in the fourth century B.C. on his way into Bajaur, the tribal land to the east. When he invaded, the local inhabitants burned their houses and fled to wage guerrilla warfare—a style of warfare their descendents would continue to use up to the modern era. In the late nineteenth century, the British found that the best way to suppress the local Pashtuns was to divide their lands artificially and place the Pashtuns of

Bajaur in British India (later Pakistan), leaving the remainder in Kunar, Afghanistan. The artificial "border" did not prevent the Kunari Pashtuns from joining their Bajauri Pashtun kin in waging guerrilla jihad against the British until the 1940s.

The vast majority of the population of Kunar are of course Pashtuns, with the Pech-based Safi tribe being the most prominent (smaller Pashtun tribes and ethnic groups include the Shinwari, Mahmund, Kuchis, Pashai, and Hisarak, as well as others). There are also Pashai and Nuristanis in the province. The Nuristanis and the Pashtuns continued to raid one another until the modern era, even though their conservative Islamic cultures eventually came to resemble one another.

By the mid-twentieth century, these two remote peoples put aside their differences and came to be included in one province known as Kunar (in 2004 Nuristan was administratively separated from Kunar and now forms its own province). Like new converts elsewhere, the Nuristanis became zealots, and the Kunari Pashtuns similarly developed a reputation for being fundamentalists. Fundamentalism came to Kunar in the 1950s via the neighboring Pakistani Pashtun province of Bajaur. Missionaries belonging to the Panjpir fundamentalist Ahl i Hadith movement imported a Wahhabi-Salafite brand of Islamic fundamentalism that took root in the Pech and other tributaries of the Kunar Valley at that time.

The Kunari Pashtuns and the newly converted Nuristianis were driven closer together in 1978 by the clumsy policies of the new Communist government that assumed power in the Saur Revolution of April of that year. Both conservative tribal groups resented the government's interference in their lives and rose up in opposition to Kabul's efforts to arrest their elders, de-emphasize Islam, empower women, and redistribute land. The first sparks of what would become the mujahideen resistance were lit in the mountains of Kunar by the summer of 1978 as local *lashkars* (tribal fighting units) began to attack regional Communist government police and garrisons. Local legend has it that the very first person to fire on the Communists in Afghanistan was a Kunari named Ghazi Yahya Khan Zamani.

The tribal rebels, who were armed with old Mausers and Enfield rifles, were led by a former schoolteacher from the Pech Valley (a side tributary of the Kunar) named Samiullah Safi Wakil. Samiullah Safi organized a Pashtun/Nuristani *lashkar* that marched down the valley from village to village gathering adherents, forcing out local Communists, and attacking government depots for weapons. This snowball effect soon led much of the valley to take up arms and send young men to join the rebels. These ad hoc fighting units initially resisted efforts to join the larger Pakistan-based mujahideen parties and were organized into the Front of the Free Mujahideen or the the Jihad Alliance of the Tribes of Kunar.

The Communist army eventually responded to these attacks by carrying out the systematic massacre of Kunari Pashtuns in the farming village of Kerala (population five thousand) in April 1979. In this tragic event that has come to define the Kunari Pashtuns' deep distrust of outside government forces, Afghan Army troops and Soviet advisors executed and bulldozed almost 1,700 men into a mass grave. The slain men's families fled over the border into the Pakistani province of Bajaur and thus became the first of millions of Afghan war refugees who would soon settle in Pakistan.

More than anything else, this bloody event drove the remainder of the population into the hands of the local *khans* who were leading the rebellion against the Communist government. By the summer of 1979, Kunar had become virtually independent, and the local government forces had been forced into their compound in the provincial capital of Asadabad. This garrison later mutinied and joined the rebels who, for a brief time, seized the provincial capital.

In response to these insurgent activities, the Afghan Communists' Soviet allies helped them shore up garrisons in key areas along the Kunar Valley at Asadabad, Asmar, and Barikot. Although the Soviets initially aimed to hold static positions and allow their Afghan Communist allies to move out into the countryside to fight, they eventually got sucked into the fighting. They launched several large-scale military operations in Kunar designed to open up the valley, including their first major Afghan operation in February–March 1980. The Kunar invasion included some 10,000 Soviet troops backed up by 7,500 Afghan Communist troops. This invasion forced as much as two-thirds of the local population to flee to Pakistan.

Although the Russian *spetsnaz* special forces did occasionally issue out from their bases to destroy mujahideen bases and groups or to launch air assaults to relieve bases, for the most part the Soviets and their Afghan Communist allies remained bottled up in their forts and under a state of siege. Their isolated garrisons were resupplied by Mil 8 transport helicopters since the roads were in the hands of the rebels. The Soviets spent most of their time fighting off local mujahideen swarm attacks and being shelled by rebels who had an almost ritualistic style of warfare.

The Communists responded to these attacks with large, clumsy sweeps and by using close air support from Mil 24 Hind attack helicopters, Sukhoi fighter bombers that led to high civilian casualties. By the mid-1980s Kunar had become, along with the Tajik-dominated Panjsher Valley and Jalaluddin Haqqani's Zadran territory in Khost, one of the "hottest" zones in all of Afghanistan for the Soviets. By this time all the major mujahideen resistance groups had established a presence in the valley, although the forces of the Pashtun fundamentalist commander Gulbuddin Hekmatyar soon came to dominate. However, the independent commander Jamil ur

Rahman from Pech, a Salafite religious leader belonging to the Safi tribe, succeeded in expelling Hekmatyar's Hezb i Islam (Party of Islam) and establishing an independent Wahhabi-style state with Saudi aid. Soon thereafter, scores of Arab jihadis made their way to Kunar via Bajaur to fight the Soviets alongside Rahman. Saudi and Egyptian fighters in particular came to consider the province their home base. One of these Arab volunteer mujahideen, Abu Ikhlas "al Masri" ("the Egyptian"), married a local woman and was to play a key role in reintroducing Arab fighters to Kunar and Nuristan after 2001. He was finally captured by U.S. forces in December 2010.

When the Soviets began to pull out their troops in 1988, the Afghan Communist government saw its position in Kunar as untenable and withdrew troops from the isolated garrisons in the spring. By November of that year, Asadabad had had been taken by the rebels, making it one of the first provincial capitals to fall to the mujahideen. With the removal of the Communists, Jamil ur Rahman set up a Salafite-Wahhabi "Amirate" (religious state) in Kunar. His government was called the Society for the Preaching of the Quran and Sunna in Afghanistan. Jamil ur Rahman crushed all other local fighting groups and struggled to fend off attacks by Gulbuddin Hekmatyar's Hezb i Islam, which aimed to control the entire northeast. Despite some initial success for Jamil ur Rahman, his foe Gulbuddin Hekmatyar (who aimed to be president of Afghanistan) could not allow the existence of an independent fundamentalist Amirate in his own backyard. In August 1991 Hekmatyar launched a major invasion of the Kunar Valley, which led to the death of fifty of Jamil ur Rahman's Arab allies and the sacking of his capital at Asadabad. In response, Jamil ur Rahman fled across the Pakistani border to Bajaur, where he took refuge. On August 30, 1991, he was assassinated by an Egyptian, presumably on Hekmatyar's orders, and the Hezb i Islam took control over most of the valley.

But in 1996, Hezb i Islam's dominance in Kunar was threatened by a new anti-mujahideen force emerging from the south, the Taliban. By late 1996 the Taliban had defeated Hezb i Islam and forced its leader Hekmatyar to flee into exile. The Taliban subsequently claimed the right to rule Kunar. But most local Salafite fundamentalists rejected the Taliban due to their insistence that Taliban leader Mullah Omar was the "Commander of the Faithful" (that is, the caliph), a claim the Salafite puritans did not accept.

The Taliban did appoint a nominal governor to Kunar (Abdul Hadi Akunzade, who served from 1996 to 2001), but his rule was limited to the southern parts of the valley below the provincial capital of Asadabad. Areas to the north remained under the de facto control of local Salafites, Hezb i Islam commanders, and a notorious timber mafia that destroyed much of the region's pristine forests and shipped the lumber to Pakistan (before-and-after satellite images of Kunar from the 1980s to today reveal the widespread nature of this deforestation).

During this period, Kunar became a battlefield between local Salafites, the Hezb i Islam, and the Taliban, with Hezb i Islam and anti-Taliban Salafites coming out on top. While the Taliban attempted to probe deeper up valleys of Kunar, they were ambushed and defeated by Hezb i Islam commander Kashmir Khan. Hundreds of Taliban were killed or captured in the battles with Khan's forces.

When the United States launched Operation Enduring Freedom in October 2001, the locals either waited on the sidelines or assisted their former Taliban and Al Qaeda opponents' escape through their territory into Pakistan; their assistance came either as a result of a feeling of Islamic solidarity or because they were bribed. Hezb i Islam commander Kashmir Khan, for example, bragged of helping Al Qaeda escape over the borders from Kunar into Bajaur. At this time hundreds of Bajauri Pashtun tribesmen crossed into Kunar through the narrow Ghahki Pass to wage jihad against the Americans, but these volunteers were defeated and retreated back to Bajaur with the Taliban governor of Kunar.

With the Taliban removed from the lower Kunar by the end of 2001, the exiled Salafite leader Haji Rohullah returned to the province and eventually participated in the first Loya Jirga (Parliament) in Kabul in June 2002. Until this time period, this prickly province seemed to be integrating smoothly with the new regime in Kabul. But this was Kunar, the land that had first raised the flag of rebellion against the Communists in 1978, and it was clear that there were anti-government elements using its mountains as a sanctuary. Many voices, including that of Pakistani leader Pervez Musharraf, began to claim that bin Laden was in the Kunar Valley, not in Pakistan. But locals who were familiar with Kunar Province's Salafites and their distrust of the Taliban disagreed.

Although it is doubtful that bin Laden was ever hiding in Kunar or Nuristan (his ties were more with the Pakistani Pashtun agencies of North and South Waziristan), locals began to turn against the government and its Coalition allies in June 2002 when an elder who was wanted by the Americans was taken to their headquarters. He subsequently died under mysterious circumstances. When his body was released two days later (one popular account said it was thrown on the side of the road), the locals decided to revolt, much as they had in the original 1978 revolt against the Communists. Rumor of the elder's death spread far and wide and drove many to see the Coalition as the enemy.

If this were not enough, the locals began to complain that policemen sent to the province from Kabul were extorting money from them. To compound matters further, the recently returned Salafite leader Haji

Rohullah was arrested by the Coalition on grounds that he was collaborating with the Taliban (although this may have been based on bad intelligence). As these events were taking place, the local Salafites began to lose power as their leaders were displaced by government professionals sent to rule the province from Kabul. This bred further resentment toward the Karzai government.

Fears that Kunar would turn on the Coalition were borne out soon thereafter. Fighting began in late 2002 as the 82nd Airborne arrived in the valley. Kashmir Khan, the Hezb i Islam commander who had earlier fought the Taliban, seemed to be leading the revolt.

In an effort to flush out Kashmir Khan's Hezb i Islam fighters as well as dozens of foreign fighters led by Abu Ikhlas "al Masri," who was declared Al Qaeda's *amir* (commander) in Kunar and Nuristan, the United States launched Operation Mountain Resolve on November 7, 2003. This operation involved a Soviet-style airdrop into the Hindu Kush mountains by the U.S. 10th Mountain Division and resulted in the killing of Hezb i Islam commander Ghulam Sakhee, a few clashes with the enemy, and the discovery of some weapon caches. The U.S. forces received close air support from A-10 Warthogs that operated in a similar fashion to Sukhoi "Grachs" (Ravens) in the earlier Soviet operations.

The next U.S. operation was Operation Red Wing on June 28, 2005. This small operation involved the insertion of four elite Navy SEALs into Kunar to track and kill Ahmed Shah Ismail. Ismail was a mid-level Taliban/Al Qaeda commander said to be leading a group of two hundred to three hundred Afghan and Arab fighters calling themselves the Bara Bin Malek. The operation failed spectacularly when the Navy SEAL team, operating on a ten-thousand-foot-high ridge known as Abas Ghar, was spotted by some local shepherds. Rather than kill the unarmed shepherds, the Navy SEALs let them go. The shepherds promptly informed Ahmed Shah Ismail, who sent roughly 140 fighters to surround and attack the SEALs. The SEALs urgently called for reinforcements, which arrived in the form of two MH-47 Chinook helicopters, four UH-60 Black Hawks, and two AH-64D Apache Longbows.

But one of the Chinooks carrying SEALs was shot down en route by a Taliban RPG (rocket-propelled grenade) round that entered the back bay door. Sixteen soldiers, a combination of SEALs and Nightstalker airmen, were killed in the ensuing crash, the single greatest U.S. death toll in Operation Enduring Freedom to date. It was also the second shootdown of a U.S. helicopter in the Afghan theater of operations.

Meanwhile, three of the encircled Navy SEALs on the ground were killed and the fourth escaped. He was saved by a local Pashtun shepherd who offered him *melmastiia* (the Pashtun code of protection) against his pursuers. The story of this tragedy, the worst loss of Navy SEALs in history, was vividly recounted in a *Time* magazine articled titled "How the Shepherd Saved the SEAL" and a book titled *Lone Survivor: The Eyewitness Account of Operation Redwing and the Lost Heroes of SEAL Team 10*. Incidentally, the target of this failed operation, Ahmed Shah Ismail, escaped his pursuers and survived a subsequent B-52 strike on his compound, but he was eventually killed two years later.

In the aftermath of this debacle, Regional Command East decided that the Kunar and neighboring province of Nuristan needed a greater military presence and launched Operation Whaler in August 2005, Operation Pil in October 2005, and Operation Mountain Lion in April 2006. Hundreds of Taliban and Hezb i Islam fighters were killed in these operations. Since then, Regional Command East has also been active in building roads (including a $7.5 million dollar road linking the Pech Valley to Asadabad), bridges, schools, and other Provisional Reconstruction Team projects as part of a "hearts and minds" strategy.

But the military has chosen to use the stick as well as the carrot and has been active in establishing forward operating bases far from the town centers controlled by the Soviets in the 1980s. This has meant establishing a U.S. presence (the Marines, 173rd Airborne Brigade, 10th Mountain Division, and 503rd Infantry Regiment have all been involved) deep inside a countryside that is hostile to the Coalition and generally supportive of the Pashtun, Pashai, Nuristani, and Arab insurgents. The new counterinsurgency strategy has involved constructing small, platoon-size outposts throughout the province. These have become magnets for local insurgent attacks, which are often filmed and posted online by U.S. troops. The Taliban also post regular online accounts of their attacks, including the following typical report, which states, "Mujahideen of Islamic Emirate of Afghanistan, with heavy and light weapons attacked a puppet police checkpoint near Asadabad city of Kunar province. In the attack the checkpoint was demolished, nine puppet terrorists were killed and their arms were booty, two Mujahideen were also wounded in the fighting." Another Taliban report states, "Mujahideen of Islamic Emirate of Afghanistan, attacked a foot patrolling unit of American occupation army in Korengal area of Kunar province. In the attack a firefight started which lasted for one hour, during which four American terrorists were killed and many were wounded." In response, the U.S. troops in these bases have also posted harrowing footage of themselves fighting off insurgent attacks.

Although this forward base policy has increased U.S. casualties in the region, it has also extended the writ of the Afghan government to places where there has been no government presence for decades. It has also helped cut off insurgent "rat lines" over the Ghahki and Nawa Passes from Pakistan into Kunar and on to Nuristan.

There has been some fascinating media coverage of life in these exposed command outposts that brings to life the daily hazards that come from regular insurgent assaults. Elizabeth Rubin's *New York Times Magazine* article titled "Battle Company Is Out There" (February 24, 2008) addresses one such base in the Salafite-Wahhabi-dominated Korengal Valley. The Korengal sub-valley, which is located in the mountains to the west of Asadabad, is inhabited by an ethnic group known as Pashais. Rubin interviewed one soldier from the 173rd at Korengal Operating Post (KOP) and wrote the following account of life in this dangerous place:

> As hard as Iraq was, he [Dan Kearney] said, nothing was as tough as the Korengal. Unlike in Iraq, where the captains and lieutenants could let down their guard in a relatively safe, fortified operating base, swapping stories and ideas, here they had no one to talk to and were almost as vulnerable to enemy fire inside the wire as out. Last summer, insurgents stormed one of the bases in a nearby valley and wounded sixteen.
>
> And unlike every other place I've been in Afghanistan—even the Pech River valley, just an hour's drive away—the Korengal had no Afghan police or district leaders for the Americans to work with. The Afghan government, and Afghans down the valley, seemed to have washed their hands of the Korengalis. As Kearney put it to me one day at the KOP (Korengal Out Post), the Korengal is like a tough Los Angeles neighborhood "and we're the L.A.P.D. kicking in the door, arresting guys, demanding information about the gangs, and slowly the people say, 'No, we don't know anything, because that guy in the gang, he's with my sister, and that other guy, he's my uncle's cousin.' Now we've angered them for so many years that they've decided: 'I'm gonna stick with the A.C.M.'"—anticoalition militants —"'who are my brothers and I'm not gonna rat them out.'"

The story of the insurgency in Korengal Valley begins with the Americans getting caught up in a feud between two tribal rivals from the nearby Pech Valley. The Americans were duped into bombing the house of a local lumber magnate named Haji Matin. Several of Haji Matin's family members were killed in the attack. To gain revenge he took his men over to the Al Qaeda commander Abu Ikhlas "al Masri" and began to fight the Americans. As more blood was spilled, Matin's *lashkar* gathered up the support of locals in the Korengal who made it their mission to destroy the U.S. forward operating post in their valley.

Since then, the Korengal has been ground zero for some of the toughest fighting in Kunar and all of Afghanistan. Sebastian Junger captured the intensity of the struggle for Korengal in his masterful December 2007 *Vanity Fair* article "Into the Valley of Death," in which he wrote:

> The Korengal is widely considered to be the most dangerous valley in northeastern Afghanistan, and Second Platoon is considered the tip of the spear for the American forces there. Nearly one-fifth of all combat in Afghanistan occurs in this valley, and nearly three-quarters of all the bombs dropped

by NATO forces in Afghanistan are dropped in the surrounding area. The fighting is on foot and it is deadly, and the zone of American control moves hilltop by hilltop, ridge by ridge, a hundred yards at a time. There is literally no safe place in the Korengal Valley. Men have been shot while asleep in their barracks tents.

The enemy in Korengal and nearby Pech consists of a variety of fighters belonging to Kashmir Khan's Hezb i Islam faction, Abu Ikhlas "al Masri's" Al Qaeda, Taliban fighters led by Dost Muhammad and Qara Ziaur Rahman, Nuristanis led by Mullah Munibullah, Arab fighters from a group calling itself Jamiat-e Dawa el al Qurani Wasouna, Pakistani volunteers, and local P.O.A.s (in U.S. military terms, "pissed-off Afghans") who resent the presence of "infidels" or any outsiders in their valleys. Between these groups, they have hundreds of fighters who routinely ambush U.S. patrols, plant IEDs, snipe at exposed soldiers, shell observation posts, and on occasion even attempt to storm forward operating bases.

This last point was vividly demonstrated in one of the boldest insurgent attacks in Afghanistan to date, the July 13, 2008, mass assault on a partially established overt observation post in the Kunar/Nuristani border village of Wanat (north of Korengal). The attack was launched by Hezb i Islam commander Maulawi Usman and involved between two hundred and four hundred Arab and Afghan fighters in a pre-dawn ambush on forty-five Americans and twenty-five Afghan Army soldiers. The U.S. and Afghan troops were in the process of setting up a base and were protected only by concertina barbed wire, earthen barriers, and a wall of Humvees when they were attacked. The attackers quickly succeeded in destroying the Coalition forces' mortar, TOW missile, and LRAS surveillance system. Then they almost overran a small observation post 50 meters (164 feet) outside of the base perimeter, killing several American soldiers stationed there. The insurgents then swarmed the post for eight hours using RPGs, AK-47s, grenades, and PK machine guns. At one point they breached the post and fighting was done face-to-face before the insurgents were repulsed. In the eight-hour firefight the Americans came close to being overrun and were only saved when A-10s, F-15s, Apaches, and a Predator drone bombed and strafed the perimeter of the base.

When the smoke cleared, nine members of Chosen Company serving in Wanat had been killed, twenty-one were wounded, and four allied Afghan soldiers were wounded. Between fifteen and forty enemy fighters were also killed in the assault. It was America's greatest firefight loss in the Afghan theater of operations to date. The cost could have been much higher, as the enemy was clearly trying to overrun the base and gain a public relations victory. The Taliban subsequently proclaimed, "Now, instead of firing at the bases from far away, the Taliban has the ability to enter the bases and kill Americans." Although the attack was a military failure, it was a strategic success. Three days later the U.S. military decided to evacuate the base. The Taliban subsequently proclaimed, "It boosted our morale and we will now plan another such attack on the enemy."

Although the United States still sends patrols to Wanat, the area has been effectively turned over to the enemy, who claim that they received support from the locals after a "collateral damage" killing of some of their people by an errant Coalition air strike. From a wider perspective, the United States has very little presence along the porous Kunar-Bajaur border, and its authority is largely limited to the Jalalabad-Asadabad-Asmar highway, the same area the Soviets tried to control in the 1980s. The arrival in Kunar of thousands of Pashtun refugees fleeing a Pakistani offensive across the border in Bajaur in the fall of 2008 also exacerbated problems. The problem may, however, be mitigated by the Pakistani army's success in taking back much of Bajaur Agency from the local Taliban in late October 2008.

Thus a pattern of revenge killing, spontaneous tribal jihad, and counterinsurgency that dates back thirty years to the original *lashkar* uprising against the Afghan Communist regime continues in the Kunar Valley and its tributaries. Although the Coalition has advantages over its Soviet predecessors in terms of surveillance, "HUMINT" (human intelligence), training, equipment, and fighting spirit, it will doubtless continue to sustain heavy losses as it fights valley by valley for control of Kunar. In Syed Saleem Shahzad's *Asia Times* article titled "At War with the Taliban: A Fighter and a Financier" (May 23, 2008), Qara Ziaur Rahman, the overall Taliban commander for Kunar, Bajaur, and Nuristan, summed up the importance of this battle for Kunar:

> From the Soviet days in Afghanistan, Kunar's importance has been clear. This is a border province and trouble here can break the central government. Whoever has been defeated in Afghanistan, his defeat began from Kunar. Hence, everybody is terrified of this region. The Soviets were defeated in this province and NATO knows that if it is defeated here it will be defeated all over Afghanistan.

Spin Ghar (Safid Koh) Mountains

Proceeding southward from the forested mountains of Nuristan and Kunar Province, one encounters a broad east-west valley carved out by the Kabul River. This river threads its way down through a narrow gorge known as the Silk Gorge where British troops were annihilated by the Pashtuns in 1842. The Silk Gorge opens as it descends toward Pakistan from Kabul to the Afghan king's winter capital of Jalalabad, which is located near the Pakistani border. From there the Kabul River flows eastward toward the Pakistani town of Peshawar (which served as the primary center for the mujahideen in the 1980s) via the Khyber Pass. There it eventually joins the mighty Indus River and flows out to the Indian Ocean.

Moving southward past this valley, one encounters a mountain chain known as the Spin Ghar (White Mountains, or Safid Koh in Persian) which extends latitudinally from west to east along the southern flank of the Kabul River. This mountain range crosses the Pakistani-Afghan border and stretches about 160 kilometers (99.4 miles) from east to west. It also has spurs going in a north-south direction parallel to the Pakistani-Afghan border. The Spin Ghar has several peaks over 4,000 meters (13,000 feet) and is less forested than Nuristan and Kunar. Most of the east-west section of this mountain range is found in southern Nangahar Province, while the north-south sections are found in Paktia, Paktika, and Khost Provinces.

The Nangahar (east-west) section of the Spin Ghar Mountains was a favorite jihadi stomping ground for bin Laden and other Arab volunteers who crossed into its peaks from the neighboring Pashtun provinces of Pakistan (namely the Kurram and Waziristan Agencies) in the 1980s. Bin Laden established a series of bases in its foothills near the city of Jalalabad at Darunta as well as a series of fallback bases in the snowcapped mountains near Tora Bora.

When bin Laden, Ayman al Zawahiri, and many other Al Qaeda Arabs fled Afghanistan in December 2001, they retreated into these mountains and crossed into the neighboring region of Pakistan. But not before they were pummeled in their caves at a place called Tora Bora in mid-December by the U.S. Air Force (contrary to media reports, there was no massive underground base at Tora Bora).

The exhausted Arabs descended into Pakistan after crossing the high peaks of the Spin Ghar and found themselves in the so-called Parchinar Beak. This is a piece of Pakistani territory that juts into Afghanistan and has long acted as a launching pad or fallback area for Pakistani-sponsored mujahideen, Taliban, and Arab jihadis.

The southern Parchinar Beak protrudes toward the south-north spur of the Spin Ghar Mountains that runs parallel with the Pakistani-Afghan border. There these mountains are known by several names, such as the Shinkay, Armal, Sodyaki Ghar, and Moghulgi Ghar Mountains. The Afghan border provinces traversed by this section of the Spin Ghar Mountains include Paktia, Paktika, and Khost. The southern spur of these mountains was used by such local Afghan mujahideen commanders as Abdul Rasul Sayyaf (a Saudi-funded fundamentalist) and Jalaluddin Haqqani as bases of operation during the 1980s.

It was in these mountains that Haqqani and the Arabs built their famous cave complexes, including the labyrinth supply depot of Zawar Kili. Zawar Kili, which lies right on a supply line to the Parchinar Beak near the Pakistani border, was heavily bombed by U.S. forces in January 2002. But it was the nearby mountain base at Jaji (southern Paktia Province) that achieved legendary status as the Arab cave complex where bin Laden received his baptism by fire in 1987. In this firefight (bin Laden's only real military action in the war), bin Laden and a group of approximately twenty-five Arabs and twenty-five Afghans held off a Russian *spetsnaz* attack and sustained heavy losses before eventually retreating back to Pakistan.

It was also in the Spin Ghar Mountains of southern Paktia Province that as many as 250 Al Qaeda Arabs regrouped after the fall of Kandahar in the winter of 2001–2002. The United States subsequently flushed them out of these mountain positions in the Shah i Kot Valley (in an operation known as Operation Anaconda) in February 2002. The entrenched Arabs used the natural terrain to fight back, much as their Arab mujahideen predecessors had at Jaji in 1987, and several U.S. servicemen lost their lives in the so-called Chinook Down episode in these high peaks.

Today the pro-Taliban Haqqani network has its base in the southern extension of the Spin Ghar Mountains and uses the cover the mountains provide to launch attacks into Khost, Paktia, Paktika, and Ghazni Provinces. Typically the insurgents wait until the snow on the mountain passes thaws in April to mount their offensives from the neighboring Pakistani-Pashtun provinces of North and South Waziristan. The tribes of this region extend across the borders and have traditionally facilitated the transfer of munitions, supplies, and fighters. To prevent such cross-border support for the insurgents, the United States constructed a "border coordination center" in a hostile area known as "Hotel Taliban" (the southern Spin Ghar Mountains at Spera, just south of Khost) in the spring of 2008.

As the mountains level out to the south toward Zabul and Kandahar, it becomes harder for the insurgents to infiltrate the border. It should also be noted that the prickly Pashtun tribes in this mountainous zone stretching from Nuristan to the southern Spin Ghar have kept their tribal identities more than their lowland kin living in the plains in the southern provinces of Helmand and Kandahar.

The Pamirs

The Pamirs, the "mother of all mountains," are located in the far northeast of Afghanistan and are so high that they are more accurately a part of the Himalayas and Tian Shan (Heavenly Mountains) chains. This remote area, which has several peaks that reach 6,000 meters (19,700 feet), is located in a strange strip of land that was artificially attached to the northeast of Afghanistan in the 1890s by the British. This narrow strip of land jutting out from Afghanistan, known as the Wakkhan Corridor, was added to the Afghan Kingdom to act as an artificial buffer or "imperial shock absorber" between the expanding British and Russian empires.

The Wakkhan Corridor is part of Badakshan Province and stretches 300 kilometers (187 miles), separating the ex-Soviet country of Tajikistan from Pakistan. It is very narrow from north to south, reaching around 20 kilometers (12.4 miles) in width in some sections.

The Wakkhan consists of mountain grazing pastures and turquoise blue lakes. It is covered by snow half the year and is the home of the Turkic highland shepherds known as Kirghiz who still live in *yurts* (portable tents). It is also the home of an Ismaili Shiite people known as the Wakhi. Afghanistan's highest peak, Mount Nurshak (7,485 meters [24,557 feet]) is found here.

Although the Soviets contemplated annexing this area directly and deployed forces here in the 1980s, thus disrupting the nomads' ancient migration patterns, the Wakkhan did not play a major role in the anti-Soviet jihad. It is also too high and remote to play a key role in the current insurgency. In addition, the people living here are moderates who have no ties to the Pashtun Taliban insurgents in the south. There are, however, reports of some drug smuggling in the region, but most of the drugs go through to Central Asia from the lands of Badakshan proper in the lowlands.

Key Strategic Areas

Afghan Turkistan

This is a roughly defined area whose borders are marked by the Murgab River in the west, the Amu Darya (Oxus) River in the north, the Kunduz River in the east, and the Hindu Kush Mountains in the south. This flatland was lopped off of the Uzbek, Turkmen, and Tajik lands of the north in the mid-nineteenth century by the Afghan government. Although it has been forcefully included in the Afghan-Pashtun state, this open plain—which is covered by hills in the south and flatlands of camel thorns and scrubs in the north—is geographically part of the vast Inner Asian *steppes* (dry plains) that extend to Mongolia, Siberia, and the Ukraine.

For centuries the Bactrian, Scythian, Hun, Turk, Mongol, Turkmen, and Uzbek horsemen roamed across this dry steppe land. Today the Turkic descendants of these nomadic nations call this realm home—hence its name Turkistan. This plain is hot in the summer (temperatures reach 120 degrees Fahrenheit) and cold in the winter as winds blow down from Siberia and Central Asia.

Although Turkistan resembles a desert, especially the stretch between the Amu Darya River and Mazar i Sharif (an area Alexander the Great crossed with great difficulty), it is rich in agriculture, natural gas, and the products of livestock grown by the local Uzbek and Turkmen herdsmen. One of Afghanistan's rare legal export commodities, natural gas, is exported from a natural gas field near Sheberghan in western Turkistan to neighboring Turkmenistan. The local shepherds' famous red Turkmen carpets and Karakul lamb's wool are also sold internationally. Agriculture is made possible on this sandy plain through the use of artificial irrigation from the Murgab, Balkhab, and Kunduz Rivers.

Generally speaking, this plain turns into a desert to the north of Mazar i Sharif and northwest of Sheberghan. This area is famous for its *khakbads*, sand tornadoes that pop up and down on the horizon and sometimes pelt you with sand if you get hit by them. In the south, Turkistan is made up of rolling hills that receive runoff water from the Hindu Kush. The locals call these sandy hills *chol*. Uzbek semi-nomads grow wheat and graze their herds in these barren loess hills and live in yurt-like tents in the summer, much as their ancestors did.

Afghan Turkistan's proximity to the former USSR and its flat, open aspect made it easier for the Soviets to control it in the 1980s, although there were Turkmen, Tajik, and Uzbek mujahideen operating in the area. General Dostum's pro-Communist horsemen, however, were effective in eradicating the mujahideen rebels in this area and protecting the roads and refineries from mujahideen rebel attacks. Today the region's local trade is with the ex-Soviet republics to the north, and for this reason many Afghan Uzbeks have adopted aspects of Sovietized (secularized) Uzbekistani culture.

It is important to note that the nineteenth-century Afghan Pashtun ruler Abdur Rahman earned his moniker "the Iron Amir" by absorbing this region in a series of bloody conquests. During the region's conquests by the Afghan-Pashtuns, local *aq saqals* (elders) were tied to cannons and blown to bits over their fellow villagers, thousands were massacred or enslaved, and Pashtuns from the south were forcefully settled across the land as "internal colonists." Not surprisingly, the northerners resent the southern Pashtuns who were planted in their midst in the regions of Bala Murgab, Sheberghan, Balkh, and Kunduz. Incidentally, the insurgent leader and head of the fundamentalist Hezb i Islam Party, Gulbuddin Hekmatyar, comes from the northern town of Kunduz, where there is a large Pashtun population.

Uzbek girls outside their yurt in the northern hills of the Hindu Kush.

In the 1990s General Dostum contemplated cutting off this area from the Pashtun-dominated land of Afghanistan. But Dostum was ultimately defeated by the Taliban in 1998 and forced to flee to Turkey and Iran. As the Taliban attacked Dostum, local Pashtuns whose ancestors had been transplanted to the north by the Iron Amir in the nineteenth century attacked Dostum from Balkh and welcomed their kin from the south as liberators. Today many of these same Pashtuns protect Taliban insurgents who are increasingly infiltrating and fighting with the German NATO contingent in Kunduz in the east and Badghis in the west.

From 1998 to 2001 Kunduz and Mazar i Sharif also served as the bases for the Al Qaeda–linked Uzbekistani jihadi-terrorist group, the Islamic Movement of Uzbekistan (IMU). Every summer this group's fighters infiltrated neighboring Tajikistan, Kyrgyzstan, and Uzbekistan to wage holy war against the region's secular governments. The IMU jihadis were, however, chased to the Waziristan region of Pakistan or killed in 2001's Operation Enduring Freedom.

Afghan Turkistan also hosts Afghanistan's most holy site, the *mazar* (tomb) of Ali, the son-in-law of the Prophet Muhammad, in Mazar i Sharif (Afghans believe Ali's body is here, not in Najaf, Iraq like most Muslims do). This shrine, known as the Rowza, is also the site of the tombs of several key Afghan rulers and is said to have curative powers. Those who wish to rule Afghanistan often gain control of this shrine to claim that they have a mandate to rule before they march on to Kabul. On two occasions in recent history (1992 and 2001) the Uzbek general Dostum has helped overthrow Pashtun governments by symbolically taking this city.

Afghan Turkistan is also home to Balkh, the birthplace of the Prophet Zoroaster and one of the world's oldest cities. Balkh was called the "Mother of all Cities" by the Arabs and was the seat of the heir to the throne of the Uzbek Khanate of Bukhara until it was annexed by the Pashtuns in the nineteenth century.

Shomali Plain

This rich plain on a plateau about half an hour's drive north of Kabul was formerly the vineyard and breadbasket of Afghanistan. Prior to the Afghan civil war of 1992–2001, it was a well-watered land of mud-walled villages inhabited by Tajik farmers. When the Taliban seized Kabul in 1996, Massoud and his Tajik army withdrew to the north and drew a defensive line across the Shomali Plain. Massoud's troops eventually dug trenches that stretched through Bagram Airfield (the base built by the Soviets) to keep the Taliban from advancing any further.

Although these static lines kept the Taliban out of the strategic Panjsher Valley and province of Badakshan, they wreaked havoc on the plain around them. As the Taliban and Northern Alliance planted land mines and shelled each other's lines, the Shomali became a wasteland. It was transformed into one of the world's largest land-mine fields in the process. One can still see red painted rocks (a land-mine warning sign) lying on the edge of the highway that runs along the western side of the Shomali. The destruction of this agrarian zone was further hastened when the Taliban cleansed much of the distrusted Tajik population from the plain from 1999 to 2001.

When the United States launched Operation Enduring Freedom in 2001, Massoud's successor, Fahim Khan, promised to move against the Taliban army in the Shomali. But his men remained in their trenches until Dostum's force of two thousand horsemen got the ball rolling and took Mazar i Sharif in November 2001. As the momentum turned against the Taliban, Fahim Khan's faction finally moved down the highway to Kabul and pushed aside a collapsing Taliban army in the Shomali.

Today this area is undergoing intensive de-mining, and tens of thousands of Tajik refugees have returned to their home villages to rebuild their lives. The Shomali is a relatively safe area for Coalition forces, with only one major attack taking place there—a suicide bombing at Bagram Air Base during Vice President Dick Cheney's February 2007 visit.

Ghazni

This Pashtun province located two hours southwest from the Afghan capital on the Kabul-to-Kandahar highway is known for its medieval walls and castle. There are ruins in the area, including the famous Tower of Ghazni, dating back to the late medieval period when Ghazni was the capital of the Ghaznavid Empire (a militant Muslim state that conquered much of India in the twelfth century). In the nineteenth century Ghazni guarded the route to Kabul, and the British took Kabul only after storming the city's seemingly impregnable fortress in 1839. When the British took Ghazni, the Afghan ruler, Dost Muhammad, saw the writing on the wall and surrendered to the British. This is a historical precedent that is not lost on the Taliban, who see Ghazni as the gateway to Kabul.

In the 1980s the mujahideen attacked Soviet convoys traveling on the Kabul-to-Kandahar highway from the region's dry hills. Today the Taliban have similarly begun to ambush police and supply convoys in this region. In July 2007 the Taliban carried out Afghanistan's largest kidnapping when it captured a busload of Korean Christian missionaries foolishly driving through Ghazni on their way to the Taliban's spiritual capital of Kandahar. Bold Taliban insurgents have also attempted to kill Ghazni's current governor and actually succeeded in killing a former one.

The Taliban insurgents in Ghazni suffered casualties in 2006's Operation Mountain Fury (a joint Canadian, British, Afghan, and U.S. assault on the Taliban in Ghazni, Helmand, Uruzgan, Kandahar, and Zabul that saw more than 1,000 Taliban killed and more than 150 Coalition troops killed in the spring of 2006). In April 2007 the Taliban took control of Ghazni's Giro District and killed the chief of police but withdrew soon thereafter. However, for all their losses, the Taliban have been able to set up checkpoints on the Ghazni sections of the Kabul-to-Kandahar Highway, and they have managed to control many districts by night. The Taliban have killed teachers and executed suspected spies throughout the province. The increasingly bold insurgents have also burned down schools, kidnapped workers on reconstruction projects, planted IEDs, burned the local government headquarters in Maqur District, and killed the district chief. The skeletons of burnt-out Coalition trucks that litter the side of the highway that passes through Ghazni are vivid testimony to the dangers of traversing this contested Pashtun province so close to Kabul.

Uruzgan

Uruzgan (whose capital is Tarin Kowt) is a hilly province in central Afghanistan. It was cut in half in 2004, and the northern half where Hazaras lived was made into a new province known as Day Khundi. The southern portion, the Pashtun-dominated section of the south retained the name Uruzgan, and has the distinction of being the former home province of Mullah Omar. For this reason it is not surprising that it has been a hotbed of insurgent activity. The Dutch, and to a lesser extent the Australians, who took over security in this region in August 2006 have been engaged in regular gun battles with Taliban insurgents who are trying to stake out a claim to the province.

Although the Dutch initially thought their task would be to engage in hearts-and-minds projects such as developing bridges, roads, and irrigation, the Taliban infiltrated the region and drove much of the population out in 2007. Without a local population to win over, the Dutch and Australians became engaged in efforts to flush Taliban insurgents out of contested districts such as Deh Rawood and Chora. The Taliban have lost hundreds of fighters in these operations.

But it has not been a one-sided affair. The Dutch have suffered casualties from suicide bombings, IEDs, ambushes, and bold assaults. And the local population has suffered casualties in the war. Uruzgan made world news in 2007 when a sixty-year-old grandmother and her seven-year-old son were executed by the Taliban as "spies" after the Taliban found a U.S. dollar on the boy. Although Operation Mountain Thrust pushed the Taliban out of some of their strongholds, they continue to harass Afghan government and NATO troops throughout the province. Efforts continue to push the Taliban out of Chora District, where there has been considerable fighting, and Gizab, which is Uruzgan Province's most dangerous district. A key objective has been to beat back Taliban who are attempting to control the strategic Baluchi Pass and take back the Chora District.

On August 8, 2007, Uruzgan again made headlines when a group of approximately seventy Taliban insurgents launched a rare frontal assault on a U.S. forward operating base known as Firebase Anaconda. In the ensuing attack, which was described as "brazen," more than two dozen Taliban were killed while the United States sustained no casualties.

If fighting off Taliban frontal and asymmetric attacks was not a sufficient task for Coalition forces in Uruzgan, poppy production in the province has increased since 2005, and Uruzgan is now a major opium-producing region. The Coalition has had some success in suppressing the trade, taking out Taliban safe houses, killing insurgents (including one ambush that is reported to have killed more than fifty), and using close air support to compensate for their lack of numbers. The Dutch contingent in Uruzgan fought well despite being hampered by a parliament back home that was afraid of casualties. In August 2010 the Dutch withdrew their two-thousand-man contingent from the province and from Afghanistan after their parliament voted to end their participation in the war.

Panjwai District (Kandahar)

The Panjwai District is located twenty kilometers (twelve miles) to the west of Afghanistan's second-largest city and spiritual capital for the Taliban, Kandahar City. The Taliban have infiltrated this agricultural zone and have fought pitched battles against Canadian, Dutch, British, and American forces to maintain their grip on Panjwai (most notably in July and September 2006 and in the summer of 2008).

In what became known as the Battle of Panjwai (early summer 2006), the Taliban dug trenches and used mud-walled complexes to wage a bloody battle against Coalition forces. Although the battle ended in defeat for the Taliban, they returned as soon as Coalition forces withdrew in late summer 2006. As the Taliban began to move on Kandahar City, the Coalition responded by launching Operation Medusa in September and October 2006. Once again the Taliban were pushed out, with losses estimated to be as high as 1,500. In the process, much of the province's population fled their homes as the Taliban were prone to use their houses to attack Coalition troops. Not surprisingly, there have been numerous incidents of civilians dying as "collateral damage" in Coalition air strikes in this close fighting.

Since then, the Canadians have worked to build a road from Panjwai to Kandahar City to help the local economy. The Taliban have fought this project with IEDs, sniping, and suicide bombers. A final operation known as Operation Falcon Summit was launched in December 2006 but met no real resistance.

Rivers

The Kabul

The Kabul River is a mere stream most of the year, but in April and May it fills with runoff from the mountain snows and tributary rivers and becomes a raging torrent. It flows from the mountains to the west of Kabul and cuts its way down through the Silk Gorge (where a retreating British army was destroyed in 1842) past Jalalabad to Peshawar, Pakistan, where it joins the Indus. It is 700 kilometers (almost 435 miles) in length, with 30 kilometers (18.6 miles) located in Pakistan. This is the main river in Kabul, although in the dry summer months it amounts to no more than a series of rivulets. A dam and hydroelectric plant have been built on the river at Darunta in the hills just to the west of Jalalabad. Incidentally, Darunta was also a notorious bin Laden base where Al Qaeda's "mad scientist," Abu Khabab, experimented on animals with sarin nerve gas.

The Arghandab

The Arghandab River starts out in the high Hindu Kush in Ghazni Province and flows 400 kilometers (249 miles) southward from the mountains into the flat deserts of the south in Helmand Province. There it eventually joins up with the Helmand River in the provincial capital of Lashkar Gah.

As it cuts its way through Kandahar Province, the Arghandab creates a narrow green valley that is filled with irrigation canals. In many ways the Arghandab and other Afghan rivers are like the Nile in the Sahara Desert—they create ribbons of green that wind through a dry, rocky wasteland that resembles Arizona or New Mexico.

In the 1950s the Americans built a dam to regulate the river and provide irrigation, and the region still benefits from this project. The Soviets (who had a garrison in Kandahar City) called the fertile area north of Kandahar City on the Arghandab the "green zone." This land of canal-watered fields and irrigation provided excellent cover for mujahideen operating in the area. The area along the river north of Kandahar City has also been the base of a powerful anti-Taliban militia led by the leader of the Pashtun Alokozai tribe, Mullah Naqibullah. It was Mullah Naqibullah who held off the Taliban until his death in 2007.

Soon thereafter the Taliban moved into his territory and even began to raid down toward Kandahar City. This culminated in a bold prison raid on the Sarposa Prison in Kandahar on June 13, 2008, when a suicide bomber drove a fuel tanker into the prison gates. Thirty Taliban insurgents then drove into the prison grounds on motorcycles, firing assault rifles and rocket-propelled grenades, and freeing more than four hundred Taliban prisoners. These prisoners then escaped into the green zone and rejoined the insurgency.

After this humiliation the Afghan Ministry of Justice rebuilt the prison and strengthened it as a symbol of its power in Kandahar. On April 25,

2011, however, the Taliban dug a 305 meter (1,000 foot) tunnel under the prison and launched a daring stealth breakout. Almost five hundred Taliban prisoners secretly crawled through the narrow tunnel which came up in a nearby house. From there Taliban cars and buses drove the prisoners to safety. The breakout, which could not have been carried out without the help of corrupt guards, was a terrible humiliation for the Karzai government and released hundreds of fighters in time for the spring campaign season.

But not all Taliban attacks were successful. There were also several incidents in which large numbers of Taliban fleeing Coalition forces drowned when their rafts sank in the river in Helmand and Kandahar.

The district of Panjwai, which is based on the Arghandab River, poses problems for the Coalition that are similar to those the green zone posed for the Soviets in the 1980s. Panjwai is just twenty miles to the west of Kandahar City. It has been the heart of the Taliban resistance in Kandahar Province, and insurgents use the villages, orchards, fields, ditches, and irrigation canals to ambush Coalition forces.

To flush the insurgents out of Panjwai and prevent them from taking Kandahar City, the Coalition has launched major operations, such as Operation Medusa in 2006 (NATO's second-largest post–Operation Enduring Freedom military mission to date), that have seen some of the heaviest fighting since the overthrow of the Taliban. In an effort to win the hearts and minds of locals, the Canadians recently built a causeway across the river linking Panjwai and Zhari Districts.

The Helmand

The Helmand is Afghanistan's longest river and flows 1,150 kilometers (714 miles) from the mountains west of Kabul into Helmand Province. From there it eventually disappears into a series of salt lakes on the Afghan-Iranian border. Like the Arghandab, the Helmand gives life to the dry lands around it and brings life to the desolate Dasht i Margo Desert.

Life was originally brought to this region, which experiences minimal rainfall, only with human help. Archaeologists believe that this region once had an extensive system of canals, but these were destroyed by the Mongol invaders in the thirteenth century, and this granary returned to desolation. It remained for the Americans to return water to the region in the 1960s. In a vast project that resembled the American construction of Las Vegas or the projects of the Tennessee Valley Authority, the American company Morrison Knudson built a series of dams, canals, and power stations on the Helmand River that helped turn this desert into one of Afghanistan's most fertile regions.

Except for the mountain streams that water a few fields in the north of Helmand, all life in this desolate province is based on the Helmand River's artificial irrigation projects. The province's provincial capital, Lashkar Gah, for example, is found on its riverbanks, as is the city of Gereshk, the economic hub of the region. Lashkar Gah, which was built by the Americans on a grid system, resembles an American suburb and was built to house Western engineers working on the dam project.

Morrison Knudson built a 320-foot dam and reservoir at Kajaki, about 80 kilometers (50 miles) north of Gereshk in the mountains of northern Helmand Province, for irrigation and flood control. The Americans also built more than 480 kilometers (298 miles) of concrete-lined canals to distribute the water held by the dam to the surrounding regions. For about 320 kilometers (199 miles) south of these dams, the Helmand forms a ribbon of green that was once used to grow fruits and vegetables. With the collapse of the Afghan central government in the 1980s, however, a local mujahideen warlord issued a *fetwa* (religious decree) which proclaimed that growing opium was no longer *haram* (forbidden in Islam). In response, opium quickly replaced other crops in the area. In the ultimate irony, the waterways the United States built in the 1960s to bring life to this region have been used to transform Helmand Province into Afghanistan's poppy-growing heartland.

By most estimates, Helmand now produces 50 percent of Afghanistan's poppy crop, making it the world's single greatest source of opium (Afghanistan itself produces over 90 percent of the world's opium). The opium mafia increasingly works with the Taliban, who protect them from the government. In 2006, Coalition troops fought to regain control of Sangin (a town in northern Helmand located on a tributary of the Helmand River), which has become the center for the province's opium trade. Coalition forces suffered considerable casualties in pushing insurgents out of Sangin District.

In 2006 the Taliban also seized control of the area around Kajaki Dam located to the east of Sangin. The British had to fight on an almost daily basis to keep the Taliban away from Kajaki so they could bring it back on line.

In early 2007 the British lost control of the town of Musa Qala (which is located on the same tributary as Sangin, about twenty-five kilometers or fifteen miles to the west of the Kajaki Dam) to the Taliban. They had hoped that they could pull out their troops and let the local elders run the city, but the Taliban quickly filled the vacuum left by the British. The Taliban then turned Musa Qala into a base for attacking surrounding regions. The British did not regain Musa Qala, the only town in Afghanistan openly controlled by the Taliban, until December 2007.

In February 2007 the Coalition launched Operation Kryptonite to flush out the insurgents from the Kajaki Dam region. The upper reaches of the Helmand River nonetheless remain one of the most dangerous regions in Afghanistan. As a result, the Taliban have had on-and-off success in preventing maintenance and improvements on the Kajaki Dam. Their aim is to prevent the Coalition from using the hydroelectric plant to provide electricity to almost two million Afghans living in the area.

The Hari Rud

The Hari Rud flows 1,100 kilometers (683 miles) in a westerly direction from the Hindu Kush, past the Minaret of Jam and down into the flatlands on the border of Iran. Along the way it creates a green oasis around the western town of Herat, which is known for its pine trees and irrigated fields. To the west of Herat, the Hari Rud finally turns northward and runs south-north along the Iranian-Afghan border before crossing into the deserts of the Kara Kum in Turkmenistan. The Hari Rud Valley has traditionally been settled by Persians or Tajiks, although it was annexed from Iran by the Afghans in the nineteenth century. In 2005 it was the scene of fighting between Tajiks led by the legendary mujahideen leader Ismail Khan, as well as Pashtuns from the south led by Amanullah Khan. The Pashtuns and Tajiks have an uneasy truce along the river, and both sides bear grudges dating back to the period of the Taliban rule in Herat.

The Murgab

The Murgab River flows 850 kilometers (585 miles) in a northwesterly direction out of the Hindu Kush toward Turkmenistan. Traditionally, this river has marked the frontier between the Persian-speaking lands of the south and the northern realm of Afghan Turkistan. The lands to the north were, as their name indicates, Turkic (most recently Turkmen and Uzbek nomads descended from the Golden Horde). The ancient gateway fortress of Bala Murgab served as the frontier to this flat steppe region in the north.

There is a Pashtun colony on the banks of the Murgab at Bala Murgab that is of interest. In the nineteenth century the Afghan ruler Abdur Rahman settled Pashtun "internal colonists" in the newly conquered lands of Afghan Turkistan to act as his representatives. This colony has been sympathetic to the Pashtun Taliban in the past and has facilitated the movement of Taliban insurgents into the northern provinces of Badghis and

Faryab. There are said to be as many as three hundred thousand Pashtuns in Badghis Province. For this reason the "Badghis Corridor" remains a weak link in the chain defending the north from infiltration by the Taliban.

In 2007 the International Security Assistance Force (ISAF) launched several large military operations designed to push Taliban insurgents out of the mountains in this area. But the western sections of Turkistan bordering on the Murgab have no proper roads linking them to Mazar i Sharif, the most important city of the north, and this isolated region remains among the most dangerous in the otherwise peaceful north.

The Balkhab

Afghan Turkistan's main river is the Balkhab. The Balkhab flows northward down from the Band i Amir lakes located high in the western Hindu Kush. It makes its way out of barren mountains onto the hot plains of Afghan Turkistan. There it eventually fans out like the Mississippi Delta only to disappear in the desert. The water from the Balkhab brought life to the ancient region known as Balkh or the Hazda Nahr (Eighteen Rivers) where the great prophet Zoroaster and the poet Rumi lived. The locals worshipped the life-giving waters as a goddess in ancient times. To this very day they venerate the waters in a pre-Islamic ceremony held every year in the blue-domed mosque of Mazar i Sharif on the first day of spring. During this ceremony a sacred pole known as the Janda is raised, locals eat special cakes, and thousands of pilgrims gather in the famous Rowza shrine complex in Mazar i Sharif to receive the blessings of Ali.

Afghan Turkistan's capital of Mazar i Sharif is located in a green, irrigated portion of the Balkhab Delta that recently became known for growing opium. But in 2007 its Tajik governor, Ustad Atta, outlawed opium production and eradicated the crop. By the end of the year, however, the province was awash in marijuana as local farmers switched from opium to cannabis. Overnight this province became Afghanistan's main marijuana and hash production center.

Historically, rebels, mujahideen, contenders to the Afghan throne, and most recently Dostum's horse-mounted Uzbeks and their U.S. Special Forces allies have also used the Balkhab River Valley and its Dar y Suf tributary as hideouts and springboards for launching attacks on the plains.

The Kunduz

The Kunduz River is found in northeastern Afghan Turkistan and flows down out of the Hindu Kush through the dune-like hills and onto the plains. It carves its way through this dry, rugged terrain before finally disgorging into the Amu Darya River in the north. Along the way it provides life to such regional hubs as Pul i Kumri, Baghlan, and Kunduz. Farmers and pastoralists have used its waters to grow wheat, rice, and various fruits and vegetables for centuries. The Kunduz River served as a demarcation line between the mini-states of the Uzbek warlord Dostum and Massoud the Lion of Panjsher during the 1990s Afghan civil war.

Today the Coalition has built a new tarmac road that runs along the Kunduz's length from Pul i Kumri up to Kunduz in the north to facilitate travel and commerce. There are Pashtun pockets along the river in places such as Kunduz City and Pul i Kumri, and these have supported the re-infiltration of the Taliban since 2008. This area made international headlines in September 2009 when the Taliban stole two NATO fuel trucks coming from Tajikistan and beheaded their drivers. When the trucks subsequently got stuck crossing a riverbed, the Germans serving in the area in a NATO capacity called in a U.S. air strike on them. A U.S. F-15E subsequently bombed the trucks with a five-hundred-pound bomb and killed more than a hundred, many of them civilians who had gathered at the site to siphon off fuel.

The Kokcha

The Kokcha River is found in the Tajik territory of Badakshan. It begins high in the snowcapped Hindu Kush near the Panjsher Valley and begins its long northward journey down past the Northern Alliance's capital of Faizabad before finally joining the Amu Darya. The remains of Ai Khanoum, a Greek city founded by Alexander the Great, are found on the northern tip of the Kokcha River where it meets the Amu Darya.

More recently it formed the final defense for Massoud's Northern Alliance in the Tajiks' battles against the Taliban. In 2001 the Northern Alliance stormed across the Kokcha River and attacked the Taliban in the city of Kunduz. Today the Kokcha River enables the Tajik farmers of the region to grow bumper crops of opium that are transported northward into Tajikistan.

Deserts

The Dasht i Margo

This desert's name is appropriate and translates to "Desert of Death." It is made up of flat, scrub-covered plains, salt flats, and sand dunes. Its only inhabitants are Baluchis, Kuchis, smugglers crossing over into Iran, and insurgents trying to avoid major thoroughfares. The Dasht i Margo is located in the south in western Helmand Province and Nimroz Province.

The Rigestan

The Rigestan Desert's name is equally appropriate and translates to "Land of Sand." This windblown expanse of dunes and salt flats in equally uninhabitable and extends from the Khwaja Amrain Mountains on the Pakistani border to the Helmand River. Some Baluchi tribes and Pashtun Kuchi tribes use the open plains as winter pastures for their flocks. Otherwise, there are few people found in this wasteland besides smugglers and insurgents.

Geographic Glossary

There are certain words in English that have topographical meanings that are recognizable to all English speakers. For example *-ville* or *-opolis* at the end of a name such as Louisville or Indianapolis indicates a town. *Mount-* indicates a mountain; *-bridge*, as in Cambridge, means a crossing; *San* or *Saint*, as in Saint Louis, indicates a Catholic saint; and of course the meaning of the addendum *Lake* or *River* is obvious to English speakers. Below are the equally obvious geographic equivalents in Dari-Pashtun, with a couple of examples:

Ab: River (Balkhab, Murgab)
Band: Dam (Band i Qargheh, Band i Amir)
Darya: River (Amu Darya, Darya ye Arghandab)
Dasht: Desert (Dasht i Margo, Dasht i Leila)
Ghar: Mountain (Spin Ghar, Sperwan Ghar)
Kalay: Village (Worzhenah Kalay, Serkey Kalay)
Khel: Tribe (Baratkhel, Musa Khel)
Khvajeh: Saint or holy man (Khvajeh Ali Oliya, Khvajeh Ali Sofia)
Koh or Kuh: Mountain (Safid Koh, Koh i Baba)
Kotal: Pass (Safid Kotal, Peiwar Kotal)

Lashkar: Army or militia (Lashkar Gah, Lashkar)
Pol or Pul: Bridge (Saripul, Pul i Kumri)
Qala or Kala: Fortress (Qala i Jangi, Musa Qaleh)
Rud: River (Hari Rud, Musa Qaleh Rud)
Spin: White (Spin Ghar, Spin Boldak)

The construction *blank* i *blank* (or *blank* e *blank*), as in *Mazar i Sharif* or *Dasht i Margo* translates to "of the." *Mazar i Sharif* means "Tomb of the Noble" or "Noble Tomb"; *Koh i Baba* translates to "Father of Mountains."

PART II

History Lessons

Chapter 3

Creating the Afghan State

If the Americans want to know Afghanistan, they should come here and sit down with us for dinner and hear our stories. It is only after they have eaten our food, visited our villages and seen how we live that they can understand us. I would assume this is the same with any people, even the Americans.
—Afghan kabob seller, Kabul, 2007

As I walked into the university secretary's office for the check to fund my summer field research, she innocuously asked where I was headed. "I hope to make my way to a lawless northern province of Afghanistan to interview an Uzbek warlord who is defined as a notorious Taliban killer. I actually hope to be one of the first outsiders to access this Northern Alliance warlord since a *Newsweek* reporter accused him of human rights abuses, such as slaughtering too many captured Taliban fighters back in 2001."

"Afghanistan?" she replied with an arched brow. "Well, try not to get yourself killed in the process . . . and remember your receipts for the reimbursement committee."

As my flight from Baku, Azerbaijan, a former Soviet republic north of Iran, descended a pass in the mountains that surround Afghanistan's (comparatively) safe capital, the enormity of my undertaking dawned on me. Somewhat belatedly, I began to question the impulses driving me to a theater of operations where just ten thousand U.S. soldiers were combating the remnants of the down-but-not-out Taliban. I was entering a land that was synonymous with war; be it the Soviet meat grinder of the 1980s, or the recent U.S.-led operation, this country had seen more suffering than any other in Eurasia.

My doubts were dispelled by the sights and sounds as I made my way to the Turkish Embassy from Kabul International Airport. Darting past camels laden with goods and taxis with riders on the roofs and in their trunks, I noticed the streetlamps festooned with ribbons of music cassette tapes and the innards of TV sets ritualistically "executed" by the Taliban's dreaded religious police as "satanic technological devices." Most women still wore the all-encompassing burqa, while armed Northern Alliance soldiers loitered on every corner due to the growing threat of Taliban urban bombers.

Yet despite such disquieting images, Kabul was as good as it got in Afghanistan that August of 2003. Dozens of Afghan civilians and several U.S. soldiers were killed in the provinces outside Kabul during my stay. This city was the showcase of the Bush administration's ambitious effort to bring peace and stability to a land that has known only war for almost a quarter of a century. When one left Kabul, there was little or no American presence except in the east. By this time, the new war in Iraq had captured most of the White House's attention, and Afghanistan was already known as "the Forgotten War."

But I had not traveled to Afghanistan to remain in the comparative "safety bubble" of Kabul. Somehow, I had to cross the heavily mined Shomali Plain and pass through the Hindu Kush Mountains of central Afghanistan to the steppes of the northern provinces, where I intended to interview the former master of northern Afghanistan, General Abdul Rashid Dostum. "But," my Turkish hosts explained patiently (and with more than a pinch of hyperbole), "you can't get to the lands of Dostum's Uzbek fighters. The mountains are filled with bandit 'checkpoints,' and practically no one has interviewed Dostum since his Northern Alliance horsemen shattered the Taliban with American forces in 2001. Dostum is a bona fide warlord who has tried to carve his lands off from the rest of Afghanistan in the past. You can't just stroll in and say 'Hi, I'm here to interview you.' Besides, you have no bodyguards. And you look like an idiot without a gun. Someone will be tempted to shoot your fool head off."

Two days later, my Uzbek guards and I began our trek out of the Hindu Kush Mountains to Dostum's inaccessible northern realm. I was thrilled to be entering the lands of the ethnic Uzbeks, descendants of Genghis Khan's Turkic-Mongol hordes. In the ultimate of historical and technical juxtapositions, Dostum's turbaned horsemen, riding on $60 horses, had united with $1.2 billion U.S. Stealth "Spirit" bombers to shatter the mighty Taliban occupation army. Among the most memorable images of the war on terror was that of Dostum's horsemen riding directly into Taliban tank fire, shooting their anti-tank grenades from the hip.

Approaching Mazar i Sharif, I thought to myself, "If I manage to carry out a rare interview with this larger-than-life warlord who captured the vast majority of the Taliban prisoners now at Guantanamo Bay (including

General Abdul Rashid Dostum posing with a Sig pistol given to him by U.S. Central Command commander General Tommy Franks.

John Walker Lindh, the "American Taliban"), it will be the coup of a lifetime."

Having traced Dostum to his compound, I was led through his bodyguards and tribal elders and introduced myself to a surprised warlord. As the bodyguards reflexively moved forward to protect him, he sized me up. I recalled that among the last Americans he had met had been Green Beret members of an A-Team and CIA SOF (Special Operations Forces) paramilitaries. These fighters had been inserted into his rugged lands by Black Hawk helicopters to help his horsemen obliterate the Taliban's powerful tank and artillery brigades. Surely I did not resemble a Green Beret. Time stood still as he considered my request for an interview, and again I wondered what had driven me from my safe home in Boston to the middle of Central Asia.

After the longest seconds of my life had passed, a perplexed General Dostum replied with the simple Turkic word "Tamam"—roughly, "Sure, let's do it." After questioning whether he could trust me or not, he agreed to the interview. I believe the fact that we were able to converse in Turkish sealed the deal.

The aftermath is a whirlwind of memories that hardly seem real now. What was intended to be a five-minute conversation became several weeks of embedded interviews. I had the extraordinary fortune of having one of the most extensive interviews ever conducted with this legendary fighter from another era. In the process, I had the unique opportunity to travel through the Uzbek lands with an actual warlord who seemed to like showing off his "realm" to a foreigner—a foreigner from the very country that helped his riders destroy the Taliban with state-of-the-art laser-guided missiles and everyone's favorite in northern Afghanistan, the awe-inspiring "beeping joe doo" ("B-52 bomber" in Dari). As a cherished American ally, northern Afghanistan was mine to tour with the man who had once claimed much of it as his own.

On a personal level I found Dostum to be a garrulous talker who loved sharing stories of his previous military exploits. As someone who fought against bin Laden and the other Afghan Arab jihad volunteers for the Communists in the 1980s, he chastised America for having allied itself with Muslim fundamentalists to wage a proxy war against the Soviets. He proudly took me to girls' schools he had built in several towns in the north (all of them featured none-too-subtle pictures of him on their walls) and proclaimed that this was his dream. This was why he had fought for the Communists in the 1980s, against the CIA-backed mujahideen, and against the Taliban in the 1990s—to free women.

Although I had no doubt that Dostum supported women and secularism, I realized that there was more opportunism behind his decision to fight for the Communists than he admitted. He was also someone who clearly enjoyed wielding power. In the evenings he held court in his compounds in Mazar i Sharif and neighboring Sheberghan where local *aq saqals* (elders) and commanders came to him to make decisions on everything from land disputes to getting new chairs for a school. Judging by the calendars on the townsmen's walls that featured Dostum's mug, billboards around town with his mustachioed face, and genuine affection with which I heard the locals speak of him, he was something of a celebrity among his own people, even though outsiders saw him as an opportunistic warlord.

Dostum certainly maintained his sense of opportunism during his service alongside the Americans in Operation Enduring Freedom. He had been held up in the mountains fighting the Taliban for months when 9/11 occurred in distant North America. For Dostum and the Northern Alliance, 9/11 was a godsend. Suddenly the world's only remaining superpower was on their side in the lonely struggle against the Taliban. Not surprisingly, Dostum spoke to me with great affection for the CIA and special forces who fought alongside him and his men in October and November 2001. On several occasions he referred to the U.S. Green Berets as "lions" and asked me to send his respect to them if I ever saw them again. He told me that when he and the American special forces victoriously rode into Mazar i Sharif in November 2001 after defeating the Taliban, they all made a pilgrimage to the blue-domed shrine of Ali in the center of the town. There Dostum said prayers for all those who had been killed fighting the Taliban in the mountains. For their part, the Americans fulfilled a promise made back in the United States by symbolically burying several burnt pieces of metal from the World Trade Center at the shrine.

On one occasion Dostum took me to his stables and showed me Surkun, the white horse he rode during the mountain campaign, and another horse ridden by the Green Beret A-Team's commander, Mark Nutsch. He also showed me a Sig pistol given to him as a sign of gratitude in December 2001 by U.S. Central Command commander General Tommy Franks. But his greatest prize was a plaque on the wall of his compound making him an honorary member of one of the U.S. Special Forces A-Teams that had fought alongside him in his drive from Mazar i Sharif to Kunduz. Dostum clearly relished the idea of fighting alongside the Americans and on more than one occasion told me he would gladly help his American "friends" again if they needed him. He also spoke in ominous terms about the re-infiltration of the Taliban in the north and decried America's decision to invade Iraq before the war in Afghanistan had been won.

Dostum seemed to have a visceral hatred of the Taliban and Al Qaeda, and I soon found out why. He told me the story of his wife, Khadija, a girl from his home village of Khoja Doko whom he had fallen in love with in his youth. After they were married in the 1980s, their house had been attacked by Arab jihadi volunteers fighting alongside the mujahideen. Dostum the pro-Communist commander had been declared an infidel by the foreign fanatics who did not respect the sanctity of the home the way the local Afghan mujahideen did.

To protect himself, Dostum had hidden several guns around his house. One day Khadija was cleaning the house when she accidentally discharged one of his guns. Sadly the bullet caught her in the chest and she died in the arms of her servants. A grieving Dostum blamed both the Arabs and himself for her death. According to several of Dostum's subcommanders, he had traveled back to Afghanistan in April 2001 to fight the Taliban from the mountains so that he could avenge himself on the fanatics and try to find absolution for his role in his wife's death. His return to fight the Taliban was described as a "one-way journey" that would lead either to his death or to victory. America's post-9/11 intervention in his feud with the Taliban and Al Qaeda assured him a miraculous victory. Clearly Dostum was a complex man with many regrets, among them the death of his wife and the death of Taliban prisoners at the hands of some of his troops in 2001. His life, like that of millions of his countrymen,

The author in a crowd of Uzbeks and Turkmen in Sheberghan in northern Afghanistan.

had been irrevocably shaped by the wars that had surged across the land for the past three decades.

As for the average Uzbeks of the north, in their simple mud-walled villages I encountered genuine hospitality of a sort I had not met in more advanced countries of the West. For example, impoverished Uzbek and Turkmen peasants, as was their custom, slaughtered their only sheep for me when I arrived unannounced for dinner. Laughing children invited me to swim with them in the muddy rivers pouring from the mountains, and shy villagers told me to send their hellos to Americans. These were simple farmers and shepherds whose lives had been terribly scarred by something unimaginable to most Americans—namely, thirty years of war fought not in a distant land (as was the case with U.S. warfare in Iraq, Somalia, Afghanistan, Kosovo, Bosnia, and elsewhere) but in their own towns, streets, and homes.

My most powerful memory is of a proud Afghan woman who looked me in the eyes without flinching and told me that her husband had been killed by the Taliban and two of her three children had been slain by an errant U.S. bomb. To my question "Do you seek revenge on the Taliban or compensation from the wealthy Americans?" she responded with a simple "No." Smiling, she pointed to her remaining daughter, an emaciated, brown-eyed four-year-old. "I want her to grow up in a land where there is no more war. That's all I want."

I turned away quickly, lest this young Uzbek woman see the pity in my eyes. The odds of her daughter experiencing such a miracle in this war-torn land were slim. Already the Taliban were taking advantage of America's distraction and beginning to launch a new war. While a mere ten thousand U.S. troops tried to patrol a country the size of Texas, the Taliban were oozing back into the country and seizing control of the countryside.

While in the plains of Afghan Turkistan, I also made a pilgrimage to the infamous Qala i Jengi, the "Fortress of a War," a mud-walled castle looming menacingly on the outskirts of Mazar i Sharif. This war-blackened fortress seemed haunted by ghosts. Hundreds of Taliban fighters captured by Dostum's Uzbek horsemen had been killed here during a desperate uprising in November 2001. Tragically, America suffered its first casualty in the Global War on Terror here when CIA agent Michael Spann was brutally slain by the revolting Taliban prisoners.

I was touched to see that Dostum's grateful Uzbeks had built a memorial to the slain American agent, thanking him for his sacrifice. I thought of Spann's sacrifice as I recalled my interviews with dozens of Taliban prisoners still held by Dostum in one of his fortress-prisons in Sheberghan. Reflecting on the fury in the faces of many of the Taliban prisoners at any mention of America, I felt truly grateful that men like Spann left their homes to defend our world from those who wanted to destroy it. For Spann, and dozens like him who ventured to distant lands to protect America after 9/11, this strangely beautiful country was a place that called them to duty. It was here that the enemy who threatened his homeland was to be found. And seeing the smiling girls in schools that had been rebuilt since the Taliban burned them down in the late 1990s, I believed that the sacrifices of Spann and countless others from the Afghan and NATO Coalition who had died fighting the Taliban had not been in vain.

As the sun set over Spann's grave, turning his monument a reddish color, a rare cool wind blew dust over me and his memorial. I shuddered—whether from the chill or from the solitude of being with someone whose life was lost on the spot where I stood, I couldn't tell.

Suddenly I felt terribly exposed and lonely in this distant corner of the globe, in a place my fellow Americans could hardly imagine. Standing on the spot where one of my countrymen had been killed, perhaps by some of the very Taliban prisoners I had recently interviewed, I felt it was time for me to return to my own world. I said a prayer for one

American hero who had no such luxury, and walked toward General Dostum, who had politely allowed me to pay my respects. "Shimdi yurduma donme zamani" (It's time for me to return to my own homeland), I said.

Only later, as I flew out of Kabul for the long journey back to Boston, did I begin to grasp the enormity of all I had experienced. I tried to make sense of the violent but beautiful land I was leaving, and the surreal, safe, modern world that I would reenter. Attempting to balance these two vastly different realities, I recalled the warm people I had encountered in the lands of Dostum's pro-American Uzbeks. I realized that the largest obstacle facing me on my return would involve explaining Afghanistan and its colorful people to my fellow Americans.

The Uzbeks who had shared meals with me, who slept outside my door at night to protect me, and who had died fighting the Taliban were not abstract figures who deserved to be killed by horrible American nuclear weapons, as many Americans had reflexively demanded after 9/11. On the contrary, the Afghan Uzbeks were—like us—a people who wanted their children to grow up in a world of no wars. Pondering these notions, I began to relax and reflect on the new hurdles facing me. Only then did I remember the university secretary's words from what seemed like a lifetime ago, and a worrisome thought struck. I began to anticipate trouble in trying to explain the impossibility of collecting receipts from my illiterate Uzbek bodyguards for everything from gas for our convoy to one fully automatic AK-47 assault rifle.

As I began to brace for the bureaucratic battles ahead, a small part of me actually became nostalgic for that rough-and-tumble world of tribal militias and warlords where problems were solved with the wave of a machine gun . . . or a simple "Tamam."

*   *   *

The United States of America is, like every other country, shaped by its history. Understanding the past can help outsiders understand its present. We Americans are our history, and those who find us quirky need to know our history to understand why we think and act the way we do.

Afghanistan has its own historical trajectories that in some ways parallel those of the United States. Like the United States, it has a history of fighting off the British Empire, expansion, and involvement in the Cold War and the War on Terror. For every American Battle of the Alamo, the Afghans have a Battle of Maiwand; and for every George Washington, they have an Ahmed Shah Durrani. To know Afghanistan's pantheon of national heroes and icons is to know the Afghans of today. To

try to fight an insurgency on Afghan soil without this crucial historical context would be the equivalent of a foreigner ignoring the importance of the American Revolution, the divisiveness of the Civil War, or
the psychological impact of 9/11 on Americans while trying to fight a
stubborn insurgency in the United States. This chapter will take the
reader through Afghanistan's turbulent military past with the aim of
introducing important developments, symbolic events, and ongoing historical trends and precedents that have ramifications for today's counterinsurgency.

Origins of the Afghan State

The Pashtuns' tribal nature, which we explored in Chapter 1, has in some
ways prevented them from unifying and creating states until relatively
recent times. They have rarely unified on the basis of an overarching
sense of Pashtun "nationalism." On the contrary, the Pashtun tribes,
who are separated by some of the world's most rugged landscape, failed
to unite like their neighbors, the empire-building peoples of the Iranian plateau, the Turkic-Mongol peoples of the steppes, and the Indians to the south. Far from creating a kingdom of their own, the quarreling
Pashtun tribes were squeezed between their neighbors' empires or conquered by them. (It is a myth that the Afghans have never been conquered.
The Persians, Macedonians, Parthians, Arabs, Turks, and Mongols all conquered and ruled them for centuries.) Until the mid-1700s, the Pashtuns
were, for example, dominated by Turkic-Mongol tribes from the north,
including the Ghaznavids, Seljuks, Il-Khanate, Timurids, and Moghuls,
or by the Iranian dynasties, including the Achaemenids, Sassanians,
Samanids, the Safavids and Iranian-Turkmen army led by Nadir Shah.

As with all history in this part of the world, the memory of this subjugation is alive and well today, although Afghans rarely admit to having
ever been conquered by outsiders. To this very day many Pashtun nationalists bear a grudge against the "flat noses" (Turkic-Mongols) from
the north and the "Farsiwan" (Farsi or Persian speakers from Iran) who
ruled them over the centuries. The Pashtuns' resentment toward the
Iranians, whose rich culture they have nonetheless emulated (much as
the English emulated the French culture of their rivals), was exacerbated
by Iran's conversion to the minority Shiite form of Islam in the 1500s. The
Pashtuns are strict Sunnis (majority Muslims), and as such their resentment of the Shiite Iranians resembled the Catholic-Protestant rivalry
and wars of seventeenth-century Europe. Seemingly minor divisions
within Islam, such as the disagreement over who should have inherited

the mantle of the Prophet Muhammad, have divided the Sunni Pashtuns and the Shiite Iranians for centuries, much as Protestants and Catholics have been divided in Northern Ireland.

The Pashtuns' enmity toward the Turkic tribes stems from the fact that their Turkic-Mongol language and nomadic culture were alien to the Pashtuns, whose language was actually distantly related to the Farsi-speaking Persians. But Pashtuns have nonetheless adopted the Uzbek-Turkmen horse-mounted game of *buzkashi* (a blend of polo and rugby first developed by Genghis Khan's troops) as Afghanistan's national sport. Pashtun chiefs also use the Turkic-Mongol title *khan*, and the current Afghan president, Hamid Karzai (an ethnic Pashtun), wears an Uzbek *chapan* (riding coat) and Turkmen *karakul* lamb hat. Pashto, the Pashtun language, also contains many Turkic loan words that point to centuries of trade and commerce between these two peoples.

Ahmed Shah Durrani, Afghanistan's Founder

Unity was not achieved by the quarrelling Pashtuns until the neighboring empires in Moghul India, Uzbek Central Asia, and Shiite Iran began to break up and lose their cohesion in the mid-1700s. It was in 1747 that Ahmed Shah Abdali, a Pashtun *amir* (commander) serving in the Persian army, led his troops home following the death of his Persian master. As the empires of Iran and India disintegrated, Ahmed Shah unified his fellow Pashtun tribesmen to fill the void caused by the neighboring states' collapse. When he was chosen to lead the disunited Pashtun clans, Ahmed Shah changed his clan's name from Abdali to Durrani ("Pearl of Pearls"). Incidentally, Ahmed Shah was from the Popalzai clan of the Durranis, the same clan that Hamid Karzai hails from.

Having unified his people, Ahmed Shah realized that the Pashtuns' propensity for feuding and raiding would sooner or later lead them to fight one another unless he directed their energies outward. For this reason he directed them to conquer their neighbors. The Pashtuns subsequently raided deep inside Moghul India and gained control of Kashmir, Sindh, Punjab, and Baluchistan (all of which are lands in modern-day Pakistan and neighboring parts of India). They also gained dominance over the east Iranian city of Herat and on-again, off-again suzerainty over the eleven Turkic-Mongol Uzbek khanates of southern "Turkistan" (that is, the flatlands of northern Afghanistan that have traditionally been dominated by horse-riding Turkic nomads). Ahmed Shah even captured the Tajik-dominated city of Kabul, and his grandson later transferred the national capital there from the previous capital of Kandahar in the south.

Although the Pashtun-Afghans refer to Ahmed Shah as "Baba" (Father) and cast him in the role of founding father of their state, Ahmed Shah's achievements did not prove to be permanent. In actuality he had not created a modern, centralized nation-state with an elaborate bureaucracy; instead, he had created a loosely organized tribal-military alliance, with himself as the dominant chieftain. Although he was first among equals, powerful Pashtun clan leaders kept much of their independence and continue to do so today. What unity that existed was maintained only by the lure of constant booty from invasions of neighboring lands. When the Afghan empire collapsed soon after Ahmed Shah's death, the various ruling elites took to squabbling among themselves. It was half-brother against half-brother fighting for control of the remaining Afghan lands. This struggle usually pitted the Sadozai Durrani clan against the Muhammadzai Durrani clan.

Ahmed Shah's "hands-off" ruling tradition was to be followed by subsequent leaders as they tried to balance their own centralizing agendas with the long-standing sense of independence that various Pashtun and non-Pashtun tribes had always cherished. Although Afghanistan's rulers dreamed of emulating the centralized-style rule of ancient Persian *Padishahs* (Kings of Kings) like Xerxes or Darius, the reality was that they could never rule without co-opting the powerful tribes that provided them with *lashkars* (tribal armies). Not surprisingly, this has led to a recurring theme in Afghan history—the effort on the part of the central government in Kabul to extend its authority to the distant provinces and to bring the semi-independent Pashtun tribes to heel.

Modern Afghan nationalists and outsiders who are unfamiliar with the loose, tribal nature of the traditional Afghan state often speak of "restoring" central rule under President Karzai. Centralization is depicted as a return to a "natural" state of affairs that has been disrupted by the breakdown of authority and the emergence of regional leaders (invariably described as "warlords"). But the truth is that there has been little central rule for most of Afghanistan's history. Afghan rulers often had little power over regional *sardars* (royal commanders and princes) or ethnic-regional-tribal leaders who assumed such titles as *mir, khan, malik,* or *amir.* Unlike the Afghan ruler who lived in distant Kabul, these local rulers often had, and still have, real grassroots support and power in their own communities, especially in the north. These local rulers often represented their communities in the face of government taxation, conscription, and forced resettlement. The struggle between tribes and the weak government of Kabul is as old as Afghanistan itself. The fact that President Karzai is estimated to control no more than 30 percent of Afghanistan today is not an anomaly—it fits the historic pattern.

Kandahar, the Spiritual Capital of the Pashtuns

For all of the reasons described above, it is not surprising that when Ahmed Shah died and was buried in the Afghan capital of Kandahar in 1772, his kingdom fell into chaos and experienced a quarter century of clan and tribal warfare. But the foundations for a vaguely defined Afghan state had nonetheless been laid by this astute leader who gave the Pashtuns the framework for constructing a loose tribal empire. Most important, Ahmed Shah established Kandahar, a city in the Afghan south, as the paramount seat of Pashtun authority. Kandahar became the seat for both political and religious authority, although the lines between these two often blurred.

Kandahar has religious significance because it is home to the Juma i Mubarek (the Great Mosque), which was said to house a hair of the Prophet Muhammad. If this were not enough, Ahmed Shah's tomb in Kandahar was built next to the shrine for Afghanistan's most sacred relic, the Kherqa, the purported cloak of the Prophet Muhammad. Ahmed Shah acquired this holy relic when his troops conquered the eleven Uzbek khanates of the north. Traditionally these Uzbek city-states had sworn fealty to the Uzbek Khan of Bukhara, a great Silk Road town found in what is today Uzbekistan. But the Khan of Bukhara recognized the Afghan-Pashtuns' growing ascendancy by giving Ahmed Shah the Uzbeks' holiest relic, the Kherqa.

Since then, many have believed that the Kherqa, which is housed in a shrine known as the Kherqa Sharif, grants the Afghan-Pashtuns the right to all the ethnic lands subsequently conquered by their people. This relic is as sacred to the Afghans as the original Declaration of Independence is to Americans or the Magna Carta is to the English. In addition, it has the religious significance accorded by many Catholics to the Shroud of Turin. In times of calamity, Afghan rulers have visited the shrine to seek the blessings of the cloak. It is said that the last Afghan king, Zahir Shah, came to visit the shrine and see the cloak, but his reverence for the relic was so great that at the last minute he turned away.

One late twentieth-century ruler had no such compunctions. In 1996, Mullah Omar, the mysterious head of the newly forged Taliban fundamentalist movement, came to the shrine, saw the sacred cloak, and actually donned it for the first time in recorded history. Not only did he wear it, he took it outside and wore it before awestruck crowds on the roof of a nearby mosque. His aim was to sanctify the Taliban's rule and gain the mandate to conquer all the other ethnic provinces of Afghanistan that had broken away during the Afghan civil war (which was fought after the Soviet invaders left in 1992). Thousands of Kandaharis came to see the spectacle and chant "Allah u Akbar!" (God is great!) as they laid eyes on this sacred relic for the first time in their lives.

This symbolic act seems to have legitimized Mullah Omar's authority. From that day forward he was recognized throughout the Pashtun south as the Amir ul Mouimen (Commander of the Faithful), an ancient term used for the caliph of Islam, the "successor" to the Prophet Muhammad.

For this reason Mullah Omar always felt that his power came from Kandahar. He preferred to govern Afghanistan from this spiritual capital rather than Kabul, a city he only visited a few times. Like many conservative Kandahari Pashtuns, he viewed Kabul, a much larger cosmopolitan city dominated by ethnic Tajiks, in much the same way many small-town Americans view New York City, with a certain amount of distrust. In contrast to Kabul, Kandahar has been renowned for its religious conservatism (it has been called the center of the "Quran belt" in Afghanistan). It stands as the polar opposite to the Afghan capital, which is seen by Kandaharis as being filled with vice, decadence, and foreigners.

For all of these reasons, today's Taliban insurgents are desperately fighting to regain control of their spiritual capital and the seat of Afghan authority. The suicide bombing rate in Kandahar is higher than anywhere else in the country, and the Taliban have repeatedly vowed that they will take Kandahar in their annual spring offensives. Although Kandahar was relatively safe from 2001 to 2005, many Western NGOs (nongovernmental organizations) have since pulled out of this city as the Taliban have extended their operations to the city itself. In Kandahar, anyone suspected of cooperating with the "infidel stooge," President Karzai, runs the risk of being assassinated by Taliban killers who stalk the city. The Taliban seem to have gained support from local Afghans who resented the corruption of the former Karzai-appointed governor of the province, Gul Agha Sherzai, and the current head of the Kandahar Provincial Council, Ahmed Wali Karzai (the younger half-brother of the president).

Although the Taliban have not been able to conquer Kandahar City itself, they have gained de facto control of many outlying regions in Kandahar Province. Kandahar, Afghanistan's second-largest city, is thus cut off from Kabul by the Taliban insurgents. The U.S.-led Coalition realizes it needs to take back this province from the Taliban in order to gain momentum in the south, and there has been talk of a major operation in this area since 2010.

Although the Coalition succeeded in building an excellent highway linking Kabul and Kandahar, the road is infested with Taliban checkpoints and is impassable to foreigners. Westerners who have to travel from Kabul to Kandahar do so on chartered UN flights or on

Ariana Airlines planes. There is a large Coalition presence just outside of Kandahar City at Kandahar Airfield (an international airport built by the United States in the 1950s and used by the Soviets in the 1980s), but this offers little protection to travelers. Thus far the Coalition has prevented the Taliban from openly taking Kandahar City proper, but the insurgents have moved to within twenty-five miles of the city from the Panjwai District in the west and from the north.

Dost Muhammad, Afghanistan's Leader During the First British Invasion

In 1826 Ahmed Shah's grandson Dost Muhammad gained control of the city of Kabul and declared himself amir (commander). Soon after gaining control of Kabul and moving his capital there from Kandahar, he found himself caught up in what became known as the "Great Game"—a Eurasian struggle for empire between the British and the Russians. His participation in this struggle is what he is most famous for.

By the time Dost Muhammad came to the throne, the Russians had already moved south from Siberia into what is today Kazakhstan and were encroaching on Uzbek territories around Bukhara (modern-day Uzbekistan). For their part, the British had gained control of Moghul India and were encroaching on territories in the vicinity of the Indus River (today's Pakistan).

To protect India, the "jewel in Queen Victoria's crown," from the encroaching Russians, the British war party commenced what became known as the "Forward Policy" toward Afghanistan. Their aim was to make sure that the unruly Afghan tribes on their northwestern frontiers were "subject-allies" with no ties to Russia. To implement this plan, the British gradually began to assume control of Pashtuns to the west of the Indus River (that is, the Pashtun tribal lands that are currently cut off from Afghanistan and found in today's Pakistan). These southeastern Pashtun lands had recently been conquered by the Sikhs, whom the British themselves later conquered, so the Brits felt they had the right to rule them.

From there, the British sought to establish a sort of protectorate over the neighboring Afghan state ruled by Dost Muhammad. Their ultimate aim was to bring the unruly Afghan tribes who raided British-claimed lands to heel, annex some of them, and then create a truncated Afghan buffer state between themselves and the fast-approaching Russian bear.

It was this project that brought the colonial British into direct conflict with the Pashtuns living in what is today's Afghanistan. The British, not content with assuming control of the Pashtun lands located near Peshawar, launched a preemptive invasion of Afghanistan itself in 1839. Their aim was to head off Russian efforts to influence the Afghan state. The British plan was to unseat the Afghan ruler, Dost Muhammad, and put a more pliant puppet named Shah Shuja (an exile who had come to the British seeking assistance) on the Afghan throne. Shah Shujah would then be forced to rely on his British masters to remain in power and would of course reject Russian influence.

The subsequent campaign is illustrative of what drives Afghan-Pashtuns to fight even today. The Afghans have a deeply ingrained sense of rallying around the banner of defense of homeland and religion. When the British invaded, they were shocked by the Afghans' ferocious defense of Kandahar and the nearby town of Ghazni. But for all their ferocity, the Pashtuns were defeated by the superior organization and weapons of the British invaders. The British subsequently took Kabul, and Dost Muhammad surrendered to them. This allowed the British to place their candidate, Shah Shuja, on the Afghan throne.

But the Pashtun tribes were far from beaten. They strongly resented the foreign "infidel" presence in their capital, and Dost Muhammad's son, Muhammad Akbar, eventually led them in revolt. It soon became apparent that Shah Shuja was not accepted by the Afghans as a bona fide ruler. On the contrary, he was seen as a puppet of the "*farangis*" (foreigners), and his credentials as a Muslim were called into question. "What kind of Afghan Muslim would allow himself to be manipulated in his own country by outside unbelievers?" they asked themselves.

Although Westerners are prone to see this sort of response as a sign of fanaticism, it should be stated that Europeans had a similar response to occupation by a foreign Muslim power. Christian Greeks, Serbs, Bulgarians, and Romanians reacted with comparable ferocity to expel Ottoman Muslim-Turkish "infidels" from their lands in roughly the same time period, and they were not labeled fanatics.

To their disappointment, the British found that the only way their candidate, Shah Shuja, could remain on the throne was through direct military support. Their conundrum was similar to the problem the West currently faces with President Karzai. To keep Shah Shuja in power, British troops were forced to establish garrisons in Kabul. This meant keeping British troops in Afghanistan longer than planned. When confronted with this news, the British General Staff decided to allow their troops to bring their families up to Afghanistan from British India to improve morale.

But the arrival of more "*kafirs*" (infidels) seemed to imply a permanent foreign occupation, and the Afghans became even more agitated. Soon the countryside was up in arms, and it became increasingly difficult for the British garrisons to get supplies up the strategic Khyber Pass from India. In 1842, as the British position became increasingly untenable due to a Ghilzai Pashtun uprising in the east, they contemplated a strategic withdrawal back down to India.

It was at this time that a mob in Kabul killed several high-ranking British officers, and this spontaneous uprising quickly turned into a total revolt. In response, the British commander, William McNaughten, went to meet with the head of the rebels, Muhammad Akbar. But Muhammad Akbar famously turned down McNaughten's offer to be made vizier (chief advisor) to Shah Shuja (Pashtuns still retell this story with pride). On his way back to the British garrison, McNaughten was subsequently killed by an angry mob, and his corpse was dragged through the streets. As the situation spiraled out of control, the British made an ill-fated decision to retreat down the Silk Gorge to safety in Jalalabad, a city located near the border of British-controlled territory.

Although Muhammad Akbar and his rebels promised not to attack the British on their retreat, the wild Ghilzai Pashtun tribes of the eastern border did not feel bound by his promise. They quickly began to pick off the retreating British soldiers as they entered the narrow Silk Gorge. As the British column, which was made up of almost 15,000 people (more than 10,000 camp followers and 4,500 soldiers), made its way down the gorge, the Afghan sharpshooters and fast-moving raiders cut them to pieces. According to popular legend, only one British soldier, Dr. William Brydon, managed to make it to safety in Jalalabad. It was the most humiliating defeat suffered by the British in their entire colonial history.

The Afghan tribes' united response proved that the bitterest rivals could put aside their differences and unite to expel a foreign invader. In the aftermath of the British retreat of 1842, Dost Muhammad returned in triumph to take control of his country, and the British-appointed puppet ruler, Shah Shuja, was later dethroned and killed. All Afghan schoolchildren are taught this story, and those who did not learn it in school during the conflict of the 1980s and 1990s (when schools were closed due to fighting) heard it from their families and clans. Just as Americans have mottoes from the Revolutionary War such as "Live Free or Die" or "Don't Tread on Me," the Afghans remember Muhammad Akbar's proud rejection of the British offer to serve as vizier to the puppet Shah Shuja. The arrogance of the British who sought to place a "stooge" of their choice on the Afghan throne is commemorated to this very day.

Not surprisingly, the Taliban have tried to cast President Hamid Karzai—whom they claim was put on the throne in Kabul with the aid of the "*farangis*"—in a similar light. They have called on Afghans to reject the latest *gaudagi* (puppet) and join them to defend their faith and their nation against the "infidel English and Americans."

In light of the Pashtuns' belief in the tribal value of *namuz* (the need to defend the honor of one's women, faith, and homeland), it cannot be doubted that such calls have resonated with those Pashtuns who see the Coalition troops through the lenses of history, Islam, and Pashtun warrior culture. Although some Taliban insurgents fight for money or out of sheer fanaticism, others fight for the same objectives that led their people to fight the British and Soviets. They are driven by a potent mixture of patriotism, fundamentalism, and xenophobia that stems from previous encounters with invaders. Taken in this light, no benefits offered by the "latest wave of infidel invaders" or their "stooge" Karzai can compensate for the perceived occupation of the Muslim Pashtun homeland by infidel outsiders. Taliban holdouts reject Western projects that aim to dig wells, construct schools, establish businesses, educate women, and build roads. They label such activities "Soviet-style propaganda" designed to lure weak Afghan Muslims from their faith and patriotism.

For such patriotic ultra-fundamentalists there is only one solution to the war—a complete withdrawal of all foreign troops from Afghanistan, of the sort carried out by the British in 1842. Although there has been talk of peace negotiations with the Taliban since late 2008, the Taliban have always stated that they will negotiate only if all "infidel" troops leave their country. Although there are moderate "village Taliban" who are not extremists, the Taliban leadership sees the war in maximalist jihadist terms and claims they will fight until the last foreigner is removed from Afghan soil.

The Second Anglo-Afghan War

History is never dead in Afghanistan, where accounts of legendary battles and past victories shape the martial expectations and traditions of the country's fighting men. Another victory that still resonates across the mountains and valleys of Afghanistan is the improbable Afghan defeat of the British in the Battle of Maiwand. This battle took place during the Second Anglo-Afghan War, which broke out in 1878 after the Afghan amir turned away a British delegation. As they had done in 1839, British expeditionary forces responded by invading Afghanistan and seizing Kabul and Kandahar. The British then put their candidate on the throne.

But despite Britain's initial success, anti-British resistance quickly materialized throughout the Pashtun heartlands. In Kabul, the British garrison was besieged but chose to ride out the storm rather than retreat to India as they had in 1842. Problems also arose in the west of the country when a royal contender named Ayub Khan decided to march on Kandahar and seize it for himself. As Ayub Khan's army approached the sacred city, local Afghan *ghazis* (tribal holy warriors) joined his army and increased its strength. Ayub Khan's army soon swelled to eight thousand soldiers and irregulars, compared to about six thousand for the British force (when local allies and support units were included).

The two forces met in a village in the southern province of Helmand known as Maiwand. What the British lacked in numbers they seemed to have more than made up for in organization and advanced Martini-Henry rifles that could fire twenty rounds per minute. By contrast, the Afghans had old-fashioned Enfield rifles that could only fire two to three rounds per minute. But the Afghans had better artillery and a sense of religious and patriotic fervor that the British of course dismissed as "fanaticism."

When battle began, *ghazi* cavalrymen dressed in white burial shrouds threw themselves on the British with fury. But they were mowed down by British Martini-Henry guns. The main Afghan army then probed the British lines but was repulsed with significant losses. The Afghan irregular forces in particular sustained many dead and wounded.

It is reported that as the Afghans reeled from their losses, a local Pashtun woman named Malalai shamed them to return to battle by raising the Afghan flag (or, more likely, a burqa that was used as a flag) and leading them into battle. Although Malalai was killed by the British, the Afghans followed her lead and attacked the British invaders with renewed vigor.

It was at this time that the British lines finally began to waver. When a unit of British grenadiers failed to hold off a fierce Afghan assault, the British center and left began to collapse. A desperate attempt to beat back the Afghans by launching a cavalry charge failed to halt their advance. In the ensuing chaos the British army quickly broke up into retreating groups. Some of these made heroic last stands before they were overrun and slaughtered by the Afghans.

Hundreds more British soldiers were killed as they retreated back to Kandahar. When the fighting was over, it was estimated that approximately 1,750 British soldiers had died in a matter of hours. It was a catastrophe for the British and one of the worst defeats of a modern European army at the hands of "Asiatics" in the entire colonial era. By contrast, the Americans lost only 244 soldiers in Custer's famous defeat by Native Americans at the Battle of Little Bighorn.

Overnight, Ayub Khan became an Afghan hero, and to this day Afghans recall the story of this military upset of the world-conquering British Empire with pride. Such major historical events have profound ramifications for today's military operations in Afghanistan. In 2006, U.S. troops that had been stationed in the vicinity of Maiwand in Helmand Province were replaced by British NATO troops. The resurgent Taliban saw this as a sign of weakness and promised to "bury a new generation of British soldiers in Afghan graves near those of their ancestors." For many Taliban who had been raised on stories of their people's earlier victories over the British invaders, the site of the Union Jack flag fluttering above British convoys in Maiwand was a sign of impending victory.

But not all of the lessons of Maiwand have such unfortunate implications. Afghans also honor the memory of the heroic Malalai, the woman who gave her life to lead the Afghans into battle. The memory of Malalai's sacrifice for her country lives on in the person of Malalai Joya, an outspoken female member of the current Afghan parliament. In 2003, Malalai Joya shocked the parliament on her first day before that esteemed body. She did so by standing before the entire parliament, which was packed with fundamentalist commanders and warlords, and roundly accusing them of having murdered thousands of their countrymen during the civil war they started in the 1990s. Calling these powerful men criminals to their faces, she held her ground against an upsurge of death threats and calls for her arrest. Her brave stand, like that of her namesake Malalai of Maiwand, captures the contradiction of this land. In this male-dominated land Afghanistan's two most prominent heroines made history simply by taking off a burqa in the nineteenth century and by challenging warlords in the twenty-first century.

Although the Battle of Maiwand gave Afghanistan two more legends for its pantheon of national heroes, the Afghans were ultimately beaten by the British. Ayub Khan was later defeated at Kandahar, and the British ultimately made a deal to put a contender of their own choosing, Abdur Rahman, on the throne. In return for British support, Abdur Rahman ceded control of Afghan foreign affairs to the British and recognized their annexation of the Pashtun lands lying to the south of the Khyber Pass around Peshawar. A large slice of Pashtun territory was thus cut off from the Afghan state and permanently added to British India. This decision was to be of crucial importance and was to shape events in the current anti-Taliban war in Afghanistan. Abdur Rahman was recognizing British control over the Pashtun tribal lands in the east that would later be included in a post-British state carved out of India known as Pakistan. In these unruly Pakistani Pashtun tribal lands (known as the FATA, the Federally Administered Tribal Agencies), Al Qaeda and the Taliban have found sanctuary today.

Although Abdur Rahman gave up an important slice of Pashtun tribal territory to the British in western India (today's Pakistan), he compensated for the loss of these historic Afghan lands by conquering his neighbors and forging the multiethnic state of Afghanistan that exists to this day.

Abdur Rahman, the "Iron Amir"

Unlike his predecessors, Afghanistan's next great ruler after Dost Muhammad, Abdur Rahman, aspired to rule as a *padishah*, a Persian-style emperor, instead of as a first-among-equals (as Afghan amirs had done in the past). He found that the best way to do rule as a *padishah* was to work with the powerful British to shore up his authority. Far from confronting the British, Abdur Rahman used them to build up a centralized bureaucracy and professional military. In the process, he began forcefully creating modern Afghanistan.

In return for Abdur Rahman's promise to recognize British control over the slice of Pashtun lands around the town of Peshawar, the British were delighted to oblige Rahman when he came to the throne in 1880. The British were also granted control of Afghanistan's foreign policy, which meant they could always prevent the Afghans from cozying up with the Russians.

But the deal worked both ways. With British gold and weapons, Abdur Rahman armed troops that were loyal to him (as opposed to employing the undependable tribal *lashkar* levies used by previous rulers) and used them to break the resistance of the restless Pashtun tribes. When the Ghilzai tribal confederation, one of the two main Pashtun groups, rose up against him, Abdur Rahman crushed them using his new army and British guns and artillery. He then forcefully transplanted many of the defeated Ghilzai Pashtun tribes to other non-Pashtun regions he was conquering at the time. These Ghilzai Pashtuns came to act as "internal colonists" when settled in the lands of recently subdued ethnic groups. Abdur Rahman's hope was that the rebellious Ghilzais would act as representatives of the very Afghan-Durrani state they were resisting once they found themselves isolated in a sea of hostile Uzbeks, Tajiks, and Hazaras.

Abdur Rahman's farsighted policy worked better than he could have dreamed, and Pashtun colonies settled in the Hazara lands of southern Uruzgan Province, in the Tajik-Uzbek lands of Kunduz, and in Uzbek-Turkmen lands of Balkh and Bala Murghab became outposts for Afghan-Pashtun central rule. To this day the local Hazara, Tajik, Uzbek, and Turkmen tribes see these Pashtun enclaves in their midst as distrusted fifth columns. During the 1997 Pashtun-Taliban invasion of the Afghan north, the tribes' fears were vindicated when the Pashtuns of Balkh and Kunduz rose up to support the Taliban invaders. Some of these Pashtun communities were subsequently attacked in retribution by the victorious Uzbek, Tajik, and Hazara members of the Northern Alliance after the fall of the Taliban in 2001. Since 2001, some members of these Pashtun settler communities of the north have offered sanctuary to the Taliban insurgents. Kunduz and Badghis Province, both northern areas with large Pashtun pockets, have seen the most Taliban insurgent activity in the otherwise calm northern plains of Turkistan. By 2009, the Taliban had begun to wreak havoc in these northern areas where they found support from local Pashtuns (the Taliban are almost exclusively Pashtun).

But Abdur Rahman's greatest military accomplishment was not the subjugation of his own rebellious tribesmen or the creation of Pashtun internal colonies in the north, but his bloody conquest of the neighboring non-Pashtun peoples. Although several of these ethnic groups had formally recognized some degree of loose Afghan sovereignty since the time of Abdur Rahman's grandfather, Dost Muhammad, most were de facto independent. Abdur Rahman was determined to crush the independence of these ethnic groups once and for all and to forcefully include them in a centralizing Afghan state. For this reason he declared war on the people who would eventually form Afghanistan.

His ambitions were, however, limited to the lands *south* of the Amu Darya River (also known as the Oxus River, the river that forms Afghanistan's northern border) since the Uzbek, Turkmen, and Tajik lands lying to the north of the river had already been conquered by imperial Russia (these lands would later form the independent republics of Uzbekistan, Tajikistan, and Turkmenistan after the collapse of the USSR in 1991).

But the free Uzbek, Turkmen, and Tajik lands lying south of the Amu Darya River were fair game. They were also rich in irrigated lands, and this proved to be a powerful lure for Abdur Rahman. Using the advanced rifles, field cannons, and wealth given to him by his British allies, he invaded the plains of Turkistan in the 1880s and definitively conquered the eleven Uzbek-dominated khanates one after another. When the Uzbeks resisted, their walled citadels, known as arks, were breached by the Iron Amir's British cannons, and their inhabitants were massacred. The Uzbeks' much-feared semi-nomadic cavalry was also decimated by the amir's advanced British field weapons.

By 1888 all of the independent Uzbek states of the north had been subjugated, which also gave Abdur Rahman total dominance over the Tajiks in the northeast (Badakshan) who had been ruled by the Uzbek khans of Kunduz. In addition, his conquests gave him control of the Turkmen tribes who lived along the banks of the Amu Darya and in towns to the west of Mazar i Sharif. Significantly, the Afghan ruler also acquired control of the most important shrine of the north, the magnificent blue-domed tomb of Ali in Mazar i Sharif.

Abdur Rahman subsequently used his cannons to march into the high mountains of Kafiristan, a beautiful forested mountain region in the east, and subdue its free pagan people who still worshipped wooden idols and mountain spirits. A jihad was declared on the multiethnic Kafirs (an Arabic word meaning "infidels"), and one after another their wooden mountain villages were subdued. Abdur Rahman painted this bloody conquest as a noble act by forcefully converting the Kafirs to the "light" of Islam and renaming their land Nuristan (the Land of Light). The Nuristanis subsequently became some of Afghanistan's most devout Muslims. Only a small group of Kafirs living across the border in British India retained their ancient pagan customs. These Kafirs became known as the Kalash and survive to this day in three remote valleys in Pakistan's Chitral Valley.

The conquest of the Kafirs left only the wild Hazara tribes of the Hindu Kush to be tamed. As he did with the pagan Kafirs, Abdur Rahman declared his war on the Hazaras to be a jihad because the Hazaras were Shiites (by contrast, the Uzbeks, Tajiks, Turkmen, and Pashtuns were Sunnis). Hazara villagers were slaughtered, their women were raped, and those living in the south in what would become known as Oruzgan were ethnically cleansed. By the end of the 1880s the Hazarajat mountain plateau had been overwhelmed by Abdur Rahman's Pashtun forces, and the region was brought into the Afghan state. In the process, Abdur Rahman tried to forcefully convert the Hazaras from their Shiite "heresy" to Sunnism, but he largely failed.

Although Afghan history textbooks gloss over the brutality of the Pashtun conquests of the ethnic regions, Abdur Rahman's subjugation of these various lands was accompanied by unimaginable horrors. Tribal chieftains were strapped to cannons and blown out of them over the heads of their families and followers, women were systematically raped, thousands were dragged to Kabul in chains and tortured to death, and many villages were burned. Hazaras could be found as slaves in Afghanistan until the twentieth century when slavery was finally abolished. Abdur Rahman's bloody conquest left tens of thousands dead and displaced and was hardly a "unification" as it is portrayed in Afghan history books. Victorian British officers at the time were horrified by the slaughter that accompanied the forceful unification of this traditionally disparate land but could do little to stop their ally's bloody rampage.

Not surprisingly, the counter-memory of this Afghan-Pashtun conquest survived through the succeeding generations, much as the memory of Union general William Tecumseh Sherman's destructive march from Atlanta to the Atlantic coast survived in the southern states of the Confederacy. However, in the case of the American Civil War, the Northern "Yanks" and the Southern "Rebs" were both English-speaking and predominantly Protestant Anglo-Saxons. In contrast to the warring parties in the American Civil War, the Pashtun conquerors in Afghani-

A typical village scene in the Pashtun belt near Gardez in Paktia Province.

stan spoke a different language, had a different ethnicity, and, in the case of the Kafirs and Shiite Hazaras, also had a different faith. For this reason, non-Pashtun ethnic groups (especially the Shiite Hazaras who formed a despised, unofficial "caste") identified with the Afghan state less than Afghan-Pashtuns who created it. It was not until the 1960s that the Afghan state began to call non-Pashtuns "Afghans," but many non-Pashtuns reject the term to this day.

When the Afghan central state disintegrated during the aftermath of the Soviet invaders' withdrawal and the overthrow of the ruling

Communist government in 1992, Afghanistan's history of brutal conquest led to the unraveling of the Afghan state. As central authority collapsed in the post-Soviet chaos, the various non-Pashtun ethnic groups rose up to regain their lost independence. The warlords of different ethnic groups carved out de facto ethnic mini-states with the weapons provided for them by the Soviets and the Americans. Guns empowered groups such as the despised Hazaras and the Turkic Uzbeks, who were both known as "flat noses" (that is, Mongols) by the Aryan Pashtuns, and allowed them to carve out autonomous regions.

But a new Pashtun fundamentalist movement known as the Taliban soon put an end to the fragmentation after 1996. The Taliban movement, which was made up of Pashtun seminary students, fought to reestablish Pashtun dominance over breakaway ethnic groups and rebuild a centralized Afghanistan. The Taliban conquests of the late 1990s thus had ethnic undertones as the Pashtun Taliban slaughtered Hazara Shiites, ethnically cleansed Tajiks from the Shomali Plain, and butchered Uzbeks in Mazar i Sharif, all in the name of returning them to "pure Islamic law." Not surprisingly, Pashtun communities in the south were much more supportive of the rule of fellow Pasthun Taliban than those non-Pashtun communities in the north.

Since 2001 Afghan president Hamid Karzai, an ethnic Pashtun, has had to walk a fine line in bringing non-Pashtun ethnic areas back under central control. Not surprisingly, many northern groups whose *jang salars* (warlords) have been disarmed as part of Afghanistan's DDR (Disarmament, Demobilization, and Rehabilitation) program are suspicious of Karzai's efforts to arm anti-Taliban *arbakis* (Pashtun militias) in the south. The northern ethnic groups also resent having their leaders, many of whom have strong grassroots support among their own *qawm* (clan, tribe, or ethnic group), labeled "warlords" by the Karzai government. They point out that Abdur Rahman, their nineteenth-century conqueror, and his Afghan predecessors were nothing more than powerful warlords themselves. Had Abdur Rahman not had the support of the British, he never could have deprived the northerners of their independence.

But for all of Abdur Rahman's initial success in expanding the Afghan state, he was eventually forced to cede major portions of his own people's Pashtun heartlands to the British Empire. In 1893, Sir Mortimer Durrand drew a 1,610-mile line through the heart of Pashtun tribal lands, permanently separating Afghanistan from the Pashtun tribal lands around Peshawar. In the name of security, those Pashtun lands lying to the southeast of the line were declared part of British India. Led by messianic religious leaders until the 1940s, the Pashtuns of this British zone rose in revolt against the British, but they never succeeded in overthrowing their "infidel" masters or rejoining Afghanistan. Until the collapse of

British rule in India, a slice of British-controlled Pashtun lands around Peshawar was governed by British agents appointed directly from Delhi. The seven provinces or agencies ruled by the British were, from north to south, Bajaur, Mohmand, Khyber, Orakzai, Kurram, North Waziristan, and South Waziristan.

When India and Pakistan achieved independence in 1947, the so-called Durrand Line became a de facto international frontier separating Pakistani Pashtuns from Afghan Pashtuns. Much to the chagrin of the Pashtuns, especially those living in Afghanistan, this artificial frontier has since taken on a sense of permanency and is now seen as an international border. The Durrand Line continues to divide the Pashtuns in Pakistan's North West Frontier Province and seven FATA from the Pashtuns living in Afghanistan.

It should, however, be stated that the Pashtun areas of the FATA are not considered to be part of Pakistan proper. Pakistan ruled this autonomous tribal area indirectly via agents and local tribal leaders known as *maliks*. The Pakistani army entered this tribal area for the first time in 2002, stirring up considerable resentment among local Pashtun tribesmen who saw the Pakistani military as trespassers. As in the 1930s, when scores of British soldiers died fighting in Pashtun tribal lands, especially in the agencies of North and South Waziristan, Pakistani troops are now dying at the hands of the fierce Waziri tribesmen who consider them invaders. It is a little-known fact that more than two thousand Pakistani troops have died fighting the Pashtun-Taliban tribesmen since 2002. Many Pakistanis resent the United States for pushing them to fight these legendary fighters who are fellow Muslims and Pakistanis.

The "Pashtun problem" is not limited to the Pakistani side of the border. Many Afghan Pashtun nationalists have demanded the return of the lost Pashtun lands that made up an integral part of the original Afghan state founded by Ahmed Shah in 1747. They claim that the 1893 Durrand Line drawn by the British to demarcate Afghanistan's eastern border is artificial and that the Pashtun lands of Pakistan actually belong to the Afghan state. Pakistanis have naturally refused to discuss the issue of giving up these lands in their state that are inhabited by three million Pashtuns. Along with Baluchistan, Sindh, and the Punjab, the Pashtun-dominated North West Frontier Province (also known as Khyber Pakhtunkhwa) is one of the four main provinces of Pakistan. Removing the Pashtun lands from Pakistan would weaken its territorial base considerably. It would also deprive Pakistan of the Pashtuns who play a major role in its armed forces.

For this reason, Pakistanis are extremely resentful of Afghan rulers who raise the "Pashtunistan" issue (that is, the matter of reuniting the lost Pashtun lands of Pakistan with those in Afghanistan). One of the reasons the Pakistani Inter Services Intelligence (ISI) supported the Taliban in the 1990s was that the Taliban were first and foremost organized around *religion*. For all of the Taliban's repression of non-Pashtun ethnic groups, Pashtun ethnicity was always the second-most important concern of the Taliban, who were principally beholden to their Pakistani fundamentalist allies (although not even Taliban leader Mullah Omar could accept the Durrand Line). For this reason, the ISI felt that the Islamically oriented Taliban would be less likely to stir up the Pashtunistan irredentism issue than Afghan nationalists who wanted to unite Pashtuns on the basis of their ethnicity.

Since the commencement of the post-2001 Taliban insurgency, the Pakistanis have offered to plant land mines along the Afghan-Pakistani border (that is, the Durrand Line) to prevent Taliban infiltration into Afghanistan. But President Karzai has adamantly refused to condone this act. He understands that such recognition of the "imaginary" Durrand Line would cost him the support of millions of his fellow Afghan Pashtuns. Every day tens of thousands of Pashtuns cross this border, and in many areas there are no frontier posts or markers to delineate it. To make this artificial border more permanent would be to recognize the division of Pashtun tribes that straddle the border and to acknowledge the colonial-era conquest of a sizable portion of the Pashtuns. Today there are more Pashtuns living in Pakistan than Afghanistan, and Pashtun nationalists still dream of "Pashtunizing" Afghanistan and making the Pashtuns, who comprise roughly 40 percent of Afghanistan's population, a majority.

Although modern-day Pashtun nationalists criticize Abdur Rahman for "selling" their lands to the British, there was actually very little the Afghan ruler could do to regain them from his powerful British neighbors. The British "compensated" Abdur Rahman's state in 1895 by adding a narrow strip of mountainous land to its northeastern border. However, this "gift" actually served the British self-interest. This mountainous addition known as the Wakkhan Corridor served as a "shock absorber" between the Russian Empire to the north and British India. It prevented these two expansionist Christian powers from grinding up against one another. The gift of the Wakkhan is the reason there is a strange land "peninsula" jutting out from Afghanistan's northeastern border toward China.

But for all of the criticism leveled against Abdur Rahman by his descendants, he left an expanded and fairly centralized state with a relatively strong bureaucracy when he died in 1901. He also established provinces ruled by *walis* (governors) responsible directly to him alone. Most important, he managed to keep his country free of British and Russian direct rule. This minor miracle was achieved, in part, by keeping the Russian and British officials, merchants, engineers, etc., out of Afghanistan. For example, when the British offered to build a railroad into his kingdom, Abdur Rahman adamantly refused. He felt it would enable the British to penetrate his lands and might excite the distrust of the Russians.

As a result, the isolated Afghan state Abdur Rahman bequeathed to his people never experienced the modernizing periods of direct European colonization that took place in British India (and Pakistan) or Russian Central Asia. For example, unlike the Uzbeks living in the plains of northern Afghanistan, the ex-Soviet Uzbeks living in Uzbekistan speak Russian, drive Russian-built Moskovitch cars, wear Western clothes, live in pre-fab concrete Brezhnev-era apartment complexes, and have comparatively secular views toward women, education, alcohol etc. By contrast, the Uzbeks in Afghanistan ride on horses, live in clay-walled compounds, are largely illiterate, and rarely allow women to leave the home without wearing a burqa. But the Soviet Uzbeks have also lost many of their people's rich cultural traditions during the process of enforced modernization. Their culture has been Russified and Sovietized to the extent that Afghan Uzbeks and ex-Soviet Uzbeks in Uzbekistan are almost different nations today.

Similarly, many Pakistanis were shaped by their British colonial rulers, and the British influence is pervasive in comparatively liberal Pakistan. This is especially true among the English-speaking Pakistani elite of the east who live in Lahore or Islamabad. It is only in the Pashtun tribal areas of the west (FATA), an autonomous area that was largely unaffected by British and Pakistani rule, that British influence was minimal. There one finds a level of tribalism and religious conservatism that is not shaped by the culture of India or the British.

Twentieth-century Afghanistan and the Pashtun tribal lands of Pakistan, in contrast to Soviet Central Asia and the rest of Pakistan, thus remained a land that time forgot. Afghanistan was a medieval anomaly where Uzbeks, Turkmen, Pashtuns, Hazaras, Afghans, and other ethnic groups lived in clay-walled fortresses without electricity; men often had multiple wives who practiced *purdah* (veiling); tribal raids were commonplace; and paved roads, hospitals, universities, and factories—all of which were found just over the border in the USSR—were almost nonexistent.

By the 1920s, however, Afghanistan's new ruler, Amanullah Khan, embarked on an ambitious project that sought to end Afghanistan's isolation and backwardness. His goal was nothing less than the modernization of his country, with the aim of bringing Islamic Eurasia's most undeveloped nation into the twentieth century. The tragic story of his fall from power is full of implications for today's internationally sponsored effort to rebuild Afghanistan and bring it into the twenty-first century.

Amanullah Khan, "Afghanistan's First Karzai"

The story of Amanullah Khan, Afghanistan's first modernizing king, is one that has eerie parallels with the struggle of the current Afghan president, Hamid Karzai. Like his modern-day successor, King Amanullah had to walk a tightrope between reactionary mullahs (religious leaders), armed Islamist rebels, and regional warlords as he strove to build schools for girls, liberalize the country, and introduce a Western-style constitution.

In the end, however, he was overthrown by reactionary rebels who overturned his "un-Islamic" reforms and modernizing projects. And although his story ended in tragedy, Amanullah Khan's reign began auspiciously enough. He came to the throne in 1919 with the aim of ending Britain's control over his country's foreign policy (which dated back to the Second Anglo-Afghan War). With this goal in mind, he launched a surprise attack on the British in the spring of 1919. The Pashtuns on both sides of the border rose up against the British, and as many as two thousand British were killed in the hill fighting.

The British, who were still recovering from their horrific losses in World War I, had no stomach for a prolonged fight. After repulsing two of Amanullah's thrusts, they agreed to peace negotiations that paved the way for Afghanistan to regain control of its foreign policy.

Despite repeated efforts, Amanullah failed to gain control of the slice of Pashtun tribal lands found inside of British India (FATA and the North West Frontier Province). The Afghans nonetheless consider the war a victory, their third straight victory in a series of wars with the British. This final twentieth-century victory has contributed to the Pashtuns' belief in their ability to repel any and all invaders, even advanced unbelievers like the "Ingliz" who used airplanes in 1919 and in today's war.

Amanullah Khan's second project was equally ambitious and was inspired by a trip he took through Europe. He dreamed of emulating the modernizing reforms inaugurated in post–Ottoman Empire Turkey by Mustafa Kemal Ataturk. It was Ataturk who transformed the Ottoman Empire from a backward Islamic empire known as "the Sick Man of Europe" into a modern republic that eventually joined NATO. Like his role model Ataturk, Amanullah Khan aspired to break the control of Afghanistan's conservative clergy, build schools for girls, inaugurate secular laws, build airports, pave roads, and empower women. He also aimed to increase the influence of the capital in provinces that had always been autonomous vis-à-vis taxation, conscription into the army, and the removal of powerful tribal leaders.

But Amanullah's reforms caused widespread resistance among conservative religious leaders in the countryside who feared and despised his policies. Among other policies, they resented his enforcement of Western-style ("infidel") clothes for government officials, the mixing of girls and boys in schools, the building of colleges in Kandahar and Kabul, the construction of telegraph poles, and the fact that his outspoken queen, Soraya, was leading by example in her effort to encourage Turkish-style unveiling. Calling his wife a whore, the mullahs led an uprising among the powerful Shinwari Pashtun tribe that began in the frontier town of Jalalabad and among the Mangal and Zadran tribes in Khost Province. (Incidentally, the Zadran tribe of Khost is currently revolting under the leadership of Taliban commander Jalaluddin Haqqani). From there, the rebellion quickly spread to other Ghilzai tribes and to the capital.

As this Pashtun uprising took place, a Tajik (Persian-Dari-speaking) rebel from the north named Habibullah "Bacha i Saqao" (the Son of the Water Carrier) attacked the capital and chased Amanullah and his "infidel" queen out of the country. Bacha i Saqao gave himself the title "The Servant of the Messenger of God" and subsequently declared strict shariah-Islamic law in Afghanistan. His followers burned down Amanullah's girls' schools, and several of the bold Afghan women who had dared to go unveiled were stoned to death.

Although the Pashtun tribes approved of the overthrow of the meddling Afghan king and his "un-Islamic" practices, they rejected the rule of the Tajik usurper Bacha i Saqao. He was subsequently attacked by Pashtun Ghilzais and other members of the royal Durrani dynasty who established the pattern of using rear-area staging bases in the Pashtun lands of British India/Pakistan to organize their forces. These Pashtun restorers of the Durrani dynasty then moved on Kabul and overthrew Bacha i Saqao, who was subsequently executed. Incidentally, it was not until the collapse of the Afghan Communist government in 1992 that another non-Pashtun "usurper" gained control of the country. On that occasion it was to be Massoud, the Lion of Panjsher, a legendary anti-Soviet Tajik resistance fighter, who rose to power. The Pashtun mujahideen faction led by Gulbuddin Hekmatyar adamantly refused to recognize Massoud's Tajik political master, Burhanuddin Rabbani, as president and instead besieged the capital. This caused the outbreak of the bloody 1992–1996 Afghan civil war. Simply put, in both the beginning and the end of the twentieth century, Pashtuns felt very strongly that theirs was the only ethnic group that had the right to run the country.

The Pashtuns clearly felt it was their right to overthrow their rulers if their conservative Islamic values were being threatened. But as in the case of the Tajik usurper Bacha i Saqao, only Pashtuns were allowed to carry out a coup d'etat. Regardless of the ethnic subtext to the overthrow of Amanullah, the king's fall from power served as a warning to subsequent rulers. All subsequent rulers would have to walk a fine line between increasing their power, secularizing and modernizing the country, and upsetting the mullahs and tribal/regional khans who represented the real center of gravity in Afghanistan. If they went too far, the tribes would legitimize their efforts to throw off Kabul's rule by declaring a jihad against the center.

Zahir Shah, Afghanistan's Last King

Although the next important ruler, King Zahir Shah, was also a modernizing and liberalizing ruler, he was nowhere near as energetic as his predecessor, Amanullah Khan. For the most part, King Zahir Shah is remembered as a rather tentative, lackluster ruler who introduced a constitutional monarchy but failed to enforce it. His power was mitigated by the fact that he was dominated by his uncles and his powerful cousin, Prime Minister Mohammad Daoud. The King's efforts to establish a parliamentary democracy and free women from the harsher aspects of *purdah* confinement met with some success, but in the end he failed to fundamentally modernize and liberalize his country.

Although his rule was not marked by major developments of his own making, Zahir Shah lived through interesting times. For example, fourteen years after his reign began, British rule in India ended, and the newly independent state of Pakistan was created next door.

During World War II Zahir Shah maintained strict neutrality and in subsequent decades tried to develop his backward country with the help of both the Soviets and the Americans. From the 1950s to the 1960s, the Soviets were involved in developing the Afghan north while the Americans led the effort in the south. In the north the Soviets built factories, gas and oil wells, and the Salang Pass over the Hindu Kush Mountains. They also helped the Afghan king modernize his army and shipped him T-35 tanks and MiG fighter bombers.

For their part, although the Americans provided considerable help in constructing dams in Kandahar and Helmand Province in addition to an airport, they did not find neutral Afghanistan worthy of arms supplies. To build an army, Zahir Shah and his cousin Daoud were therefore forced to rely on the Soviets, who thus made inroads into the Afghan army. Their inroads were especially extensive among those Afghan officers who had been exposed to Soviet modernization while they were undergoing training in military academies in the USSR. Afghan officers who trained in the USSR were impressed by the country's modernity and dreamed of similarly modernizing their backward homeland.

Afghanistan's relations with Pakistan proved to be equally fraught with dangerous implications, despite their shared Islamic cultures. Tensions were caused by Zahir Shah's cousin Daoud, who continued talk of reuniting the Afghan and Pakistani Pashtun lands into a greater "Pashtunistan." On occasion this issue flared up and led to border closings, skirmishes, economic embargoes, and brinkmanship, but it never came to full-scale war.

Thus Afghanistan tried to play off the three powers—Pakistan, the USSR, and the United States—that would subsequently involve themselves in the anti-Soviet Afghan jihad of the 1980s. One of the results of this balancing act was the creation of the People's Democratic Party of Afghanistan (PDPA), a party that was, despite its name, Communist and linked to Moscow. By the 1970s, college students and officers in the army who joined the PDPA began to grow frustrated with their timid king's pace of reform. They bemoaned the fact that the Afghan countryside was largely dominated by conservative mullahs and powerful khans. They claimed that these entrenched voices of conservatism worked to thwart the government's modernization policies. The PDPA's solution was to rip their country out of the Middle Ages by force. The PDPA Communists dreamed of modernizing Afghanistan much as the Uzbek, Turkmen, and Tajik lands of the USSR had been forcefully brought into the twentieth century by the Soviets during Stalin's *hujum* (an "assault" on Islam that saw mosques closed, mullahs executed as "parasites," and women forcefully unveiled by KGB security services).

While the PDPA Communists gained adherents among liberal modernizers, conservative religious students were drawn in an entirely different direction. They were drawn to a political movement that came from Egypt known as the Muslim Brotherhood (Ikhwan al Muslimun or simply Ikhwanis [Brothers], as many Afghans called them). Far from emulating European-style modernization, the Muslim Brotherhood called for the expulsion of "infidel" Western colonial rulers in Egypt (the British) and other Muslim lands colonized by Western Christian powers. They also called for the introduction of shariah Islamic law and the politicization of Islam in the Arab world.

It should be noted that these calls stood in stark contradiction to Afghan tradition, through which secular rulers, not mullahs, had always governed. Although village mullahs or local religious figures could exert power locally or rally the people on the basis of Islam (as in the case of a foreign invasion or intrusion by an "infidel" king), they were not the rulers of the land. The real rulers were local tribal or village landed elites, the khans or *maliks*, who were nominally under the control of the Afghan amir, *walis* (governors), or *serdars* (princely commanders).

The Ikhwanis' calls for politicizing Afghan Islam also flew in the face of Afghanistan's Sufi-mystical tradition, which was marked by its lack of political fanaticism. The three main Afghan Sufi (mystic) brotherhoods were the Naqshbandi, Qadiriyah, and Cheshtiya. All of them had a tradition of borrowing from and accepting other religious traditions. In Afghanistan, Muslims were as likely to make pilgrimages to local magical shrines and ask for amulets to protect them from the evil eye as to make the pilgrimage to Mecca in Arabia. Such Sufi mystical traditions were of course frowned on by the Ikhwanis, who called for a literal interpretation of the Holy Quran. Unlike the Arabs, the Sufi-moderate Afghans had also never been conquered and colonized by Europeans. For this reason, they had no chip on their shoulder toward the West. Their Sufi traditions were not as radical as the Muslim Brotherhood or the Saudi Wahhabi fundamentalists who were at war with Sufi mysticism.

But the ancient Sufi brotherhoods were losing their influence among young conservatives, who had become increasingly politicized in the 1970s. As this process continued apace, Afghanistan's first Arab-style religious party, the Jamiat i Islam (Community of Islam), emerged. This fundamentalist party was led by a Tajik named Burhanuddin Rabbani who had been trained in Cairo's prestigious Al Azhar Islamic university. Another rival party, known as the Hezb i Islam (Party of Islam), led by an Ikhwani-inspired fundamentalist Pashtun named Gulbuddin Hekmatyar, was also formed at this time.

These conservative Afghan Muslim parties began to clash with the liberal Afghan Communists and with secularists who sought to import Western traditions in the 1970s. In particular, fights between Hezb i Islam followers and Communists regularly broke out at Kabul University. And as a sign of things to come, the fundamentalist followers of Hezb i Islam founder Gulbuddin Hekmatyar were said to have thrown disfiguring acid in the faces of bold women in Kabul who wore short skirts or went unveiled. It was an internal culture war.

As the Communist-secularists and Islamic-fundamentalist parties began a series of clashes that would culminate in tit-for-tat murders, King Zahir Shah was engaged in a battle of his own. His was a battle to break out from the control of his domineering cousin, Prime Minister Daoud, who was the real power behind the throne. But in 1973, while the King was in Italy having eye surgery, Daoud deposed Zahir Shah and overthrew the monarchy. Afghanistan was declared a republic and Daoud its president. During his five-year rule from 1973 to 1978, Daoud sought to acquire weapons from the Soviets to strengthen his army. On occasion he also stirred up the "Pashtunistan" issue, which caused problems with Pakistan.

Domestically, Daoud tried to balance Afghanistan's competing political parties, playing off the Communist reformists against the Islamist conservatives. Anyone who challenged his authority was treated with brutality, and he had members of both Islamic and Communist groups arrested or killed when they plotted against him.

During this period of political fermentation, foreigners began to visit Afghanistan, many of whom were backpackers passing through this colorful tribal land known for its *buzkashi* (polo), mountain hiking, spectacular ruins, colorful tribes, hospitality, and modernizing capital. Visitors to Kabul found a predominantly Tajik-Farsi-speaking city that was a mixture of ancient and the new. Backpackers could stay in hotels, buy cheap carpets and hash, see Afghan women walking the streets in Western-style skirts, and go to the city's movie cinemas. They could also see poverty, open sewage, women in burqas, men riding donkeys, and beggars.

But in the countryside, life continued as it had for centuries. In the provinces, khans controlled the destiny of illiterate villagers, and there were few of the modern amenities that one could find in neighboring Uzbekistan or Iran. Although President Daoud passed laws freeing women from veiling, burqas were still prevalent, especially in the Pashtun south and east (contrary to popular belief, the Taliban did not introduce the burqa, or *chadri* as it is more commonly known—it had been around for centuries). Although there were some improvements, such as the building of new schools; a ring road linking Kabul to the major cities of Kandahar, Herat, and Mazar i Sharif; and electricity that was brought to most towns, much of Afghanistan remained stuck in the Middle Ages. Girls were married off at young ages, literacy rates and life expectancy were among the lowest in the world, Kuchi Pashtun nomads clashed with Hazaras, and villagers turned to local mullahs to cure them from *jinns* (demons) that they believed caused their illness.

It was this backwardness, and the perceived role that the entrenched khans and reactionary mullahs played in preventing modernization, that led the PDPA Communists to finally contemplate overthrowing Daoud by 1978. They dreamed of speeding up the modernization process. In addition, they wanted to end the inequality that caused most peasants to spend their lives farming lands for their rich landlords and living in debt.

But the Communists' April (Saur) 1978 overthrow of Daoud and their attempts to enforce Communist-style modernization on the rural population led to a mass uprising. It was this uprising that led to the Soviets' fateful 1979 invasion to support the beleaguered Afghan Communist Party in its struggle with the rebels. Although many Americans believed at the time that the Soviets were invading Afghanistan to annex it and move closer to the strategic Persian Gulf, we now know that their objectives were actually much more limited. They were simply trying to save an allied Communist regime that had bitten off more than it could chew. History would show that the Soviets got in over their heads in this untamed country.

Chapter 4

Soviet Rule, the Mujahideen, and the Rise of the Taliban

While some U.S. high school students in the early 1980s had pictures of sports or music heroes on their walls, my walls were covered with news images of Massoud the legendary Lion of Panjsher. Massoud was the Tajik mujahideen guerrilla who had humiliated the Soviet Union and become an icon for millions of Afghans and many Cold Warriors in the West. For me, the image of Massoud with his trademark *pakol* hat was as iconic as any image of Che Guevara. After all, it was the Cold War, and Massoud, an outgunned Afghan "freedom fighter," was doing what any *Rambo* aficionado dreamed of doing—fighting off the "red wave" of Communism in defense of his people, his faith, and his homeland.

Later, when I went to college at Stetson University in Florida, I was given a chance to meet Russian soldiers a few years older than me who had fought against Massoud in the Panjsher during a winter semester in the USSR. The Russian soldiers I met in Moscow in 1987 spoke with awe and fear of fighting Massoud's *basmachis* (bandits) in the mountains of the Panjsher and plains of Shomali. They truly considered him and his men to be half *dukhi* (ghosts). When Massoud was killed on September 9, 2001, by an Al Qaeda suicide bomber, I lost a hero, no matter how flawed he may have been.

On my second trip to Afghanistan, I was therefore determined to make a pilgrimage to the Panjsher Valley to see the famous mountains from which my Tajik idol had fought an empire to a standstill. Unfortunately, my hosts were Uzbeks and Turkmen, and they did not see Massoud as a hero. They revered General Dostum and were therefore reluctant to venture into Massoud's Tajik province.

My guide, Seracettin Mahdum, the son of a famous Turkmen holy man known as the Kizil Ayak (Red Foot) Sheikh explained to me: "There is nothing in Panjsher. Just mountains, goats, a dirt road, and more mountains."

I patiently explained to him that this was exactly why I wanted to go to this forlorn spot—to see the natural terrain. Seracettin reluctantly agreed to drive me there from our residence in Kunduz. Kunduz was a nondescript Uzbek-dominated town located in the northeastern plains of Afghan Turkistan. Its bazaar was lively and filled with kabob stands, the occasional German NATO patrol, numerous Uzbek villagers, Pashtuns who had been settled in the region in the nineteenth century by the Iron Amir, and donkeys and camels. It was, by Afghan standards, a relatively peaceful place, although the Taliban had recently begun making some inroads into the region and would soon conquer many outlying districts.

It was at Kunduz that the Taliban army of the north made its last stand in Operation Enduring Freedom. By mid-November 2001 Dostum had crushed the Taliban in Mazar i Sharif, and the Taliban had retreated to Kunduz to fight to the finish. In Kunduz the Taliban were mercilessly pummeled by Tajik forces from the east, Dostum's forces from the west, and the U.S. Air Force from above. The United States even brought in a new weapon—AC-130 Specter gunships to militarily "degrade" the Taliban force in Kunduz. The U.S. B-52 and Specter bombings broke the spirit of the Taliban, and they began to surrender and join the Northern Alliance. Although many of the Al Qaeda foreign fighters were determined to fight to the death, the Taliban were Afghans who had much more pragmatic views of ritualistically surrendering to erstwhile enemies. They decided to surrender not to the Tajiks whom they feared, but to Dostum who had a reputation for being a rather flexible moderate.

Thousands of Taliban then did as Dostum ordered and marched into the desert hills west of Kunduz to a Taliban-controlled position called Ergenek to surrender. Dostum gave me a video of the surrender, which featured columns of bedraggled Taliban, Arabs, and Pakistanis being loaded into trucks for a journey eastward to the fortress of Qala i Jengi (where they later revolted). We visited the Taliban's former positions at Ergenek and found them filled with spent artillery shells, bombed-out trenches and shelters, and the occasional destroyed vehicle. It was a graveyard and memorial to the collapse of Taliban rule in the plains of Afghan Turkistan.

But for all of Dostum's importance in capturing Mazar i Sharif, it was Massoud, not Dostum, who had resisted the Taliban with the greatest determination, and we decided to set out from Kunduz to cross the mountains and see his home terrain. We crossed the Hindu Kush Mountains, which make up the "spine" of Afghanistan, via the spectacular Salang Tunnel going south, and we descended to the Shomali Plain on the southern side.

Having crossed the mountains, we drove eastward across the northern fringe of the Shomali Plain toward a wall of mountains looming before us. Although the mountain wall appeared to be impenetrable, the road ultimately took us to a narrow gorge carved out by the Panjsher River that led directly into the peaks. The frothy river at this point was no more than ten yards wide with a narrow dirt road carved into a ledge on the northern bank. The entrance to the gorge was guarded by several Kalashnikov-toting Tajik soldiers who sat beneath a billboard featuring a picture of Massoud. There was no doubt whose lands we were entering. We were passing into the Panjsher, the lair of the legendary Massoud.

We drove along the dangerous ledge road as the sun set and saw dozens of destroyed Soviet tanks and armored personnel carriers rusting on the banks of the river. We also noticed abandoned villages on the mountainsides that a local told us had been bombed by the Soviets in the 1980s. By then the sun had set, and we drove cautiously along the banks of the river through a series of villages that were closed down for the night.

Finally we arrived in Jangalak, Massoud's home village and site of the green-domed tomb over his grave. We decided to try to find a place to stay for the night. Unfortunately, there were no inns in the town, but some curious villagers directed us to Massoud's former headquarters. There we found a couple of bearded Tajik mujahideen fighters (one missing an eye) who had served alongside Massoud for years. When I told them that I had come all the way from the United States to pay tribute to their former commander, they were deeply touched. Their leader kindly offered to let our party stay in Massoud's former headquarters for the night, and I was thrilled.

We were then led into the very building from which Massoud had run his operations, and his presence still lingered. His office was left almost untouched, with his books of Persian poetry scattered around, a pair of his military boots in the corner, an Afghan flag on the wall, and a wreath with his picture on it in his chair.

We were then directed to a room in which we were told he had slept, and we were allowed to sleep on pallets by the wall. But as our guards left, we witnessed a sight that made us think twice about staying in the Lion's headquarters. No sooner had the door to our room been closed than a fist-sized scorpion crawled under it and began to scuttle about like some deadly crab. I instinctively yelped in shock, and the mujahideen guards ran back in and began chasing the scorpion. One of them used his military boot to crush it with relish—at least most of it. Parts of the scorpion still writhed around for a few seconds, and I decided at that moment that I was not sleeping in Massoud's bed, no matter how much of an honor it might have been.

When I asked one of the guards if the scorpions were deadly, he took great pleasure in telling us that on occasion people survived their stings, but only with the prayers of a mullah and the help of an evil eye amulet. With that, we retreated to our dusty SUV and had a fitful sleep until the bleak mountains began to come to life in the pre-dawn light.

As the sky turned from black to blue, I stretched my legs and decided to go up the hill to see Massoud's tomb before everyone else awoke. The tomb itself was situated on a windy hill overlooking the idyllic riverside village of Jangalak. Next to the tomb were a couple of destroyed Soviet tanks and other remnants of the Russian outpost that was temporarily established there in the 1980s—that, and the barren mountains whose rocks make an eerie whistling sound in the wind as if the ghosts of past battles haunted the valley.

As for the tomb itself, it was a simple, round edifice no larger than a room with a lighted green dome atop it. In the center of the tomb lay the carpet-covered gravestone of Massoud, the man who did more than any other to free his homeland from the Soviets and to defend it from the Taliban. I was touched by its simplicity. It was a monument for a man who did not live ostentatiously and was content to live like the lowliest of his soldiers despite his fame.

As the morning winds howled outside and the sun rose, I said a prayer for the soul of my childhood hero and noticed a guest book that some-one had placed on a stand by the mausoleum entrance. Leafing through its pages, I saw many testimonials in Tajik-Dari but was most moved by one I found in English written by a rare American visitor. Referencing Massoud's desperate attempts to alert President George W. Bush to the Al Qaeda threat emanating from the Arab terrorists in his country in the months prior to 9/11, the simple message read, "Thank you for try-ing to warn us. Sorry we didn't listen to you sooner."

The Communist Coup and Soviet Invasion

The famous 1978 Saur (April) Revolution (or, more correctly, coup d'etat since it was not actually a mass revolution) that overthrew President Daoud began when Daoud moved to arrest key Afghan Communist Party leaders. One of those leaders whom Daoud targeted for arrest, Hafizul-lah Amin, managed to get word out in advance to Communist members in the army. He ordered them to initiate a coup against Daoud, and they led their army units in attacking the president at his palace in Kabul. In response, Daoud decided to fight back like the Pashtun heroes of old. But he and as many as one thousand of his followers were killed in the ensuing tank, aircraft, and ground assault on his palace.

The Communists then proclaimed one of their own, a Pashtun named Nur Muhammad Taraki, as president of the "Democratic Republic of

Afghanistan." They then began a series of reforms designed to modernize and secularize Afghanistan in Soviet-style "five-year plans." But the Communists were a small minority in Afghanistan (there were no more than twelve thousand Communists in Afghanistan at the time). The cadres of young ideologues they sent out to the countryside to teach Marxism, increase literacy, empower women, and establish health clinics were often met with hostility by suspicious villagers who were very conservative.

For their part, the PDPA Communists had no tolerance for the "backward" traditions that dominated the countryside, and they tended to treat respected khans and mullahs as "bourgeois exploiters" and "reactionary social parasites." Needlessly provocative measures, such as changing the color of the Afghan flag from green (a color that symbolizes Islam) to red (for Communism) and the using women in educational cadres sent to remote villages, further angered the conservatives of the countryside.

When the Communists moved to redistribute land from khans (who owned most of the country's property) to poor peasant sharecroppers who worked it, the landed elites were infuriated. And when the Communists interfered in such traditions as the giving of dowries and marriages of young girls, they infuriated the mullahs. In addition, a rumor began to spread throughout the countryside that the Communists were empowering women only to send them to Russia to work as prostitutes. As the Communist government brutally forced itself on the provinces, which had never before had a government influence, the semi-autonomous regions rose in revolt.

The spark that set the countryside on fire was lit in the eastern regions of Nuristan and Kunar, and from there the inferno began to spread throughout the land. Soon, schools and clinics were being burned, and Communist teachers were being killed. The Communist Party exacerbated matters by launching a wave of terror of its own. Thousands of innocent Afghans suspected of having links to the "*ashrars*" (rebels) were arrested, tortured, and killed in the notorious Pul i Charki Prison near Kabul. By the summer of 1979, the rebels were no longer using the term *ashrar* for themselves. They had declared their struggle a jihad (holy war) and called themselves mujahideen (singular, *mujahid*, one who wages jihad). This was an ominous sign, for the last time the countryside had risen up in jihad against the meddling of an "infidel" ruler, it led to the overthrow of the reformist King Amanullah by the Tajik rebel Bacha i Saqao in 1929.

As they had done in 1929, the local khans and mullahs led their followers into the hills, where they began to form local fighting fronts known as *sangars* (trenches). These units then launched haphazard tribal attacks on local government bases and police stations. Rarely did a *sangar* range beyond its own locale. If it did, it had to gain the permission of the leaders of that valley or tribe who might fight trespassers.

The rebellion was initially rather spontaneous, local, and ad hoc. A rebel group might consist of a *qawm* (clan, village, or local ethnic group) that had decided to rise up in response to the arrest of a local khan/mullah or the intrusion of some meddling "infidel" policy. As such, the mujahideen developed a reputation of respectability, and they were fed and housed by the local population. As men who had given up their work in the fields to fight injustice, the mujahideen were held to high moral standards and were considered holy warriors in the finest of Islamic traditions.

The leaders of these groups were for the most part local khans, but this would soon change. The local nature of the resistance began to change when Islamic parties, such as Rabbani's Jamiat i Islam and Hekmatyar's Hezb i Islam, began to run trans-regional mujahideen operations from across the border in Pakistan. As hundreds of thousands of Afghans became displaced by fighting between the Afghan Communist Government and Afghan mujahideen rebel forces, the above-mentioned parties began to recruit and finance full-time fighters who were loyal not to their clan, khan, or region, but to their party. These full-time mujahideen, known as *maslaki* (professionals) or *mutaharek* (mobile fighters), were recruited into seven mujahideen parties that were based in the Pashtun border city of Peshawar in Pakistan. Gradually, the Islamic parties' commanders displaced most of the local khans who had initially led the uprisings. In the process they began to indoctrinate their fighters and teach them fundamentalism of the Egyptian Islamic Brotherhood and Islamist parties found in Pakistan. The rebellion thus led to the radicalization of many of the mujahideen rebels.

Pakistan's role in these developments was key. Pakistan, which had always borne the brunt of Afghan-sponsored insurgent rebellions in its Pashtun provinces (namely, Daoud's efforts to create "Pashtunistan"), was only too eager to pay back Afghanistan for its interference. The Pakistanis sponsored the formation of seven mujahideen parties, among them a royalist party that sought the return of King Zahir Shah, a Sufi moderate party, a single Tajik party, and the Hezb i Islam, which was led by the fanatical Gulbuddin Hekmatyar. Ultimately, the Pakistanis chose to support Gulbuddin Hekmatyar, the most fundamentalist of all the major rebel leaders, for the simple reason that his party was Islamist first and foremost. The Pakistani Inter Services Intelligence was confident that Hekmatyar and his highly organized fundamentalist followers would rally fighters on the basis of Islam, not their common Pashtun identity. Arming Pashtun nationalist fighters who might one day turn their guns on the Pakistani government to carve out a Pashtunistan was clearly not in the Pakistanis' interests.

In addition to Hekmatyar, there were several great mujahideen leaders who fought the Communists in the 1980s jihad. These commanders, who were based in Afghanistan, were often distant from the political parties based in Peshawar. Several of them are discussed below.

Ismail Khan, the Amir of Herat

As exile parties in Pakistan were developing, several key commanders began to emerge inside of Afghanistan itself. The first of these was a Tajik *toran* (captain) named Ismail Khan. Khan was an officer in the Afghan government army who was sent to suppress a rebellion in the western Tajik city of Herat in March 1979. But when he was commanded to fire on his protesting countrymen, he refused to do so. Instead, he attacked the Soviet advisors and their families who had been dispatched by the USSR to assist their Afghan Communist allies. The Soviets and teachers sent by the Communist government were all slaughtered, and the rebels were said to have paraded their decapitated heads through the streets of Herat.

As vengeful Afghan Communist army forces were dispatched to Herat, Khan and his men fled eastward into the Hindu Kush Mountains to wage a guerrilla war. Ismail Khan subsequently became a legend among the Tajik mujahideen in the west for his struggle against the Afghan Communists and Soviet invaders. As a Tajik, he naturally joined the mujahideen party of fellow Tajik Burhanuddin Rabbani (the Jamiat i Islam Party, to which Massoud the Lion of Panjsher had also belonged). But despite his nominal allegiance, Khan, like Massoud, remained largely independent of Rabbani's leadership. Ismail Khan and other commanders in the field in Afghanistan typically had little respect for party political leaders living safely in exile in Pakistan.

After Ismail Khan's retreat to the mountains, the Communist government used Soviet-supplied MiGs to bomb Herat. In the process, much of this ancient Silk Road city that had been the capital of the ancient Timurid dynasty of Tamerlane was destroyed. In the ensuing inferno as many as twenty-four thousand Heratis were massacred. But despite his best efforts to come to the aid of the people of Herat, Khan was unable to break out of the mountains and liberate the city, which had a large Communist garrison guarding it.

As a Persian-speaking Tajik, Khan turned to Persian-speaking Iran for assistance, but it should not be forgotten that the Iranians were first and foremost Shiites, whereas Khan was a Sunni. For this reason, the

Iranians initially gave only limited assistance to Khan and instead directed most of their aid to the Shiite Hazara factions (although this would later change). The Iranians were always circumspect in their shipment of aid to the anti-Soviet rebels for fear of overly antagonizing their powerful Soviet neighbor and pushing Moscow into the arms of their archenemy, Iraq (Shiite Iran and Socialist-Baathist Iraq were fighting a war of their own at the time).

When the Afghan Communist government of President Najibullah finally collapsed years later in 1992, Ismail Khan seized the oasis of Herat and the surrounding regions and ruled them as an autonomous Jamiat i Islam fiefdom. Although he was a fundamentalist, his rule was nonetheless stable and the region prospered under his control. It is a common myth in the West that *all* warlords in the 1990s preyed upon their own people and destroyed civil society. Although this was certainly the case in the fractured Pashtun south where dozens of warlords, raped local women, set up checkpoints on roads to rob people, and levied "taxes" on villagers, it was less the case in the Tajik, Uzbek, and Hazara lands. The peoples of the north often benefited from the rule of such warlords as Ismail Khan, Dostum, and Massoud. As such, a new movement known as the Taliban was warmly embraced and its members were considered liberators when they arrived in the chaotic Pashtun south; but they were rejected in Herat, the Uzbek north, northeastern Tajik, and the Hazara highlands. Simply put, the northern ethnic groups did not mind their mujahideen warlords, while the groups in the Pashtun south despised theirs.

When the newly emerging Taliban began to encroach on Ismail Khan's territory from the Pashtun belt, he fought back ferociously in 1995. But his offensive drive from the strategic Shindand Air Base to the south became overextended, and the Pakistani-trained Taliban were able to defeat him. The comparatively cosmopolitan town of Herat, which had benefited from its proximity to the Iranian border, was then taken by the Pashtun Taliban. The Taliban despised the Farsi-Dari (Persian-Tajik) speakers of Herat, forcing them out of power positions and enforcing draconian Taliban laws in Herat. Herat, a vibrant city of poets, was plunged into darkness.

For his part, Ismail Khan fled to Meshed in northeastern Iran to regroup his forces and eventually crossed back into northern Afghanistan to fight the Taliban alongside his former enemy, the pro-Communist Uzbek leader General Dostum. Dostum used Khan's forces to help hold his southwestern Faryab front against the Taliban. But Dostum's second in command, Abdul Malik, betrayed Dostum and Khan, and went over to the Taliban in the heat of battle. In the process, Malik arrested Ismail Khan and gave him to the Taliban as a "gift." Khan was subsequently thrown into jail and humiliated by his jubilant Taliban captors who had captured their first major mujahideen opponent (although many Westerners erroneously conflate the mujahideen with the Taliban, the Taliban actually emerged as a response to the abuses of Pashtun mujahideen in the south and fought to destroy them).

But in a turn of events that could only take place in Afghanistan, one of Ismail Khan's captors, a Taliban defector named Hekmati, secretly planned Khan's release from prison. During one of Hekmati's shifts as guard at Khan's prison, he smuggled Khan out of his cell and into a waiting SUV, which then drove them out of Kandahar. However, on their way to the Iranian border, the fleeing Khan and Hekmati hit a land mine and both of them broke their legs. Both injured men eventually limped to the safety of Iran ahead of their Taliban pursuers. Khan later returned to Afghanistan in the spring of 2001 to help the Tajik opposition commander, Massoud the Lion of Panjsher, establish opposition enclaves in the western Hindu Kush Mountains. When the United States invaded Afghanistan in 2001, Khan and his men poured out of the mountains, seized the Chaghcharan area, and moved down to Herat, which they succeeded in liberating from the Taliban.

Bizarrely enough, Khan's savior from the Taliban prison, Hekmati, was later arrested by the United States upon his return to Afghanistan in 2003. He was then taken to Guantanamo Bay on false charges and kept there for five years. Ismail Khan tried to get him released and made it clear that Hekmati was the enemy of the Taliban, not their friend. But Hekmati's U.S. captors at Guantanamo Bay ignored Khan's pleas. Tragically, Hekmati died of cancer in jail before his name could be cleared.

Khan fared somewhat better than his savior Hekmati. From 2001 to 2004 he ran his old fiefdom in Herat as a personal Amirate. He used the money from Herat's lucrative trade with Iran to develop and beautify the city. Today Herat has beautiful parks, monuments (including one to Khan's slain son), and a thriving economy. But Khan's policy of keeping all tariffs and taxes from trade with Iran for himself caused tension with President Karzai's central government. This was compounded by his promulgation of fundamentalist laws, such as his policy of enforcing virginity checks on women.

When Khan's men began to clash with Amanullah Khan, a powerful Pashtun warlord from the south, the central government was faced with the threat of a major interethnic war from 2002 to 2004. The problem was compounded when Ismail Khan's son was killed in a shootout with government forces. The Americans also believed rumors of his ties with Iran, which, as mentioned earlier, were probably exaggerated given that Khan is a Sunni and the Iranians are Shiites.

For all of these reasons, Khan was removed from his governorate of Herat in September 2004 (amid riots by his followers) and transferred to Kabul. There he was given the portfolio of minister of energy, a position he appears to have managed effectively in light of his previous experience in running Herat. In 2009 Khan threw his support behind President Karzai to help him in the contested presidential elections of August of that year. Khan thus seems to have tied himself to the Karzai government for the time being.

Massoud, the Lion of Panjsher

Ahmad Shah Massoud was a Tajik whose father was an officer in King Zahir Shah's Afghan army. When he was young he attended a French-speaking high school in Kabul and led his classmates in soldier games. By the time he was in college at Kabul University, he had become a member of Rabbani's Jamiat i Islam Islamist Party. Like other Muslim youth, he resented the emergence of Communist Party youth groups in his university and in the government. Massoud, Rabbani, Hekmatyar, and other Islamists also decried the creeping secularization that had accelerated in Afghanistan since the overthrow of King Zahir Shah in 1973.

In an effort to overthrow President Daoud, the Islamists attempted an uprising in 1975, and Massoud was sent to the Panjsher Valley to rally his fellow Tajiks. But the local peasants did not come over to his side, and Massoud and his followers were forced to flee to neighboring Pakistan. There they were given refuge by the Pakistani Inter Services Intelligence (ISI). The ISI sought to use these Islamist exiles as proxies against President Daoud, who was stirring up the "Pashtunistan" issue against Pakistan.

Massoud returned to the country in 1978 after the Communist Saur Revolution and joined rebel groups operating in the mountains of Nuristan. He later fought against Afghan Communist Army troops in his native valley of Panjsher (Five Lions), a scenic, river-fed mountain valley that carves its way down from the Hindu Kush to the lush Shomali Plain north of Kabul. Although Massoud was initially defeated, he found it easy to gather support from his fellow *qawm* (Panjsheri Tajiks) and returned to the fray.

Massoud then began to lay the foundation for the creation of what was to become the mujahideen's most professional and effective fighting force. While many of the Pashtun mujahideen factions were made up of poorly disciplined, part-time tribal fighters, Massoud's troops were made up of local militiamen known as *mahallis* (locals), mobile fighters known

Ahmad Shah Massoud, the legendary "Lion of Panjsher."

as *muhtahereks* (mobile fighters), and professional shock fighters known as *zarbatis*. Massoud studied the campaigns of Che Guevara, Mao, and other guerilla leaders and waged a systematic form of asymmetrical warfare against the Communists that differed from the haphazard attacks of most of the Pashtun mujahideen in the south. While the Pashtun commanders tended to engage in a seasonal, almost ritualistic tempo of warfare (such as shelling government outposts and bases every afternoon to chants of "Allah u Akbar!" [God is great!]), Massoud's troops carried out large-scale, complex operations.

The Soviets estimated that Massoud was responsible for as many as two-thirds of those killed in action in Afghanistan. Massoud's fighters were also able to carry out devastating strikes on Soviet supply convoys coming down from the Salang Pass across the Shomali Plain to Kabul. Massoud's *muhtahereks* wreaked havoc using anti-tank weapons, RPGs, machine guns, recoilless rifles, and land mines. In the process they turned the Doroga Zhizn (Russian "Road of Life") supply line, which ran from the Soviet border of Uzbekistan down to Kabul, into the Road of Death.

In response, the Afghan Communist forces and their Soviet allies launched nine full-scale invasions of the Panjsher Valley prior to 1986. As Soviet mechanized units and heliborne troops moved up this narrow valley, Massoud's troops known as *dukhis* (Russian "ghosts") ambushed them and retreated up side valleys. In frustration the Soviets carpet bombed the valley with long-range Tupolev bombers based in the USSR. The bombings were so intense that clouds of dust drifted hundreds of miles across the border into the Soviet republic of Tajikistan.

But for all their efforts to annihilate Massoud, the tens of thousands of Communist troops sent to flush out the famous Lion of Panjsher failed to kill him. To this day the Alpine-like scenery of the Panjsher Valley is marked by the ruins of bombed-out villages and the rusting hulks of destroyed Soviet tanks.

Such feats earned Massoud an almost mythic status, and he was called Milli Kahraman (National Hero), Amir Sahib (Lord Commander), and of course Sher i Panjsher (the Lion of Panjsher) by his grateful people. In the process he demonstrated that the Tajiks, not the legendary Afghan-Pashtuns, were the most effective warriors in the battle against the Soviet atheist invaders.

Although Massoud was an Islamic warrior and a dedicated anti-Communist, he was not a fanatic like the Pashtun leader Gulbuddin Hekmatyar. On one occasion he even made a truce with the Communists, although he did so in order to replenish his supplies and regroup his badly damaged forces so they could continue to bear the brunt of Soviet attacks. Resentful critics in the mujahideen parties based safely across the border in Pakistan nonetheless called him a "sellout" and labeled him a traitor. But within months Massoud's men were back at it again, destroying Soviet columns crossing the Shomali Plain and storming Communist bases in the northeastern parts of the country.

Ironically, this Tajik jihadi warrior, whom the Soviets labeled their greatest enemy, also became an enemy of the Pashtun fundamentalist commander Gulbuddin Hekmatyar and his Arab jihadi volunteer allies (including Osama bin Laden). While Massoud lived in the war zone and rarely left Afghanistan, the Arab jihad volunteers who were living safely in Pakistan had the luxury of holding a court to "try" Massoud for being an "apostate." The fanatical Arab Wahhabis and Salafites (two Arab fundamentalist strains that seek to return Islam to its "pure" roots, as they define them) clearly resented Massoud for his fame. They sought to promote the Pashtun fundamentalist Hekmatyar as a "good Muslim" alternative to Massoud.

Interestingly, the Pakistanis also found Massoud unworthy of the sort of support they directed to the fundamentalist Hekmatyar. While Hekmatyar received the lion's share of the weapons, funds, and Stinger anti-aircraft ground-to-air missiles supplied by the United States, Massoud claimed he was only given six of these anti-aircraft missiles and limited funds.

The ISI distrust of the legendary Tajik commander stemmed in part from the fact that he was not fanatical enough for Pakistan's fundamentalist military leader, General Zia ul Haq. Zia ul Haq had seized control of Pakistan in 1977 by executing Benazir Bhutto's father, Prime Minister Zulfikar Bhutto, and was trying to Islamify Pakistan. Zia's ISI had full control of the distribution of CIA funds and chose to direct them to only the most fundamentalist mujahideen commanders. This meant that U.S. tax dollars were not being sent to the moderate and effective fighter Massoud, but to Hekmatyar, whose followers were rabid extremists known for throwing acid in the faces of unveiled women, not for fighting the Soviets. In addition, the ISI was dominated by Pakistani Pashtuns who siphoned the money to fellow Pashtun commanders such as Hekmatyar and Haqqani, not to Tajiks or other groups.

For his part, Hekmatyar actually damaged Massoud's jihad against the Soviets by attacking his supply columns and ambushing and killing his commanders. The Soviets were of course delighted by this mujahideen on mujahideen violence. Such internal cleavages also demonstrated that there were deep conflicts between moderate mujahideen leaders such as Massoud and ISI-Saudi–funded extremists such as Hekmatyar. Ironically enough, it was the extremist commanders Hekmatyar and Haqqani—not moderates like Massoud (whom the United States did not support)—who received U.S. money and would later turn on their American patrons and join the Taliban-led insurgency.

Although Massoud's moderate Islam and his Tajik ethnicity cost him the support of the wealthy Arabs, the Americans, and the powerful ISI, it won him support among his own people. For this same reason, he was also able to reach moderates in the Afghan Communist government. Many of these moderate Communists (especially Tajik Communists who belonged to the comparatively moderate Parcham Communist faction) defected to his side when the war finally came to an end in 1992. In that year Massoud was able to seize Kabul from the defeated Communists with the help of General Dostum, a pro-Communist Uzbek commander who joined him.

But it should be noted that although Massoud was the most powerful of the various mujahideen field commanders, he did not seek to hold the highest power in the land. Instead, he accepted the portfolio of defense minister, given to him by his political master, President Burhanuddin Rabbani. During his tenure as defense minister, Massoud's most important job was defending the people of Kabul from the vicious attacks of the Pashtun leader Hekmatyar. Hekmatyar felt that he should be president and shelled the city mercilessly for years during the post-Communist civil war, killing thousands of innocents.

Massoud's own reputation was, however, damaged in the subsequent Afghan civil war of 1992–1996. In particular, his troops are blamed for massacring Hazara opponents in western Kabul in 1993 during the Afshar Massacre (which was carried out in conjunction with a fundamentalist commander named Sayyaf and his troops). His men also shelled Karte Sei and other neighborhoods in their battles to control the city during the civil war.

Although Massoud's image was tainted by these events, he offered the best hope for defeating a new force called the Taliban that set out to conquer Afghanistan in the mid-1990s. Massoud clearly had greater vision than the other quarreling anti-Taliban mujahideen warlords and sought to organize a united front against the Taliban. This front was called the United Islamic Front, and it eventually included the Hazaras of central Afghanistan and Tajiks, as well as the Uzbeks of the north. The United Islamic Front was nicknamed the "Northern Alliance" by the Pakistanis, who tried to depict it as being strictly limited to the north.

When his former enemy Hekmatyar was defeated by the Taliban in 1996 (thus opening the eastern approaches to the capital), Massoud was forced to abandon Kabul to the seemingly unstoppable forces of Taliban leader Mullah Omar. Massoud strategically withdrew to the northeast and created an Afghan government enclave that extended from the Tajikistan border through Takhar Province to the Shomali Plain (north of Kabul), then eastward over to the Pakistani border. Although Massoud made several attempts to retake Kabul from the Taliban, his Tajik forces were largely pinned into a shrinking, mountainous enclave that represented no more than 10 percent of Afghanistan. As his fellow warlord allies in the Northern Alliance, including Ismail Khan, Sayid Naderi, Karim Khalili, and Dostum, were defeated one after another, Massoud was left as the last man standing against the Taliban by 1998.

From 1998 to 2001, Massoud desperately fought a lone battle to keep the Taliban at bay and to protect the moderate society that thrived in his endangered sanctuary. But Massoud's lonely struggle was not just against the Taliban. The Pakistani ISI openly supported his Taliban opponents, and in the summer months thousands of Pakistani madrassa (religious seminary) students and noncommissioned officers swarmed across the border to bolster the Taliban's campaigns. The Pakistani Frontier Corps and ISI also supplied the Taliban with fuel, weapons, funds, and training.

If this were not enough of an advantage, the Taliban's wealthy Saudi guest, Osama bin Laden, supported his Taliban hosts with his wealth and contacts among Arab veterans of the 1980s anti-Soviet jihad. To help Mullah Omar's Taliban conquer Massoud, bin Laden created the world's largest jihad foreign legion, the dreaded 055 Brigade. The 055 Ansars (Companions) came from all over the Arab world and spearheaded the Taliban's thrusts. In the late 1990s the foreign fighters came in the thousands to Afghanistan to train in the camps that bin Laden had established in a swath of Pashtun tribal territory extending from Kandahar up to Jalalabad. When the Taliban stalled, bin Laden's Arab shock troops would storm across land-mine fields and throw themselves on the Northern Alliance Tajik enemy with hand grenades strapped to their bodies.

Not surprisingly, Massoud, who was armed by Tajikistan, India, Russia, and Iran, began to lose ground despite this last-minute assistance. His forces included fewer than twelve thousand men, while the Taliban army was estimated to have around forty-five thousand to fifty-five thousand fighters and a much greater supply of tanks, artillery, aircraft, and logistic support. As the odds against him increased, Massoud's World War I–style defensive lines began to waver under enemy assaults. In 2000 his hard-pressed troops were forced deeper into Takhar Province when a 055-led attack captured his capital at Taloqan.

With his back against the wall, Massoud desperately struggled to get U.S. presidents Bill Clinton and George W. Bush to support his war with the Taliban and Al Qaeda. But neither administration had the foresight to train and equip his anti-Taliban forces. In 2001 he warned: "If President Bush doesn't help us, then these terrorists will damage the United States and Europe very soon and it will be too late." But his warning went unheeded. Some members of the CIA and Counterterrorism Chief Richard Clarke's office circulated a memo from Massoud warning that Al Qaeda planned to "perform a terrorist act against the US on a scale larger than the 1998 bombing of the US embassies in Kenya and Tanzania." But the CIA had its hands tied by the White House and the Department of State. Nobody wanted to antagonize the Taliban government. By 2001 the Bush administration was focused on the war of words with China and Saddam Hussein's Iraq, and Afghanistan was forgotten.

But Massoud found help elsewhere. To head off what the Taliban–Al Qaeda were touting was to be their triumphant summer offensive of

2001, Massoud convinced two legendary warriors, General Abdul Rashid Dostum (the Uzbek) and Ismail Khan (the Tajik Amir of Herat), to return from exile and join the fray. These two commanders were able to ignite what he called "distractionary brush fires" in the high mountains of the central Hindu Kush that summer. Thousands of Taliban troops had to be diverted from Massoud's front lines in Takhar and Shomali Provinces to put down Khan and Dostum's uprisings.

This diversion in Taliban resources relieved the pressure on Massoud's lines and enabled him to survive into September 2001. Sadly, on September 9, 2001, the famous Lion of Panjsher was assassinated by two Arab reporters who had a bomb hidden in their camera. They entered his headquarters, took advantage of his legendary hospitality by drinking tea he served them with his own hands, then asked him a rude question about his dislike of bin Laden. Before he could answer, they detonated their bomb and killed the Northern Alliance's last hope. Massoud's death was a signal for the Taliban and Al Qaeda to launch a vast assault on his defensive positions.

Massoud's commanders kept the news of the Lion's death hidden from the men manning the front lines. They announced that he had only been wounded in the cowardly attack. This message inspired his men to fight for revenge, and they managed to survive until the morning of September 12. On that day news arrived from the distant United States about Al Qaeda's attack on New York and Washington, DC. Everyone knew that this would change the dynamic of the war. Sadly, Massoud, who had fought for over two decades to see his country freed from the Soviets and Taliban, died too early to see this new era.

As the Americans sent special forces to liaise with Massoud's less-than-charismatic successor, Fahim Khan, it became obvious that Massoud had been killed in order to weaken the Northern Alliance. Bin Laden correctly foresaw that a U.S. military response to his bold attack on the American mainland would force the United States to use the Northern Alliance as a proxy force against the Taliban–Al Qaeda army. During the war, Fahim Khan proved to be no Massoud, and he waited until Dostum had already taken much of the north before belatedly moving on Kabul. There Fahim Khan gained wide notoriety for trying to keep international forces out of the city and for keeping power in the hands of his Panjsheri Tajik faction. He also abused his position as minister of defense in the Karzai government and used it to push people out of their homes and buy real estate. Eventually these actions led to his removal from power. He is currently vice president.

Massoud remains an icon for his people, the Tajiks. His tomb in the Panjsher village of Jangalak is a shrine and a national monument. The day of his assassination, September 9, is a national holiday. Today one can find Massoud's pictures on calendars, billboards, cars, and stickers throughout the Tajik lands where he is remembered as a national hero.

Abdul Haq

Abdul Haq was a portly Pashtun mujahideen commander from the province of Nangahar (Jalalabad area) who was a head of a sub-clan of the Ahmadzai tribe. He was responsible for mujahideen actions in his home district and for launching attacks on the well-defended Afghan capital. During the anti-Soviet jihad, his fighters successfully lobbed mortars into Communist government bases and destroyed power networks and electric grids. During one of his forays into Afghanistan, however, Haq slid off the trail and stepped on a Soviet land mine. The mine blew off his foot and crippled him, but he bravely returned to the jihad riding on a horse.

Unlike Hekmatyar, the fundamentalist who famously refused to meet with President Ronald Reagan during a White House visit, the English-speaking Haq was seen as an ally by the Western leaders who contributed to the anti-Soviet jihad. He met with both Reagan and British prime minister Margaret Thatcher. Fundamentalists criticized him for this and called him a CIA "stooge," which was hypocritical as the fundamentalists had received funds from the CIA.

Interestingly enough, Marc Sageman, Haq's CIA field officer (who was also Massoud's field officer) during the time of the jihad, cut him off from U.S. funds when he was caught claiming credit for operations he did not carry out in order to get funding.

When the Afghan Communist government was overthrown in 1992, Abdul Haq chose not to partake in the struggle for power that tainted the reputations of Massoud and many other mujahideen leaders. Instead, he moved to Dubai to run a business and remained widely respected by the Afghans.

But when the Taliban swept into the country imposing their puritanical version of Islam in the mid-1990s, Haq returned to politics and became an active opponent. He subsequently paid a high price for his opposition to the Taliban. In 1999 assassins broke into his house in Peshawar, Pakistan, and murdered his wife and son.

Haq paid an even greater price when he himself entered Afghanistan in October 2001 to try to stir up the eastern Ghilzai Pashtun tribes against the Taliban after 9/11. The Taliban learned of his arrival and surrounded his small team. As Haq desperately called the Americans for assistance, they sent helicopters and remote-control Predator drones to rescue him. But they were too late, and Haq and his followers were all executed by the Taliban. Had Haq not been killed, he would have been an obvious contender for the Afghan presidency, which was subsequently taken by Hamid Karzai. Incidentally, Karzai later succeeded where Haq had left off and galvanized a southern Durrani Pashtun front to fight the Taliban within weeks of Haq's death.

Jalaluddin Haqqani, the Pashtun Extremist

Jalaluddin Haqqani is a legendary Pashtun mujahideen commander from the Zadran (or Jadran) tribe whose territories lie in the eastern Afghan provinces of Khost, Paktia, and Paktika, and across the Pakistani border in North Waziristan. He was trained as a mullah in Peshawar in the 1970s and later became known as a *maulvi* (a higher rank than mullah). Haqqani joined an Islamist uprising in 1975 against the Daoud government and gained fame for luring a government minister of tribal affairs to a meeting then slaughtering him and his entire staff. He later fought the Communists when they came to power in 1978 and, as was often the case in the war when Islamists and mullahs took power, he ousted the local tribal khans of the powerful Barbrakzay clan. At this time his fighters joined the fundamentalist party of Gulbuddin Hekmatyar, the Hezb i Islam. But Haqqani later left Hekmatyar and joined a less extreme faction of the Hezb i Islam led by Yunus Khalis.

Haqqani gained fame in the 1980s for besieging isolated Communist garrisons in the eastern provinces of Khost and Paktia and cutting off the road from the city of Gardez to Khost. His operations forced the Soviets to launch major operations to bring supplies to these garrisons, including 1987's Operation Magistral. Haqqani's fighters fought back ferociously against the Soviets, who sustained casualties at a level they were more used to seeing in the Panjsher.

Haqqani's success was facilitated by his close ties to both the Pakistani ISI and the Arabs. The Pakistanis funded his fighters using cash distributed by the CIA and provided him with shoulder-fired Stinger anti-aircraft missiles. Like Hekmatyar, the Arab-speaking Haqqani also worked closely with Arab volunteers who came to Pakistan in the late 1980s to partake in the anti-Soviet jihad. Haqqani's tribe controlled the passes leading from Pakistan's Waziristan tribal agencies into neighboring Khost and Paktia provinces in Afghanistan. This area was located just south of the Parchinar Beak, a strategic "peninsula" of Pakistani land jutting into Afghanistan that served as a springboard for mujahideen (and later Taliban) operations.

Haqqani's greatest accomplishment was his conquest of the city of Khost in April 1991, the first Communist city to fall to the Pashtun mujahideen. His troops, however, gained notoriety for sacking the town.

When the war ended the following year, Haqqani took the post of minister of justice in the mujahideen government. Like Abdul Haq, he did not engage in the fratricidal struggle of the 1990s civil war, and for this he was respected.

When Osama bin Laden was expelled from his sanctuary in Sudan, where he had lived from 1992 to 1996, he also renewed his contacts with Haqqani. Bin Laden and his family settled in territories near Jalalabad that were controlled by Yunus Khalis, Haqqani's political chief in the Hezb i Islam Party. Later, when the Taliban began to move into Haqqani's territory after 1994, bin Laden talked Haqqani into joining them instead of fighting them, as Hekmatyar subsequently chose to do. Haqqani's decision to join the Taliban was important, because he brought his powerful tribe with him. This helped facilitate the Taliban's expansion into the Ghilzai Pashtun tribal areas of eastern Afghanistan. This mountainous area is far more tribal than the flat Pashtun lands of the south around Helmand and Kandahar. Even though the Taliban were a supra-tribal movement that frequently displaced tribal khans and overthrew mujahideen commanders, they wisely accepted Haqqani into their ranks. He subsequently became the first non-Kandahari mujahideen leader to be accepted into the Taliban's upper echelons. In light of his influence over the tribes of the frontier, the Taliban made him minister of tribes and borders.

But Haqqani's job description changed when the Taliban's Arab guests attacked the United States on 9/11 and invited the wrath of the Americans on themselves. As the Taliban state collapsed and the hard-core Taliban leadership fled eastward toward the safety of Pashtun tribal areas in neighboring Pakistan (most notably into the Parchinar Beak), Haqqani was named commander of the Taliban armies. He seems to have been ideally suited to help lead the Taliban in shifting from frontal warfare to the asymmetrical tactics of his former mujahideen guerrilla days.

Haqqani's followers facilitated the retreat of Osama bin Laden and many other Arabs through the Spin Ghar Mountains into Pakistan's Khyber and Kurram Agency and then down to Waziristan. There he offered them *melmastiia* (sanctuary) in and around the North Waziristan capital of Miram Shah. Haqqani had deep roots in this area and had even established a madrassa, the Manbaul Ulom, in this Pashtun city. Although the United States tried to woo Haqqani away from the Taliban in 2001, he rejected them on the grounds that he was a Muslim. He claimed it was his duty to wage jihad against "infidel invaders" just as he had in the 1980s.

Lest there be any ambiguity about his view of the Americans, Haqqani made the following statement to a Pakistani newspaper *Jang* on October 19, 2001: "We will retreat to the mountains and begin a long guerilla war to reclaim our pure land from the infidels and free our country again like we did against the Soviets. We are eagerly awaiting the American troops to land on our soil. The Americans are creatures of comfort."

Haqqani and his sons subsequently helped the Taliban regroup, recruit new followers, and shift to guerrilla tactics. Their headquarters was just outside Miram Shah, in the small village of Dande Darpa Khel. They also had a base in Afghanistan's Khost Province in the village of Zambar.

The Haqqanis then began to lead insurgent operations against the Karzai government and U.S. troops in the neighboring Afghan provinces. As they had in the 1980s, they slipped across the border from Waziristan and began to attack targets in neighboring Khost, Paktia, and Paktika Provinces. Their aim was to cut the Gardez-Khost road as they had in the 1980s and overwhelm government bases. Eventually their infiltration extended even farther into Ghazni, Loghar, and Wardak Provinces. From there, the network attacked Kabul itself three times in 2008. These attacks included a suicide bombing gun assault on the luxurious Serena Hotel, a suicide bombing with the help of the Pakistani ISI on the Indian Embassy, and a sniper attack on a VIP stand where President Karzai was watching a parade.

As the Taliban's fallback base in Pakistan's North and South Waziristan became a de facto Taliban Amirate, Haqqani began to shift some of his responsibilities to his three sons. One of these sons, Sirajuddin, appeared to play a key role in integrating new Al Qaeda–inspired terrorist tactics into the Taliban's strategy. As a new branch of Al Qaeda appeared in Iraq in response to the overthrow of the Baathist regime in 2003, the Iraqi insurgents began to share their new tactics with Sirajuddin and his brothers Naseruddin and Badruddin. Sirajuddin (also known as Khalifa) and his father appear to have been among the first Taliban commanders to embrace the alien Iraqi jihadi tactic of suicide bombing. This is best demonstrated by the fact that their primary "jihad zone," the tiny and rather inconsequential frontier province of Khost, ranked second and third in overall suicide bombings for the years 2006 and 2007 (behind Kabul and the spiritual capital of Kandahar). As the so-called Haqqani network fused with bin Laden's Al Qaeda Central and learned from Zarqawi's Al Qaeda in Iraq, it played a key role in transforming the Taliban insurgency into an Iraqi-style terrorist movement.

Along with kidnappings, beheadings, the killing of women, and assassinations, the semi-independent Haqqani network is said to have been behind the killing of Hakim Taniwal, the governor of Paktia Province, and a subsequent attack on his funeral in 2006. They also played a role in the 2009 kidnapping of *New York Times* reporter David Rhode. Such actions have increased Haqqani's control over the "Eastern Zone" of Afghanistan, and for some time there have been rumors that he resents being subordinate to Mullah Omar.

Although the United States has offered sizable rewards for the arrest of the Haqqanis (and has tried killing them with missile strikes, one of which killed several of Haqqani's family members in the fall of 2008 and one of his sons in 2009), they have proven to be untouchable in their Pakistani tribal sanctuary in North Waziristan. For their part, the Pakistanis have been equally unable (or unwilling) to capture or kill the Haqqanis, although they have killed or captured several high-level Haqqani commanders. There have been many voices that have argued that the Pakistani ISI has safeguarded its old ally Haqqani against efforts to destroy him. In December 2009 the U.S. government asked the Pakistanis to wage military operations against Haqqani, but the Pakistanis pointedly refused. As of the spring of 2011, there has been talk of a Pakistani offensive in Haqqani's base in North Waziristan, but this has yet to materialize.

At one time coalition troops held out hope that Jalaluddin Haqqani, who was in his 70s in 2001, had died when he was not seen or filmed once in the seven years after 2001. But in April 2008 such hopes were dashed when he appeared with his trademark red-dyed beard in a video that appeared on the Arab Al Jazeera network. His message provided considerable insight into the worldview of the man who is the Taliban's most powerful field commander. It demonstrated that he is operating out of a combination of religious and Pashtun-nationalist motives of the sort that have inspired the tribes to resist invaders since the British invasions of the nineteenth century. According to Haqqani:

> All 37 (NATO) allies will be humiliated and driven out of Afghanistan. Jihad is compulsory and will continue until the end of time; we are without resources, but we have the support of God. Bush and his allies have decided to kill us or arrest us—they consider us as weak and think of themselves as all powerful. They think we have no place left in the world to survive—they think we are destined either to die or to be captured . . . they think they are wealthy nations, with their money and with half of the world behind them. They think they can enslave poor Afghans—bomb us with their planes and gunship helicopters—they think they have everything and we are voiceless—the media are with them and they belittle our resistance. We kill 80 and they report two or one. I promise the Afghan nation that soon we will be victorious.

Haqqani and his followers clearly believe that time is on their side and that they can outlast the latest wave of "infidel invaders" and disrupt their efforts to build a strong Afghan state. They also aim to extend their influence to tribal regions of Afghanistan that are disaffected with the Karzai government and distrustful of the presence of foreigners in their homeland.

In this last endeavor they have had less success than hoped. Many of the tribes in the Khost, Paktia, and Paktika regions have rejected Haqqani and the Taliban. The tribal khans see him as a threat to their power and have sided with the Karzai government to keep the northern areas of these three frontier provinces relatively stable. The inherent tensions between the Taliban (which is opposed to tribes) and the tribal chieftains are highlighted in the case of a tribal chieftain from Khost. The khan fell out with Haqqani when the latter recruited one of the khan's sons for a suicide bombing mission without his father's permission. The furious khan threatened to launch a war against Haqqani and the Taliban unless his son was returned. To prevent bad blood, Haqqani returned the khan's son with the admonition that he had denied his son the glory of "martyrdom."

Haqqani and his sons clearly represent a destabilizing influence in the Pashtun tribal regions of the east and North Waziristan, but they are unable to cause the same level of disruption they did with the Soviets in the 1980s. Perhaps the best thing Haqqani has going for him is the Karzai administration's inability to protect tribal khans who stand up to the Taliban. It remains to be seen whether the tribes, the real center of gravity in the eastern region, can be coerced, intimidated, or made to join the Taliban out of Islamic-Pashtun solidarity. Killing Haqqani would go a long way in preventing this sort of defection to the Taliban and convincing the border tribes that momentum is on the Coalition's side. It would also disrupt a network that is to a large extent based on family and *qawm* ties and loyalties that are hard to penetrate.

Gulbuddin Hekmatyar, the Fundamentalist Warlord

Gulbuddin Hekmatyar is a Pashtun belonging to the Kharrut (Ghilzai) tribe, much of which was forcefully settled among Uzbeks in the north by Amir Abdur Rahman, the "Iron Amir," in the late nineteenth century. Hekmatyar's tribe was settled in Kunduz and Baghlan Provinces (in the northeastern territories of Afghan Turkistan) and it was here, in the northern village of Imam Sahib, that Hekmatyar grew up before attending Kabul University in the early 1970s. While studying to be an engineer, Hekmatyar joined the Communist Party (the People's Democratic Party of Afghanistan) for four years. He later abandoned the Communists after he was convicted of murdering a Maoist student.

After two years, Hekmatyar was released from jail and he joined the Muslim Youth Organization. He and his followers soon gained notoriety for spraying acid in the faces of girls who did not wear veils. When King Zahir Shah was overthrown in 1973, Hekmatyar fled to neighboring Pakistan to resist President Daoud's secularization policies. There he established a splinter Islamist party known as the Hezb i Islam (the Party of Islam) in 1976.

Today Hekmatyar's followers reject accusations that he was once a Communist, and they are forbidden from mentioning this dark past in his presence. Hekmatyar nonetheless runs his party using the same sort of rigid party hierarchy, discipline, and cells that he witnessed among the Communists. This made the Hezb i Islam unique among the loosely organized jihad parties. Like the Communists, Hekmatyar also established a cult of personality around himself, and he purged or executed anyone suspected of disloyalty. His organization was the most organized of all the mujahideen groups when it came to the harvesting, smuggling, and refining of opium in laboratories. This trade further enriched the leader, who was already receiving the lion's share of the money offered by the U.S. and Pakistani governments.

Hekmatyar's Hezb i Islam cadres used the money from drugs to gain adherents among the thousands of Pashtun refugees who fled to Pakistan in the 1980s. The main refugee camp Hekmatyar recruited from was the Shamshatoo Camp (fifteen miles south of Peshawar), which became home to as many as twenty thousand refugees. Even prior to the advent of the Taliban, the refugees in Hekmatyar's camp lived by a strict Islamic law that forbade television sets, men without beards, or unveiled women. But these draconian laws were made more palatable by a functioning social service that helped provide rations, schools (with Islamic content), and housing for refugees. In this respect, Hekmatyar's party gained adherents in much the same fashion as Hezbollah and Hamas in Lebanon and Gaza, respectively. The irony is that Hekmatyar used U.S. funds to create this fundamentalist enclave in Pakistan that still exists today.

This story of U.S. boomerang-style "blowback" stems from the pact the United States made with the devil in using Pakistani territory to arm the anti-Soviet insurgents in the 1980s. As previously noted, when the Soviets invaded Afghanistan, the Pakistani ISI turned to Hekmatyar to help fight the atheist invaders. They chose Hekmatyar rather than the monarchist jihad parties for the simple reason that he, like the Taliban, operated on a strictly Islamic platform. This meant that he would not turn against his Muslim neighbors and try to carve out a larger "Pashtunistan" from Pashtun lands in Pakistan. The Pakistanis disliked Massoud because he was too moderate and was an ethnic Tajik.

When the Americans subsequently offered tens of millions of dollars to Pakistani leader Zia ul Haq to support the mujahideen "freedom fighters," he agreed to assist them, but with one key caveat: the Pakistani ISI, not the CIA, would have to control the distribution of resources so as to prevent the jihad from being tainted in the eyes of Muslims.

There was also the question of national sovereignty. The Pakistanis did not want the distrusted Americans, who had recently sanctioned them for their nuclear weapons program, running covert operations from their soil unmonitored. And at the end of the day the Pakistanis' objectives were vastly different from the Americans'. The Americans wanted to turn Afghanistan into a quagmire for their Soviet adversaries and prevent the spread of Communism. But the Pakistanis wanted to weaken the Pashtun nationalists in Afghanistan and create a fundamentalist neighbor next door that might assist them in their wars with India.

Forced to let the ISI act as the distributor for U.S. funds and weapons, the CIA allowed the Pakistanis to support the most fundamentalist of all the mujahideen commanders, Hekmatyar. In the process, moderate Afghan mujahideen commanders, such as the Qadiriya Sufi *pir* (master) Sayid Ahmed Gaylani, Sebghatullah Mujadidi (a leader of the Naqshbandi Sufi order), and the aforementioned leaders Abdul Haq and Massoud, lost out in the race for arms and followers. Not surprisingly, this led to a marked increase in radicalization among the mujahideen as Hekmatyar, Abdul Rasul Sayyaf (a Saudi-funded Wahhabi), and Haqqani gained followers from the more moderate mujahideen groups.

Incidentally, Hekmatyar's group had the prestige of having the most Stingers, and one of his followers shot down the first Soviet Mil-24 armor-plated helicopter gunship, a scene captured in the movie *Charlie Wilson's War*. But this did not make Hekmatyar a friend of America. In a sign of his lack of gratitude to the Americans, Hekmatyar famously refused to shake hands with the "infidel" president Ronald Reagan when he visited the White House in 1985. Later, when the United States launched a war against Iraq's Saddam Hussein in 1991, Hekmatyar came out against the United States and offered to send volunteers to help Saddam Hussein fight the Americans.

But for all of his external funding, Hekmatyar's power base in Afghanistan was weaker than Massoud's base among his own *qawm*, the Panjsheri Tajiks. Geographically, Hekmatyar's de-tribalized followers were found scattered in the regions of Kunduz, Kunar, Nuristan, Takhar, and Baghlan in the north, in the greater Jalalabad region in the east, and in the Kabul vicinity (incidentally, these are the regions in which they operate today as part of the anti-Coalition insurgency).

Ironically, Hekmatyar appears to have been more effective at ambushing Massoud's troops and killing his commanders than fighting the

Soviets. Yet despite his lack of success in fighting the Soviets, Hekmatyar was the Pakistani ISI's choice, and he received one-fifth of the U.S. funds for the jihad. When the Afghan Communist government began to weaken in 1990, the Pakistani ISI pushed Hekmatyar to stake his claim to the government. Hekmatyar launched a bold armored assault on Kabul with the aim of knocking out the Najibullah regime. However, Najibullah's Communist forces shattered Hekmatyar's "Army of Sacrifice" and forced him to retreat back to Pakistan.

Hekmatyar later allied himself with a hard-core Pashtun Communist general named Shahnawaz Tanai and attempted to launch a coup against the Najibullah Communist government, but this also failed. Hekmatyar subsequently failed in his effort to take the key eastern city of Jalalabad from the Communists in 1989. Although the ISI and Hekmatyar's Arab allies (including bin Laden) proclaimed that this frontier city would easily fall to their troops, the Communists resisted bitterly and held off Hekmatyar through the spring of 1989. The Communists fought back ferociously, in part because Arabs fighting alongside Hekmatyar had massacred and cut to pieces dozens of their troops who surrendered to the mujahideen. The fate of their comrades inspired the besieged Communist garrison to fight back even harder against Hekmatyar's men. Hekmatyar's siege of Jalalabad was also undermined by the other mujahideen factions' distrust of Hekmatyar. When he asked them for assistance and reinforcements, they ignored him and thus doomed the siege of this major Communist-held Afghan city to failure.

But these losses did not deflate Hekmatyar's ego or his desire to be the leader of all the mujahideen groups. His fighters even took the step of ambushing and killing some of Massoud's top commanders as they returned from a meeting. Massoud responded by attacking Hekmatyar and catching and executing the Hezb i Islam commander responsible for the ambush.

But Massoud was not the only mujahideen commander who detested Hekmatyar. Besides Abdul Rasul Sayyaf (a Saudi-sponsored fundamentalist who had no real following inside Afghanistan), none of the other predominantly Ghilzai Pashtun commanders trusted Hekmatyar. His unpopularity would subsequently prevent him from achieving dominance in post-Communist Afghanistan.

When the Communist president Najibullah finally stepped down in 1992, a triumphant Hekmatyar marched on Kabul with thousands of his followers who expected him to be the next ruler of Afghanistan. But it became apparent that none of Hekmatyar's fellow mujahideen parties supported his drive on Kabul. When his forces arrived in the capital's suburbs, they were cut off by an unlikely alliance of Massoud and the pro-Communist Uzbek commander Dostum. As the alliance between the

Tajik Massoud and Uzbek Dostum demonstrated, these northern peoples could on occasion unify in opposition to the southern Pashtuns.

With no support from his fellow Pashtun mujahideen, Hekmatyar could not displace the two powerful northern commanders, who also allied themselves with the Hazaras. Massoud subsequently became the master of Kabul. Hekmatyar was further infuriated when Massoud's Tajik master, Burhanuddin Rabbani, was chosen to be the new Afghan president. The old order, in which only Pashtuns ruled the country, was being overturned by Hazaras, Uzbeks, and Tajiks who had not ruled the country since the Tajik Bacha i Saqao's overthrow of King Amanullah in 1929.

As was to become glaringly obvious in the ensuing Afghan civil war, there were much more complex ethnic and religious undercurrents in the anti-Communist jihad than most Americans were aware of at the time. It was these powerful ethnic currents that led Afghanistan into a bloody post-Soviet civil war.

The war began when Massoud and Rabbani offered Hekmatyar the post of prime minister in an effort to mollify him. Hekmatyar rejected the offer and suddenly turned his guns on Kabul. In a move that shocked the world, he unleashed an indiscriminate bombardment of the civilian-packed capital that would continue on and off from 1992 to 1996. The destruction inflicted on Kabul far surpassed that which was unleashed during the much-hyped Serbian siege of the Bosnian city of Sarajevo from 1992 to 1995.

In the process of callously shelling Kabul, which had been spared the horrors of the war thus far, Hekmatyar killed thousands of innocent Kabulis. Although other warlords later took part in the urban fighting in Kabul (most notably Massoud and the Hazara leader Mazari who battled for the Karte Sei district, as well as Dostum who attacked in the winter of 1994), the vast majority of damage inflicted on the city was caused by Hekmatyar. Whole neighborhoods were flattened, and tens of thousands of innocent people lost their lives or limbs in the sickening carnage he inflicted. What made this slaughter more unforgivable was that it was Afghanistan's own prime minister who was unleashing it on his nation's capital. If anyone bears the responsibility for the Hiroshima-esque destruction of Kabul and the wanton killing of between twenty thousand and forty thousand of its inhabitants, it is Hekmatyar. Many felt that the callousness of his actions made him a war criminal and an ideal candidate for a crimes-against-humanity trial at the Hague.

Despite the fact that Hekmatyar had the ability to destroy Kabul, it gradually became clear to the ISI that he did not have the means to capture it. And it became obvious that the Pakistanis had bet on the wrong horse. Therefore, when a new, vibrant religious movement known as the Taliban appeared in the Pashtun south in 1994, the ISI quickly began to support it as an alternative. By 1995 the Taliban had spread from Kandahar and had even defeated Sarkateb, one of Hekmatyar's commanders in the south.

This conflict between two fundamentalist Pashtun factions did not initially bother the Hazaras, Uzbeks, and Tajiks, who initially viewed the mysterious Taliban movement as an ally. But the Taliban became more alarming when they gained momentum. Then the Afghan "snowball effect" kicked in, and tribes and local leaders began to defect to the Taliban. Declaring Hekmatyar a war criminal, the Taliban attacked his base at Charyasab (southeast of Kabul) while he was besieging the Afghan capital. In response, Hekmatyar belatedly made peace with the Rabbani government and joined Massoud in defending Kabul from the Taliban. He did so, however, only after the government agreed to enforce a strict ban on veiling of women and other fundamentalist edicts that would presage the draconian laws of the Taliban.

But Hekmatyar was too late, and his struggle for the presidency had weakened both him and Massoud. After the Taliban united with the Zadran mujahideen leader Haqqani, the Pashtun tribes of the east abandoned the Hezb i Islam en masse and went over to the Taliban. Soon thereafter, Hekmatyar's positions near the strategic Silk Gorge Pass were overrun by the unstoppable Taliban army, and he was forced to flee to Iran in 1996. In a display of the increasing importance of ethnicity, many of his men who were Pashtuns defected to the Pashtun Taliban rather than defend the Afghan government, which was dominated by Massoud's Tajiks. Hekmatyar's retreat doomed Massoud, who was subsequently forced to surrender Kabul to the Taliban.

After fleeing Afghanistan, Hekmatyar established the headquarters for his Hezb i Islam in Iran, a country that had given refuge to other Sunni mujahideen leaders in the past. After the U.S.-led invasion of Afghanistan in 2001, however, Hekmatyar came out in support of the Taliban. He also claimed that one of his commanders, Kashmir Khan, had helped bin Laden and Zawahiri escape from Tora Bora to Pakistan in December 2001. When President Bush subsequently declared Iran a member of the "Axis of Evil," the Iranian Pasdaran (Revolutionary Guard) responded by facilitating Hekmatyar's return to Afghanistan to stir up trouble. Hekmatyar subsequently claimed that he met Osama bin Laden and Zawahiri, a claim that cannot be substantiated.

Although the Karzai government entertained hopes that Hekmatyar, an early victim of the Taliban's expansion, might not take up arms against the government alongside Mullah Omar, their hopes were soon dashed. In 2002 Afghan police arrested dozens of Hezb i Islam terrorists planting bombs in Kabul, a tactic Hekmatyar's followers had earlier used against the Communists. Hekmatyar later explained that he and his fighter-terrorists were only targeting foreign forces. He called on Afghans to "cut off the hands of meddling foreigners." Hekmatyar promised that "Hezb i Islam will fight our jihad until foreign troops are gone from Afghanistan and Afghans have set up an Islamic government," which put him squarely in the crosshairs of the Coalition. The Americans and their former proxy from the anti-Soviet jihad were now at war with one another. Thus began a hunt to kill or capture Hekmatyar who has been recognized as a terrorist by the State Department. In 2002 U.S. forces narrowly missed killing Hekmatyar with a predator drone missile in Kunar. Soon thereafter, Pakistani forces succeeded in arresting his son Ghairat in Pakistan.

Hekmatyar's followers (known in U.S. military terms as Hezb i Islam Gulbuddin or HIG) are currently operating in the north near his home province of Kunduz as well as in Kabul and the Pashtun lands of the east. Suspected Hezb i Islam terrorism has included suicide bombing attacks on German International Security and Assistance Force troops and the devastating suicide bombing attack in Baghlan in 2007, which killed as many as one hundred people (Afghanistan's largest suicide bombing to that date). His fighters are also thought to have mortared German positions and to have engaged in fighting in Nangahar, Kunar, Wardak, and Nuristan Provinces. Hekmatyar's influence is strongest in the northeastern region. His forces form the majority of what the U.S. military calls AGEs (Anti-Government Elements) around the capital and adjacent provinces. His commander, Haji Ghafour, is also said to be the most powerful insurgent leader in Nuristan, and his followers are to be found in neighboring Kunar under the control of Kashmir Khan.

But Hezb i Islam appears to be under pressure as the United States deploys thousands of troops to this previously neglected northeastern region. In March 2006 U.S. troops attacked a compound in Kunar where one of Hekmatyar's commanders was hiding and killed him in a shootout. Then, in April 2007, a group of Hekmatyar's commanders in Nuristan were killed in a U.S. air strike on the village of Doab. In that same month, Coalition troops killed Fateh Gul Haqparas, a Hekmatyar commander who had been planting IEDs in Laghman Province. These losses compounded the earlier defection of dozens of Hekmatyar's commanders to the Karzai government in 2004 and 2005 as part of the government's amnesty plan. There have also been reports of Hekmatyar loyalists engaging in gun fights with Taliban in Baghlan and Kunduz Provinces in northern Afghanistan.

As the pressure mounted on Afghanistan's third-largest insurgent group (after the Taliban and the semi-independent Haqqani network), there were questions about Hekmatyar's ties to the Taliban. This is a complicated issue. It should be recalled that there is bad blood between the two groups going back to the Taliban's conquest of Hekmatyar's realm from 1995 to 1996. Many Taliban still see Hekmatyar as a mujahideen war criminal and do not want their movement to be tainted by association with him. The Taliban's codebook, known as the Lahiya, was created by Mullah Omar in 2006 and explicitly states that "Anyone with a bad reputation or who has killed civilians during the Jihad may not be accepted into the Taliban movement."

Although there appears to be some coordination between the Taliban and Hekmatyar, they essentially operate among different types of followers with radically different command structures. Hekmatyar summed up the ambiguity: "The process of negotiation with the Taliban has been disconnected, but if they feel the need then we are ready." Although Hekmatyar's group has been weakened by arrests, he has not lost his audaciousness.

Hekmatyar, the warlord who did his utmost to destroy the Rabbani government in the Afghan civil war, is clearly bent on trying to do the same to the Karzai government today. It remains to be seen whether this failed engineer, murderer, ex-Communist, mujahideen-terrorist can maintain his authority and following in the northeastern regions he has haunted since 1975.

Osama bin Laden, Saudi Jihadi Volunteer

While much has been written about Al Qaeda's amir (commander) and his terrorist activities, bin Laden's Afghan experiences are less documented than his attacks on the West. In a nutshell, bin Laden first came to take an interest in the struggle of the Afghan mujahideen in the early 1980s under the influence of a Palestinian-Jordanian jihad recruiter named Abdullah Azzam. Like thousands of other young Arabs who grew up in the 1970s chafing from repeated Arab defeats in the wars with Israel, bin Laden was drawn to the notion of political, religious, and military salvation through jihad. Jihad, this new generation was told, would return the Arabs and the entire *umma* (the trans-ethnic community of global Islamic believers) to their former glory.

Many young Arab Salafites believed that the cause of the Muslim world's decline since the days of the glorious caliphs of medieval Baghdad lay in its straying from the path of pure Islam. Holy war would expel both creeping infidel influence and Western invaders from the Dar al Islam (the borderless Realm of Islam). The Western-inspired policies of Arab nationalism, the secular-socialist Baathism of Saddam Hussein, and the leftist liberation ideology of the Palestinian Liberation Organization would be replaced by a return to the holy war of the great anti-crusader

Saladin. In the process, Islamic law would be returned to the land, and the Western powers that had pulled the strings for the Arab rulers since the 1920s would be expelled.

But the first order of the day was to ignite the jihad revolution, and this could only be done by expelling the hated atheist Soviet invaders from the frontiers of the Dar al Islam. By the mid-1980s the fiery rhetoric of Abdullah Azzam, who called for Arabs to "join the jihad caravan" to Afghanistan, had been answered by thousands of Egyptian, Saudi, Algerian, Yemeni, and Sudanese Arabs (but few secular Iraqis, who were involved in a war with Iran at the time). These volunteers made their way to neighboring Pakistan. There Abdullah Azzam organized them to provide medical, logistic, and financial help and morale to Afghan mujahideen fighters and refugees from the town of Peshawar.

In the process, these Arab relief workers engaged in *da'wa* (missionary work) among the Sufi Muslims from Afghanistan who had not seen the light of "pure" Saudi-style Wahhabi-Salafite fundamentalism. As they distributed Saudi riyals and U.S. dollars, the Arab fundamentalists proselytized and tried to instill their puritanical form of Islam among the easy-going Afghans.

But their role was not limited to missionary work or fund-raising and logistics support. By the mid-1980s some Arabs had taken to joining the mujahideen fighters of Hekmatyar, Haqqani, and Sayyaf to fight in Afghanistan. Most of these young Arabs were placed in Afghan mujahideen units, but this caused innumerable problems. The Arab puritans often destroyed the local Sufi-mystic shrines that the simple Afghan villagers considered holy. Many Arabs also disliked the almost ritual rhythm of Afghan hit-and-run warfare and seemed to be bizarrely focused on their own martyrdom. By contrast, Afghan tribesmen fought to fight another day and loved to brag of their exploits. This invariably caused bad blood between the Afghans and Arabs. Arabs caught destroying Sufi shrines, ridiculing local Muslim leaders who did not speak Arabic, or executing prisoners of war were killed by angry Afghan mujahideen on several occasions.

But not all Arabs were hell-bent on martyrdom or eradicating the Afghans' ancient Islamic traditions. Others became known as "gucci jihadis" for coming to Afghanistan for a few months, lobbing some mortar shells at a Communist base, getting their picture taken, then returning home as "mujahideen." This generation of "Afghan-Arabs" proudly wore their Afghan *pakols* (round felt berets) to prove their jihad credentials, and many subsequently waged terrorist war against their own "un-Islamic" governments in Algeria, Egypt, and Jordan after they returned home. Tens of thousands of people died as the so-called Afghan-Arabs waged a war to overthrow their home governments in the 1990s.

Although not all Arabs who came to Pakistan in the late 1980s went on to become terrorists, it should be stated that an increasing number were extremists escaping the authorities in their own countries. As Azzam traveled from Brooklyn, New York, to the Arab Gulf recruiting Arab adventurers, fanatics, or those who were inspired by the plight of their fellow Muslims in Afghanistan, a new wave of Arabs began to arrive in Pakistan. This wave was more militant than the first wave and was dominated by a group of Egyptian Islamic Brotherhood Ikhwanis who had been inspired by the militant writings of the fanatical Egyptian scholar Sayid Qutb. Before his execution in Egypt in 1966, Qutb had called on Muslims to cleanse their societies of Westernism and remember the forgotten *fard* (obligation) to wage purifying jihad. The new wave of Arabs took his words seriously. The Pakistani frontier city of Peshawar gave them a safe haven to gain experience with weapons and explosives and to prepare for jihads against their own "*munafiq*" (apostate) governments.

These extremists quickly found a wealthy benefactor in Osama bin Laden, the most famous of all the Arab volunteers. Although bin Laden initially fell under the spell of the relatively moderate Abdullah Azzam, he gradually drifted into the shadow of Ayman al Zawahiri, an Egyptian follower of Qutb. Zawahiri and his Egyptian followers supported bin Laden in his dream of creating an all-Arab *jund* (fighting force) that would wage jihad in Afghanistan independently of the Afghans. Although Azzam wanted the Arabs to fight in the ranks of the Afghans, the Egyptians rejected his decision and turned against him for his support of Massoud the Lion of Panjsher. Instead they began to work with the extremist Pashtun leaders Sayyaf, Hekmatyar, and Haqqani to create Arab brigades.

In 1987 bin Laden led one of the first of these units into the Spin Ghar Mountains just over the Afghan border. His objective was to build a base known as Al Masada (the Lion's Den) in the Afghan tribal regions controlled by Haqqani's Zadran tribe. Bin Laden settled on an easily defended position in a place called Jaji, where fighters loyal to Sayyaf and Haqqani had bases of their own. There bin Laden and his men patiently dug an elaborate mountain bunker and waited for the Soviets to come to them. It did not take the Communists long to realize that a group of bold mujahideen had created fortifications to guard the supply lines from Miram Shah in Pakistan to Khost in Afghanistan. In April 1987, the Soviets hit bin Laden and the neighboring Afghan groups with everything from napalm to mortars and tank fire. Then they sent in *spetsnaz* (Soviet Special Forces) to clean them out. Bin Laden had a mental breakdown during the siege and led his men in retreat, but Sayyaf ordered him back, and bin Laden made his legendary stand. Of the approximately twenty-five Arabs with bin Laden in the final assault, roughly half were killed.

This small border skirmish did not radically alter the dynamics of the war in Paktia Province, and eventually the Soviets overran Al Masada and the larger mujahideen-controlled region. In the grand scheme of things, it paled in comparison to the large-scale mujahideen activities in the Panjsher and elsewhere. It is therefore erroneous to state, as many observers do, that bin Laden "defeated" the Soviet Union. His contribution to the war was too little and too late (the war lasted just one more year after Jaji) and paled in comparison with the efforts of the more than 150,000 to 250,000 Afghan mujahideen operating throughout the country.

What *was* of seminal importance was the impact that the war made on bin Laden and his "Afghan-Arab" volunteers. For bin Laden, surviving a Soviet offensive proved to be an epiphany, and his followers disseminated the news of the glorious Arab victory at Jaji throughout the Middle East. Thousands of young Arabs were inspired by the stories of bin Laden's heroics. He became an icon for a new generation of voiceless, devout, or disenfranchised Arab militants who subscribed to *Jihad Magazine*. For these young men, returning to Islam was a means for rebelling against the old order and expressing their frustration at life under U.S.-sponsored Arab dictators.

And speaking of the United States, there are many critics of the United States who take a certain glee in the fact that America was attacked on 9/11 by bin Laden, its former jihadi "Frankenstein." The belief is that the American CIA funded, trained, and indoctrinated bin Laden, who then turned on the Americans with devastating results (this is paralleled by the misconception that the United States also supported the rise of the Taliban, which it did not). The truth is far more prosaic. Although it is true that the United States financed and equipped many local *Afghan* fanatics who set back women's rights in Afghanistan and went on to become terrorists (most notably Hekmatyar and Haqqani), the United States never trained or financed the Saudi millionaire bin Laden. On the contrary, bin Laden deeply loathed the United States for supporting Israel and for daring to interfere in "his" holy war. For bin Laden, the war in Afghanistan was a God-ordained jihad, not a subplot to Washington's Cold War against the Soviets. Far from embracing the United States, bin Laden actually tried to have American and Western war correspondents in Afghanistan killed as "infidel trespassers" in the 1980s.

Not surprisingly, when the war ended in 1988 bin Laden began to work with his new mentor, the Egyptian extremist Ayman al Zawahiri, to mobilize the Arab volunteers to topple the "Near Enemy" (the Iraqi, Kuwaiti, Jordanian, Egyptian, Syrian, Algerian, and Saudi "secular puppet dictator" regimes) and create a new caliphate. But this was not all that bin

Laden envisioned. The Egyptians around bin Laden were increasingly dominated by an extremist ideology called Takfirism (from the Arabic, to label someone a "*kafir*" or "infidel"). The Takfiris declared jihad on those they defined as "bad Muslims" and sanctioned terrorism against them.

As mentioned earlier, the Takfiris demonstrated their propensity to terrorize "apostate" Muslims when they helped the Afghan mujahideen besiege the Communist-held town of Jalalabad in 1989. When sixty captured Afghan (Muslim) government troops were given to them, the Arab Takfiris physically cut them into pieces instead of engaging in the Afghan tradition of embracing their former enemies. The massacred prisoners' body parts were then sent back to Jalalabad where, far from intimidating the defenders, they inspired them to resist the mujahideen for another three years.

Bin Laden's former inspiration, Abdullah Azzam, was adamantly opposed to this sort of fanaticism and Takfiri terrorism against fellow Muslims. He also rejected bin Laden's plans for creating a legion for launching terrorist attacks on Muslim regimes in the Middle East. Instead, Azzam envisioned the creation of a mobile rapid reaction force that could be deployed to wage frontal combat in areas such as Indian-controlled Kashmir where Muslims were endangered.

But Azzam's ideas were no longer radical enough for bin Laden and his group. As the Egyptian extremists turned on Azzam, the original "patron saint" of the modern jihad movement, they began to criticize his links to the relatively moderate Massoud. Just as the split began to widen, Azzam and his sons were mysteriously assassinated in a November 1989 bombing in Peshawar. Azzam's surviving son blamed the killing on bin Laden and Zawahiri.

With the removal of Azzam, bin Laden was recognized as the paramount leader of the Arab veterans of the Afghan war. Although bin Laden's dreams of establishing an Al Qaeda al Jihad (Base for Holy War) in Afghanistan were put on hold by the 1992 defeat of his local host, Hekmatyar, he never forgot Afghanistan when he moved to Sudan. For bin Laden, Afghanistan was "Khurasan" (an ancient name for western Afghanistan), a land that had been sanctified by the blood of Arab *shaheeds* (martyrs).

There are deeper spiritual attractions to Afghanistan as well. Bin Laden and his followers seem to have believed in a *hadith* (saying of the Prophet) of dubious authenticity which predicted that "From Khurasan will emerge black flags, whom none will be able to turn back and they, the flag bearers, will continue moving forward till they reach Illya [Jerusalem] and embed their flags into its earth." They also proclaimed, "If you see the

Black Banners coming from Khurasan go to them immediately, even if you must crawl over ice, because amongst them is the Caliph, Al Mahdi (the Messiah)." Clearly, it was in the cloud-covered mountains and caves of "Khurasan" that bin Laden, a rather inconsequential son in a large Saudi family, had fulfilled his self-proclaimed destiny. Afghanistan would always be sacred to bin Laden, and it was here that he would build his terrorist organization and fighting force.

When he returned to the Jalalabad region in 1996 (after being expelled from his temporary refuge in Sudan), bin Laden worked hard to create the 055 international jihad brigade to help his Taliban hosts crush the Northern Alliance opposition (a front composed of Uzbeks, Tajiks, and Hazaras). It came as a surprise to none that the Arab 055 Ansar (Companion) fighters chose to fight in this unit under a black banner known as the Rayah instead of the white banner of the Taliban. Bin Laden the exile clearly saw himself as playing a role similar to that of the Prophet Muhammad who was exiled from Mecca to Medina in the sixth century. From his Afghan "Medina," bin Laden dreamed of rallying tens of thousands of Muslims to march out from Khurasan under black flags to topple the apostate regimes of the Middle East and liberate Jerusalem and Mecca.

To achieve this goal, bin Laden and his newly reconstituted Al Qaeda declared a war on America in a series of *hukums* (edicts that have less clout than a fatwa issued by a religious scholar) from 1996 to 1998. Their ultimate goal was to force the United States to withdraw its troops from holy Arabian soil and leave the unpopular Saudi regime to its fate. Interestingly enough, Mullah Omar and many moderates in the Taliban movement tried to muzzle bin Laden, but they failed. In many ways, bin Laden betrayed his Taliban hosts by hosting terrorists in their land and making decrees against the United States. The issue of the Taliban hosting terrorists (combined with their treatment of women and destruction of the ancient Buddah statues of Bamiyan) led the United Nations to initiate sanctions against Afghanistan.

By this time it became apparent that bin Laden was no longer content to wage war against the so-called Near Enemy (the Saudi dynasty and other American "puppet" Muslim regimes in the Middle East). It was time to attack the Far Enemy (the United States) directly. Thus was born the attack on the U.S. embassies in Kenya and Tanzania in 1998 and the USS *Cole* in Yemen in 2000. Bin Laden's obsession ultimately led to the 9/11 attacks on New York and Washington, DC, that would come to be known in Al Qaeda circles as the "Holy Tuesday attack."

As the Americans prepared to strike back at Al Qaeda after 9/11, bin Laden dreamed of transforming Afghanistan into a quagmire that would galvanize public opinion against the United States throughout the Muslim world. But bin Laden's glorious guerrilla war in the mountains of Afghanistan failed to materialize in 2001. In fact, average Afghans across the country turned on the arrogant Wahhabi *Araban* (Arabs) and killed them from Kandahar to Kabul. The 055 brigade was annihilated by Northern Alliance troops who were supported by U.S. close air support. Thousands of them were killed or captured and sent to Bagram Airfield or Guantanamo Bay. In Kabul the Afghans rose up, slaughtered the Arabs, and stuffed Afghani banknotes in their mouths as a sign of contempt. As his dreams collapsed around him, a shocked and humiliated bin Laden subsequently fled to his hideout in Tora Bora, a frontier mountain complex he had used in the 1980s south of Jalalabad. Here he was forced to bribe mujahideen commanders in the area to allow his men to escape across the border into the Parchinar Beak in Pakistan in December 2001.

Once safely in Pakistan, bin Laden continued to make threats against the West. Much to his joy and amazement, he watched as the great jihad quagmire that he had envisioned for Afghanistan began to materialize not in Khurasan, but in the ruins of Baathist Iraq. Although the fanatical jihad warrior Abu Musab al Zarqawi and his Tawhid wal Jihad (Unity and Jihad) fighters in Iraq stole the headlines from 2003 to 2005, bin Laden and Zawahiri patiently worked to revive what became known as Al Qaeda Central. Although many Western analysts prematurely wrote him off, it soon became obvious that bin Laden's role as both an inspiration and a terrorist leader was not over.

Indicators that Al Qaeda Central was still in business came on many levels. Bin Laden was, for example, recognized as the overall amir of Zarqawi's Iraqi insurgent group (which was symbolically renamed "Al Qaeda in Iraq" in December 2004), and bin Laden's followers began to reestablish smaller training camps in the forested mountains of Pakistan's Waziristan agencies. Several Al Qaeda international terror plots have been linked to these camps, including the July 7, 2005, bombings in London, a subsequent plot to blow up multiple airplanes flying from London using liquid explosives, and the plot to set off a bomb in Times Square in 2010. There are also Al Qaeda affiliates in the Magreb region in North Africa, Somalia, and Yemen that have the potential to strike at the United States. The Yemeni affiliate known as Al Qaeda in the Arabian Peninsula in particular has shown itself to be most capable of carrying out strikes on the U.S. mainland.

Although bin Laden appears to have been considered too high-value a target to actively run Al Qaeda operations himself, Al Qaeda's number two, Ayman al Zawahiri, and a new generation of leaders, including the charismatic Abu Yahya al Libbi, stepped in to run the show. It was al Libbi, for example, who produced Al Qaeda's media branch Sahab (The Clouds) and helped the Taliban manufacture their own video and Internet production known as Labaik. Al Qaeda also played a key role in assisting the technophobic Taliban (who banned the Internet in August 2001) in adapting to everything from the Internet to suicide bombing. In the summer of 2008, Al Qaeda Central also played a role in convincing their native Pakistani Taliban hosts to turn on the Pakistani government, their former sponsors, and wage a terrorist war that eventually led to the killing of the presidential candidate Benazir Bhutto.

Although many of bin Laden's friends and colleagues (including Al Qaeda's number three, Muhammad Atef) were killed during 2001's Operation Enduring Freedom, Al Qaeda Central appears to have survived and regrouped. With the rise of the Taliban insurgency, bin Laden, who first cut his teeth leading his men in the mountains of Afghanistan in 1987, was clearly determined that the Arabs play a similar role to the Arab mujahideen volunteers of the 1980s in the current conflict. Bin Laden, who was confined to a compound for about six years, in Abbottabad, northeastern Pakistan, far from the battle front in Afghanistan and the FATA, does not, however, seem to have been able to run the organization he created. The images the Obama White House later released of a frail-looking, gray bearded bin Laden watching a younger version of himself on television from the walls of a compound/prison paint a picture of a man who had been forced to be an observer to history. His self-imposed imprisonment in the Abbottabad compound was cut short on the fateful day of May 1, 2011, when a U.S. Navy SEAL team killed the man whose journey to the region had begun back in the early 1980s with the Soviet invasion of Afghanistan. Soon thereafter the body of the world's most famous terrorist jihadi icon was dumped off a U.S. aircraft carrier into the Arabian Sea. The man responsible for the deaths of more than five thousand U.S. soldiers in Iraq and Afghanistan and hundreds of thousands of Afghans and Iraqis simply disappeared from the face of the earth.

General Abdul Rashid Dostum, the Secular Uzbek Warlord

No Afghan warlord is more colorful than Abdul Rashid Dostum, an Uzbek commander who defies stereotypes. Dostum's origins are in many ways unique. As it happens, not all of Afghanistan's regional, tribal, or ethnic leaders joined the anti-Soviet jihad in the 1980s. Indeed, some, such as Dostum, actively fought *against* the mujahideen Islamic rebels. Although the Americans defined the war in black-and-white terms as a struggle of freedom-loving Afghans against Soviet atheist invaders, many oppressed ethnic groups saw the war in gray terms. They saw it as an opportunity to settle old scores, achieve autonomy, and escape Pashtun dominance. The Afghan Communists and their Soviet backers were quick to exploit such ethnic cleavages and use them to their advantage (much as the Americans belatedly did with anti–Al Qaeda Sunni tribes in Iraq's Anbar Province in 2008). In the invasion of Iraq, the Americans made use of Kurdish resentment of Sunnis to establish a northern front and later won over many Shiites who were disenfranchised by the ruling Sunnis.

Pro-Communist groups included the long-suffering Ismaili Hazaras of Baghlan Province led by Sayid Naderi, as well as disgruntled Pashtun tribes in the south. These groups took arms to fight the mujahideen and created pro-Communist government pockets in the north and southeast. Naderi's Ismaili Hazaras, for example, guarded Soviet convoys traveling over the first leg of the Salang Pass through the Hindu Kush Mountains. In the south, an ex-mujahideen Pashtun commander named Ismatullah Muslim took his tribe over to the Communists and guarded the road from Kandahar to the Pakistani border at Spin Boldak. Other "*arbakis*" (pro-government militias) were formed by the Jaji, Tanai, Shinwari, Arghandabi, Mohmand, Wadir Safays, and Afiridi tribes.

But the most powerful group co-opted by the Afghan Communist government to fight the mujahideen were the Uzbeks who lived in the flatlands of the northern Afghanistan region known as Turkistan. The Uzbeks were not definitively conquered by the Afghan-Pashtuns until 1881, and the memory of their former independence just one hundred years earlier was not lost in the 1980s. Many Uzbeks resented their despised status in the Pashtun-dominated Afghan state. The Uzbeks, who were known as "flat noses" by the Pashtuns, also remembered their glorious past as horse-mounted warriors in the Mongol Golden Horde.

Many secularized Afghan Uzbeks had also grown to trust the Soviets since Russian engineers had been working among them in the north on various construction projects for two decades. For many of these Uzbeks, the Soviet Union meant progress, jobs, roads, and factories of the sort found just across the border in the Soviet ethnic republic of Uzbekistan. The Soviet engineers who brought this progress with them to Afghanistan were often Soviet Uzbeks who told the comparatively backward Afghan Uzbeks about the glories of their modern home republic of Uzbekistan. In the USSR, they were told, Uzbeks were not a despised race of Turkic "flat noses"—they were masters of their own Soviet republic. The Uzbek Soviet Socialist Republic had a modern capital called Tashkent and special prerogatives for native Uzbeks.

For this reason, when the calls for jihad against the Soviets rang out in 1979, many Afghan Uzbeks chose not to join the mujahideen guerrillas. Although there were Uzbek mujahideen in the north (who fought under the command of Hekmatyar's Pashtuns or Rabbani's Tajiks), they were never as numerous as the mujahideen among the Tajiks and Pashtuns. This was in part dictated by geography. The Tajiks and the Pashtuns of the east had cross-border sanctuaries in neighboring Pakistan and mountainous terrain from which to fight, whereas the northern two-thirds of Afghan Turkistan consisted of a flatland that bordered the USSR.

But the comparative lack of jihadi activity in the north was also due to the efforts of a pro–Communist government Uzbek commander named Abdul Rashid Dostum. Abdul Rashid grew up working in the northern gas and oil fields built by the Soviet engineers. He later served as a member of the special forces in the Daoud-era Afghan Army in 1977. When the 1978 Saur Communist Revolution took place, he was an ideal candidate for guarding the oil and gas facilities around his native region of Sheberghan, located in the deserts of northwestern Afghanistan.

While local mujahideen recruited for the jihad, Abdul Rashid recruited tough Uzbek and related Turkmen oil workers to guard the plants that they themselves had built with Soviet help. As the Afghan Communist army began to collapse due to defections in 1979, Abdul Rashid's *qawm*-based militia force (which was recruited from his native district of Jowzjan Province) grew in strength. Many of its soldiers were impoverished Uzbeks who received good salaries, weapons, prestige, and power from the Communist government in return for their service. For this they adored Abdul Rashid, who led them from the front and called everyone *dostlorum* ("my friends," in Uzbek)—hence his nom de guerre "Dostum" (My Friend).

By the early 1980s Abdul Rashid Dostum had been able to use his Jowzjani militia to pacify their province, which became known as Little Moscow. As the mujahideen insurgency grew stronger in the northern foothills of the Hindu Kush, his horse-mounted Jowzjani fighters were used to clear the rebels out of the mountains as well. By the mid-1980s the north was pacified and Soviet troops could move through it with relative safety until they entered Massoud's territory on the other side of the Hindu Kush.

As Dostum's successes mounted, so did the size of his militia, which was upgraded to division strength and became known as the 53rd Division. As thousands of Uzbeks and related Turkmen defected from the mujahideen to join Dostum's "snowballing" force (which was organized as one of the Afghan Communist government's new Tribal Divisions), the government decided to use it to fight the Pashtun mujahideen in the south. There Dostum led his men in fighting in Kandahar, Wardak, Laghman, Khost, Nangarhar, Paghman, and other Pashtun provinces. His

Uzbek and Turkmen soldiers earned a reputation as fearless fighters. They came to be hated by Hekmatyar, Haqqani, bin Laden, and other mujahideen leaders who called them *"gilamjams"* (carpet thieves) for their tendency to plunder.

It should be noted that although ethnicity and full-blown nationalism never played the same role in tribal Afghanistan that it did in, say, the Balkans, mounting ethnic differences certainly contributed to antagonism. As the centralized state brutally created by Amir Abdur Rahman in the late nineteenth century dissolved into quarreling tribal and regional militias, it was only natural that ethnicity became an increasingly important focus for allegiance. It was at this time that local groups first began to rally around the concept of nationality, a term now defined by the word *qawm*.

The Soviet withdrawal contributed to the process of ethnicization. When the Soviets withdrew from Afghanistan in February 1989, they bolstered Dostum's pro-Communist ethnic forces with tanks, attack helicopters, Scud missiles, and artillery. As the Jowzjani Division soared to as many fifty thousand men, Dostum became the strongest *qawm*-military leader in Afghanistan. Although he seems to have loyally served his Pashtun Communist master, President Najibullah, many Pashtun Communists nonetheless distrusted him. For his part, Dostum soon developed reasons to distrust Najibullah as Soviet funds dried up.

As the writing appeared on the wall for the Afghan Communist regime following the collapse of the USSR in December 1991, ethnic Pashtuns began to defect from the Communist government to join Hekmatyar's Pashtun mujahideen. To prevent this, President Najibullah, himself a Pashtun, began to emphasize his government's Pashtun and Islamic nature. He also contemplated removing his powerful Uzbek praetorian guard, Dostum, and demobilizing his tribal army to make amends with the Pashtun mujahideen.

But when Najibullah began to remove non-Pashtun commanders allied to Dostum in the north, the Uzbek commander reacted first. Dostum warned the Russians that he and his people would not give up their guns or autonomy and would never again be relegated to the role of second-class citizens in a Pashtun-dominated state. To keep his grip on power, Dostum engaged in a quintessential Afghan preemptive betrayal. In a move that few could have foreseen, he met with Massoud the Lion of Panjsher and concluded an alliance between the Uzbeks and the Tajiks. The two northern allies then took Mazar i Sharif, the largest city in the north, and moved on Kabul itself. A panicked Najibullah tried to flee but was stopped by Dostum's men at the airport. Then, to prevent Hekmatyar from taking the capital, Dostum flew his and Massoud's men into the city on his transport planes and pushed Hekmatyar's advance guards out of the city. Dostum then seized many key points in Kabul, including the Bala Hissar Fortress overlooking the city.

Dostum clearly expected that he, as the commander of the largest army in Afghanistan, would play a major role in the new mujahideen government that subsequently took control of Kabul. Dostum even made the hajj pilgrimage to Mecca and had himself declared a mujahideen. But Hekmatyar refused to serve in the same government with Dostum the "Communist." The other mujahideen factions distrusted him as well, and he was pointedly excluded from the new post-Communist mujahideen government.

Incensed at his exclusion and frustrated by the growing fundamentalist nature of the new mujahideen government, Dostum returned to the north. There he created the first political party dominated by Uzbeks, known as the Jumbesh i Milli i Islami, the National Islamic Party (recall that the Uzbeks did not have a mujahideen party of their own as the Tajiks, Pashtuns, and Hazaras did, so many Uzbek mujahideen joined Dostum when the jihad ended).

Although dominated by Uzbeks, the Jumbesh party also united ex-Communists of all ethnic backgrounds, as well as Uzbek mujahideen, in one political bloc. In the process of uniting these various factions, Dostum created an autonomous realm that extended across six northern provinces. Although Massoud and the Tajik commander of Herat, Ismail Khan, both attacked Dostum to prevent this de facto secession of many of Afghanistan's richest and most stable provinces, Dostum countered by besieging Kabul in January 1994. He did so in conjunction with his former enemy, Hekmatyar. Faced with an attack on the capital, Massoud and Khan ended their own efforts to crush Dostum, and he was left free to run the north until the emergence of the Taliban.

From 1992 to 1998, Mazar i Sharif, the capital of Dostum's northern mini-state, remained a stable, secular bastion in contrast to the Pashtun south, which was torn apart by competing fundamentalist mujahideen warlords. The university in Mazar i Sharif, for example, hosted as many as 1,800 women at a time when women, who had been liberated in the Communist-controlled cities, were forced into the veil in the mujahideen-dominated south. Thousands of secularists, teachers, ex-Communists, Muslim moderates, and women fled to Mazar i Sharif at this time to live in freedom under Dostum the secularist. They did so to escape Kabul, which began to suffer from mujahideen violence and the enforcement of fundamentalist laws.

But Dostum's secular bastion in the north was plagued by internal dissension between regional commanders. Although Dostum personally led his tank and cavalry forces in crushing all attempts by the mujahideen (and later the Taliban) to take the north, he was weaker than he appeared on paper. This weakness stemmed in part from the fact that the various Uzbek commanders of the north were very divided and engaged in constant power struggles among themselves.

The Taliban exploited this weakness in the spring of 1997 when they convinced one of Dostum's commanders, a half-Uzbek, half-Pashtun named Abdul Malik, to defect in the heat of a battle. The Taliban's truck-mounted "cavalry" then swept across the north and overran Dostum's positions before taking the cosmopolitan city of Mazar i Sharif. For his part, Dostum fled to Turkey to escape certain death. In his absence, the horrified people of Mazar i Sharif were told that strict shariah law would be enforced and that the city's large Shiite Hazara population would be defined as "heretics." To make matters worse, the Taliban also began to disarm the troops of Malik, the very Uzbek commander who had betrayed Dostum and assisted them in the first place.

In response, Malik "the Traitor" and the Shiite Hazaras together attacked the dispersed Taliban who had incautiously spread themselves thin throughout the city. What had started out as a Taliban triumph ended in disaster. Thousands of Taliban were killed in the mazes of Mazar i Sharif or were executed in the desert by Malik (a crime many non-specialists have erroneously attributed to Dostum). Malik then fought to repel the Taliban from the north, but it quickly became obvious that he lacked Dostum's leadership skills.

After Malik requested his assistance, Dostum returned in triumph from exile in Turkey to fight the Taliban. He quickly succeeded in crushing a Taliban drive to retake his former "capital" of Mazar i Sharif. But his army had been fatefully weakened by Malik's betrayal, and Malik seems to have continued to undermine him. By the spring of 1998, Dostum's forces were overrun and he again fled to Turkey to plot his revenge on the Taliban and Malik. In his absence, the Taliban brought the horrors of their puritanical laws to the north and began executing female "adulteresses," vengefully slaughtering thousands of Hazaras, and taking land from Uzbeks. Dostum's pride and joy, the university in Mazar i Sharif, was also closed, as was the Rowza, the holy Sufi shrine of Mazar i Sharif. For three long years Taliban darkness descended on the people of the north.

During my own visits to the north, I collected numerous horror stories of female schoolteachers being executed for teaching girls, of Hazaras having their throats ritualistically slit, and of refugee columns being shelled by Taliban gunners. One Uzbek tried to explain it to me in terms Americans could understand: "If 9/11 was the day the world will never forget, then 1998 to 2001 were the *years* that we Uzbeks will never forget."

Dostum, a large, energetic man who went by the nickname "Pasha" (Commander), followed these events with fury from his place of exile in Ankara, Turkey. Unable to stay away from the battle, he finally returned to Afghanistan in April 2001 at the request of his old rival Massoud. In the finest of Afghan traditions, these former enemies embraced, and Dostum swore that he would either liberate his country from the Taliban or die in his famous green *chapan* (riding coat) trying to do so. Dostum, the feared Uzbek Pasha was now a member of Massoud's Northern Alliance opposition.

But for all of his eagerness, Dostum's task was difficult, and many felt his mission was suicidal. An old Soviet Mil 8 "Hip" helicopter placed him in the high, barren peaks of the Hindu Kush behind Taliban lines to raise a distractive rebellion. There he rallied roughly two thousand Uzbek *cheriks* (raiders) to join him in waging a horse-mounted campaign against a much larger Taliban occupation army. His skilled Uzbek horsemen used the hit-and-run tactics of their ancient Mongol forebears to kill Taliban and Al Qaeda fighters. By summer Dostum was even able to liberate the mountain district of Zari and launch raids down in the lowlands.

But the Taliban responded by sending five thousand men into the mountains to repulse him. Outgunned and outnumbered, Dostum's small force of less than two thousand riders was beaten back. Nonetheless, Dostum's activities served their main purpose, namely to divert desperately needed Taliban troops from the front lines against Massoud's embattled enclave in the Panjsher region. This reprieve allowed Massoud's Tajik component of the Northern Alliance, who were fighting trench warfare, to survive until 9/11.

But Dostum's rebellion was ultimately doomed, and the Taliban began to push his turbaned riders deeper into the mountains by September 2001. With supplies running out and his men dying in daily Taliban air raids (the Taliban maintained a fleet of aging MiG and Sukhoi fighter bombers), the odds of his survival seemed slim.

It was in the midst of this desperate battle to the finish that Dostum was informed of the events in distant North America on 9/11. Dostum, a committed secularist who had been fighting *against* the likes of bin Laden, Hekmatyar, and Haqqani for two decades (while America had been supporting them), lost no time in offering his services to America's Central Command. In late October 2001, the U.S. Special Operations Command's Fifth Group sent a twelve-man A-Team known as Tiger O2 (Operational Detachment Alpha 595) to act as a "force magnifier" for Dostum and his horsemen. The U.S. Air Force also introduced

Operational Detachment Alpha 595, also known as Tiger 02, the Green
Beret team that fought alongside General Abdul Rashid Dostum's horsemen
in 2001.

close air support specialists from the 23rd Special Tactics Squadron. Their
job was to strike at nearby Taliban targets during the winter while United
States Central Command (CENTCOM) mobilized the 10th Mountain
Division, 101st Airborne, and the Marines to launch a full frontal invasion
of fifty thousand soldiers in the spring.

But the always energetic Dostum pushed his A-Team and Air Force close
air support controllers to go on the offensive before winter, and they
quickly developed that most important of Afghan factors—momentum.

In November 2001 Dostum and his horse-mounted A-Team launched
a weeklong cavalry charge down the Dar y Suf Valley (located on the
northern flank of the Hindu Kush Mountains) and out onto the plains
of Afghan Turkistan. Their charge was bolstered by close air support,
including two strikes by Daisy Cutter, the world's largest bomb. As the
American JDAMs (Joint Direct Ammunition, i.e. satellite-guided bombs)
wreaked havoc on Taliban positions in their path, Dostum's Uzbek
horsemen charged through the bomb clouds firing AK-47s and RPGs.
Against all odds, Dostum's riders overran one enemy line after another.
This campaign revolved around a remarkable synergy between medieval-
style Uzbek cavalry charges and twenty-first-century U.S. military technology. The "first war of the twenty-first century" was being fought by B-52

bombers working in conjunction with horsemen descended from Genghis Khan.

During the campaign Dostum regularly taunted the Taliban on his radio and threatened them with the "death rays" that he claimed came from Azrail the Death Angel (in actuality, he was referring to a deadly AC-130 Specter gunship and satellite-guided bombs). Dostum's threats and his deadly cavalry charges broke the fighting spirit of more than one Taliban unit, and many Talibs began to surrender to his small force.

In one of the most stunning developments of the stalemated Afghan campaign, Dostum succeeded in breaking through the much larger Taliban army guarding the approaches to Mazar i Sharif at a place called the Tangi Gap. Then, with fellow Northern Alliance commanders Ustad Atta (Tajik) and Karim Khalili (Hazara), his small "army" liberated the holy shrine in the center of Mazar i Sharif. This represented a tremendous symbolic victory, because the possessor of Mazar i Sharif and its famous blue-domed shrine is said to have the mandate of Allah to rule the plains of northern Turkistan. The Taliban army of the north collapsed soon thereafter, and its remnants fled eastward to Kunduz where it was quickly surrounded. In Kunduz the Taliban and die-hard Al Qaeda elements were mercilessly pummeled by B-52 bombers and AC-130 gunships, and they finally surrendered at a place called Ergenek.

Dostum subsequently captured thousands of Taliban and Al Qaeda 055 fighters at Kunduz, and his small force was overwhelmed by prisoners of war. He then incautiously had these captives transported to his former headquarters, a nineteenth-century fortress located to the west of Mazar i Sharif known as Qala i Jengi (the Fortress of War). Putting their trust in the Afghan tradition of surrender, Dostum's guards did not carefully check their prisoners, which led to disaster. Many of the prisoners were not fellow Afghans but Arab 055 Ansar fanatics. They were somehow able to overwhelm and kill their incautious guards as well as a CIA agent named Michael Spann who was interrogating them (he became the first American casualty of the global war on terror). They then seized control of the fort's arms depot and launched a breakout attempt with the objective of retaking Mazar i Sharif. Had the Taliban retaken the shrine of Mazar i Sharif, Dostum's momentum would have been destroyed and a long winter war may have been inaugurated.

In desperation, the remaining CIA agent, David Tyson, called in U.S. air strikes by F-18s, and British and U.S. Special Forces helped bolster Dostum's outgunned men. After two days the fighting was over and hundreds of foreign fighters were killed. Incidentally, among the survivors, Dostum's men found an oddity no one had expected to find in the bombed-out ruins of the fort. As they entered the fort's ruined basement, they found an *American* jihadi volunteer named John Walker Lindh who had traveled from California to Afghanistan to fight in bin Laden's field army. Lindh became an instant cause célèbre and was subsequently transported to the United States and sentenced to twenty years in prison as an "American Taliban."

When news of the uprising got out, some of Dostum's men who were guarding another column of Taliban prisoners fired shots into several of their transport containers. Somewhere between one hundred and two hundred Taliban prisoners may have been killed in the process. Some of those killed may have died from wounds and from asphyxiation. Critics of the United States have tried to use this incident to portray Dostum, America's "Mongol warlord" ally, as a bloodthirsty slaughterer. They have tried to suggest that as many as four thousand were killed in the massacre (which is almost the total number of prisoners captured). But local Pashtuns I interviewed, as well as Taliban prisoners of war, refuted this high number (no more than five thousand prisoners were taken at Kunduz, and these were released in well-publicized waves in subsequent years). Efforts to undermine Dostum, who was not present at the time of his men's attack on the prisoners, are also meant to undermine America's moral high ground in Afghanistan. They aim to vicariously link not only Dostum, but the United States itself, to a fictitious Bosnian- or Rwandan-style massacre of thousands of prisoners of war.

Regardless of the true number killed, the death of one to two hundred Taliban fighters in the midst of a war meant little to the oppressed people of the north who had lost thousands of their kin during the Taliban's conquest and oppressive rule. Thousands of Taliban were actually killed in the rout of their northern army, and this went unnoticed by all but a few critics of U.S. foreign policy. For the Uzbeks of the north, Dostum the Pasha was seen as a liberating hero, and tens of thousands of them came out to welcome him on his victory tour of the northern plains. Dostum the secularist, who had always supported women and a relatively moderate Islamic vision, had returned to free his people from their Taliban and Al Qaeda tormentors.

Some of the newly liberated northerners later took revenge on the Pashtuns in their midst who had sided with the Taliban from 1997 to 2001 and pushed them off their lands. Dostum, however, put an end to this. He wanted to make the northern Pashtuns his allies in his turf war with his former Northern Alliance ally, Tajik commander Ustad Atta. Atta, a member of Rabbani's Jamiat i Islam Party, had powerful friends in the government, and he was eventually able to seize control of Mazar i Sharif. The fact that Atta rules Dostum's old capital as governor of Balkh Province is still a bone of contention between these two powerful northern warlords who waged tank battles in 2003. Dostum cannot, however, move too forcefully against Atta for fear of being portrayed as an unscrupulous warlord. Dostum has been weakened by this defeat and by his exclusion from the government, which gave him the purely symbolic positions of deputy minister of defense and chief of staff of the Afghan Army.

Although Dostum was able to garner 10 percent of the vote when he ran for president of Afghanistan in 2004 (roughly the size of the Turkmen and Uzbek population of Afghanistan), he has continued to see his power erode. President Karzai sees Dostum as a warlord relic, and many of his detractors have painted him as a threat to Afghanistan. Uninformed observers in the West have also linked him to Malik's massacre of the Taliban in 1997 and to the fabricated massacre of four thousand Taliban prisoners. To make matters worse, in his best seller *The Taliban: Militant Oil, Islam and Fundamentalism*, Pakistani journalist Ahmed Rashid conveyed a secondhand account of Dostum using a tank to run over one of his men who was caught pillaging. This single story of dubious authenticity has been retold over and over again by journalists who have exaggerated it and spoken of Dostum running over "enemies," "prisoners," "ethnic opponents" (always in the plural) with tanks (plural). The legend of Dostum "the Tank Killer" who has "laughed men to death" has thus shaped U.S. policy toward this former ally.

In my own time spent with Dostum, I found him building schools for women, meeting with local Pashtuns, and offering to fight his old enemies the Taliban. As stated earlier he cherishes the Sig pistol given to him by former U.S. CENTCOM commander General Tommy Franks and has a plaque on his wall declaring him an honorary member of a U.S. Special Forces A-Team. But as an ethnic Uzbek who has tried to maintain his power base among his well-organized Jumbesh Party followers, Dostum is seen as a centrifugal threat to the Afghan central government.

Dostum's February 2008 dismissal from his post as chief of staff of the Afghan Army followed an incident in which he beat and kidnapped Akbar Bei, one of his enemies. In 2009 Dostum was exiled to Turkey by President Karzai. But in August of that year, Dostum was invited to come back to the country if he could garner Uzbek support for Karzai in the August 20 election. Four days before the election, Dostum returned to a hero's welcome in Kabul as thousands of his Uzbek followers beat drums and chanted "Long live Dostum!" The Uzbeks subsequently did as Dostum asked and voted in large numbers for Karzai. Today Dostum is back in the good graces of the Karzai government and is working to rebuild his power base in the north. As the Taliban have begun to reinfiltrate the plains of Turkistan, Dostum has repeatedly asked the Karzai government to let him fight them. There may yet be a role for the Pasha Dostum in fighting a newly resurgent Taliban in the north.

Afghan Mujahideen Flexibility and the Afghan Culture of Defection

The larger-than-life story of Dostum the ex-Communist, pro-American warlord is a quintessential story of Afghan political flexibility and alliance building and breaking. Although the Americans and Soviets were incapable of seeing the Afghan conflict in anything but stark black-and-white terms in the 1980s, the Afghans were much more pragmatic and flexible in their views of the war. Many Afghan families had sons fighting in both the Communist and mujahideen forces during the Afghan war of the 1980s. Defections from "red" (Communists) to "green" (Muslim) and vice versa were not uncommon in the war.

Soviet forces naturally distrusted their Afghan Communist allies, and for good reason. Many of these allies were giving information to the mujahideen. Massoud himself was warned of impending Soviet attacks on more than one occasion by moles in the Communist army. On other occasions, Afghan mujahideen warriors, such as the forces of the famous Pashtun commander Ismatullah Muslim, defected to their Communist "comrades" when offered the right money. Ismatullah fought the mujahideen for a while and then defected back to them when they appeared to be winning. The Communists were also able to buy off whole districts. They were quite effective at recruiting tribal militias (*arbaki*) to fight the mujahideen and interdict rebel supply columns moving through their territory.

Such blurring of loyalties inspired one frustrated Pakistani ISI officer to comment, "You can rent an Afghan, but you can never own him." The Afghans have a tradition of "jumping ship" at the right moment, and the art of timely defection and opportunistic betrayal is as old as Afghanistan itself. Its roots go back to the fluidity of alliances among nomadic groups that settled in the north and in the Pashtunwali code of the southern tribes. The Afghans' traditionally moderate Islam and tribal culture lent themselves to this sort of flexibility and made them poor recruits for ideological indoctrination. Far from being ideologically driven, most average Afghans keep their finger to the wind to sense which side has the momentum in any struggle. Their ultimate aim is to survive in their unstable land by joining the winning side.

In Afghanistan the concept of momentum is key and often leads to "snowball effect" defections. The importance of defections was eloquently demonstrated in 2001's Operation Enduring Freedom. When Taliban troops sensed that the Northern Alliance opposition had the momentum, they quickly joined the victors. The "tipping point" came when Dostum seized the holy city of Mazar i Sharif on November 9, 2001. At that moment Taliban troops, who were incorrectly defined by many Western journalists as "die-hard fanatics," threw down their weapons and rushed to embrace their former Northern Alliance foes. Many more simply shaved off their beards and went home.

However, there are of course hard-core believers in Afghanistan, and many of the Taliban's more fanatical elements have kept up the struggle. Today's Taliban extremists have been effective in exploiting the concept of momentum in such southern and eastern provinces as Uruzgan, Helmand, Zabul, and Kandahar. By killing pro-government mullahs who stand up to them, overrunning police posts, burning schools, and publicly assassinating government officials, they have given the impression that momentum is on their side. Many of their tactics, including the distribution of *shabnames* (threatening "night letters"), were perfected by the CIA-backed mujahideen in the 1980s. If the Taliban can create the impression that they have gained the momentum, then tribes or whole districts that are "on the fence" will come over to them just as they did in the 1980s.

But the tradition of defection continues to work both ways, just as it did during the anti-Soviet jihad. When British International Security Assistance Forces moved to take back the southern town of Musa Qala, which was occupied by the Taliban in 2007, a local Pashtun leader named Mullah Salaam sensed that the wind was turning against the Taliban. He then defected to the Karzai government with his Alizai tribe, the largest tribe in the province. The Karzai government has also continued the Communist government's tradition of hiring tribal *arbaki* militias to fight insurgents. Today the Mangal tribe in the southeast and various tribal militias in Helmand and Kandahar have essentially been paid off to fight the Taliban or to guard convoys.

The Soviet War and Its Lessons

Although many observers glibly predicted that the United States would be defeated in the Afghan "graveyard of empires" as the Soviets were, such prognostications demonstrate a lack of awareness of the differing natures of the two wars. First, it should be noted that the Soviets did not, as many alarmist Cold Warriors suggested at the time, invade Afghanistan in December 1979 as a springboard for invading the Gulf. They invaded it to remove a highly unpopular Afghan Communist leader named Hafizullah Amin and to install a more pragmatic Communist government in his place. As Amin's brutal actions drove his countrymen to rebellion, the Soviets repeatedly cautioned him to moderate his policies and felt he had to be removed. To head off an armed overthrow of Afghanistan's unpopular Communist government, the Soviets believed it was necessary to remove Amin and replace him with a more moderate Communist leader.

With this goal in mind, the Soviets invaded Afghanistan from December 25 to 27, 1979. In the process they killed President Amin and made a Communist leader named Babrak Karmal president. The Soviets then placed troops throughout the country to bolster the embattled Afghan Communist government forces. Their goal was to guard the cities and roads and allow the Afghan Communist Army to retake the countryside. Their mission was not meant to be permanent, and some optimists in the Kremlin believed they could finish the task in a year or two.

But the Soviets were quickly sucked into the fighting in the countryside since the Communist Afghan Army was clearly not up to the task. The Soviets were soon launching massive sweep offensives up the Kunar and Panjsher Valleys to secure their supply lines, clashing with mujahideen, and trying to interdict mujahideen supply columns coming over the mountains from Pakistan. The Soviets' problems were compounded by the fact that the Soviet 40th Limited Contingent in Afghanistan was a conscript army that had been trained to fight NATO in the plains of Western Europe. It was not prepared to wage a counterinsurgency in the mountains of Afghanistan. For this reason, the Soviets' initial operations were clumsy and often led to high casualty rates due to mujahideen ambushes.

But the Soviets had learned from the U.S. experience in Vietnam, which taught them the value of helicopters in carrying out counterinsurgency operations. To keep casualties down, the Soviets began to move their troops in fleets of Mil 8 Hip transport helicopters and Mil 24 Hind attack helicopters. This enabled them to place troops on mountaintops to fire down on mujahideen, strafe supply columns coming from Pakistan, and transport soldiers to battlefields without having to face ambushes on the ground. The armor-plated Mil 24 Hinds became the iconic fighting machines of the war. These fearsome gunships had a nose-mounted Gatling cannon and wing-mounted missile pods that allowed them to direct tremendous firepower on enemy villages, supply columns, or mujahideen positions. The armored Mil 24s (known as *sheytan arabas*—"devil's chariots"—by the mujahideen) were almost impossible to shoot down with machine guns and could destroy an Afghan village in a minute or two.

The Soviets also relied on such workhorses as the Sukhoi 24 Frogfooter (a dive-bomber known to the Russians as a Grach or Raven; it played the same ground-support role as the American A-10 Warthog),

T-62 main battle tanks, and armored personnel carriers. For their part, the mujahideen fought with a combination of old Enfield rifles, captured AK-47s and PK machine guns, Oerlikon anti-aircraft guns, RPG-7 rocket-propelled grenades, Blowpipe anti-tank missiles, land mines, and recoilless rifles.

But clearly the Soviets had the advantage in firepower, and they were not constrained by the same dread of civilian casualties that U.S.-led Coalition troops face in Afghanistan today. When their forces were attacked in a district, the Soviets thought nothing of bombing surrounding villages in retaliation or driving out the area's inhabitants. While today's Coalition is concerned with winning the Afghans' hearts and minds, the Soviets were driven more by the concept of collective punishment. As the Soviets indiscriminately bombed and strafed villages, millions of Afghans fled their homeland for refugee camps in Iran and Pakistan. As many as one in three Afghans fled the country, making them the world's largest refugee population. Whole districts that had offered shelter and support to the mujahideen were depopulated by the vengeful Soviets (by contrast, today's Afghans have come back to Afghanistan in the millions).

While this mass displacement might have seemed like a farsighted policy, in actuality it radicalized tens of thousands of displaced men who chose to join the mujahideen and fight back. By the mid-1980s the Soviet "recruitment drives" had driven the number of Afghan fighters up to 250,000 (by contrast, the Taliban insurgents have between 20,000 and 25,000 men under arms). And despite their lack of training or organization, these hardy mujahideen guerrillas were able to take control of most of the countryside. Although the Soviets controlled the roads (at least by day) and the major cities (Kandahar, Herat, Bamiyan, Mazar i Sharif, Kunduz, Khost, Taloqan, Sheberghan, Kabul, and Jalalabad), the mujahideen controlled the areas outside the cities. To combat them, the Soviets and their Afghan Communist allies were forced to leapfrog from district to district confronting mujahideen fighters who incessantly sniped at them, planted mines, attacked exposed bases, and overran distant garrisons.

This leapfrogging became more difficult after 1986 when the CIA took off its gloves and began to export Stinger heat-seeking anti-aircraft missiles to the mujahideen. These shoulder-fired missiles allowed illiterate Afghan peasants riding donkeys to shoot down multimillion-dollar Soviet aircraft flown by Soviet "Top Gun" flyers. As the Soviets' invincible Hinds went up in spectacular fireballs and their Sukhoi dive bombers were shot down by rebels, the Soviets lost their total air superiority. The Stinger acted as an equalizer and forced the Hinds and Sukhois to fly higher to avoid being shot down. In so doing they lost much of their effectiveness in supporting Soviet ground troops. It became increasingly dangerous to transport soldiers in slow-moving Mil 8 transport helicopters, so Soviet troops had to move on the ground in convoys. This made them easier targets for mujahideen ambushes. By this time the Soviets were losing more than two thousand troops a year in a war that had increasingly become a quagmire.

As the Soviet High Command kept insisting that they needed just one or two more years to quell the insurgency, the Soviet public began to see through its propaganda. Thousands of their young men were coming home in "black tulips" (zinc coffins), and tens of thousands more were coming home maimed, wounded, or psychologically damaged. And the economy began to suffer from the continued war expenditures.

As these events took place, a new liberal Soviet leader named Mikhail Gorbachev became president of the USSR. Unlike his hawkish predecessors, Gorbachev was critical of the continuing rationale for the war and described it as a "bleeding wound." Gorbachev began to search for a way out of the war and eventually held talks with U.S. president Ronald Reagan about withdrawing Soviet troops. But as the Soviets talked of retreat, the Americans smelled blood and talked of continuing the war. The Americans ratcheted up the money they were giving to Hekmatyar and encouraged their Saudi allies to do the same. It was at this time (1986) that the Arab volunteers began to make their appearance on the battlefield as the Saudi government offered its citizens discounted fares on flights to Pakistan. Tragically, it was this ratcheted-up U.S. and Saudi involvement that led to the creation of the Afghan-Arab jihad alumni that would later become known as Al Qaeda.

Unable or unwilling to keep up the costs of the war as he tried to focus on stimulating the faltering Soviet economy, Gorbachev decided to begin pulling out Soviet troops in 1988. By February 1989 the Soviets had conceded defeat and brought their *malchiki* (boys) home. Their costly blunder had officially cost them the lives of roughly 14,000 soldiers and had led to the death of over one million Afghans (by contrast, the United States lost just over 1,400 soldiers—one-tenth of the Soviet losses—in Afghanistan in roughly the same time period). Far from bolstering the cause of Communism in Afghanistan, the Soviets' preemptive invasion had backfired and radicalized the local Afghan culture. It had also led to the creation of a transnational jihadi movement that would later take the form of Al Qaeda. Instead of spreading Marxism to Afghanistan, the Soviet invasion gave birth to the modern fundamentalist jihad that led to 9/11 and terrorist attacks in London, Madrid, Nairobi, Sana, Dar as Salaam, Mumbai, Istanbul, New York, Washington,

Bali, and elsewhere. Thousands across the globe were to die in Al Qaeda's transnational terrorist jihad.

Meanwhile, without their Soviet sponsors to protect them (only a few advisors were left following the February 1989 Soviet retreat) President Najibullah's local Afghan Communist government fought on after the Soviets left. While the Soviets and post-Soviet Russian Federation succeeded in keeping the Afghan Communists in power for three long years after their departure, the government finally fell in the spring of 1992. Although many Soviet hawks had scared the Russian people by predicting that if the Soviets withdrew, the mujahideen fundamentalists would march through Soviet Central Asia and up the Muslim Tatar lands on the Volga, their prediction proved to be alarmist. Far from marching on Moscow, the mujahideen fought among themselves in the Afghan civil war of 1992–1996 and destroyed Kabul. Into this mess came a new anti-mujahideen force—the Taliban.

With the Taliban's overthrow of Dostum's defensive "shield" based in Mazar i Sharif in 1998, the ex-Soviet states of Central Asia (Uzbekistan, Tajikistan, Kyrgyzstan, Turkmenistan, and Kazakhstan) were confronted with the arrival of tens of thousands of fundamentalist Taliban warriors on their southern borders. The Taliban then hosted Uzbekistani Islamic dissident-extremists known as the Islamic Movement of Uzbekistan (IMU). The IMU jihadis aimed to overthrow the dictatorship of the secular "Red Khan," Uzbekistani president Islam Karimov. For three years the Taliban allowed the Uzbek jihadis to launch raids into Uzbekistan and Kyrgyzstan from their territory in Afghan Turkistan. It was not until the fiery destruction of the Taliban army of the north in 2001 that the Uzbek jihadists from the IMU were destroyed or dispersed to the tribal zones of Pakistan. In the process, their fearsome leader Juma Namangani, an ex-Soviet paratrooper, was killed by U.S. bombs and his place was taken by the IMU religious chief Tohir Yuldushev (who was later killed in a CIA Predator drone strike in Pakistan). Today the remnants of the IMU are found fighting alongside the Taliban in the Waziristan provinces of Pakistan.

As for the Afghan people, they were no longer useful to the Americans once the Soviets departed. U.S. funds dried up and the West quickly forgot about the Afghans whose blood had been spilled in helping bring down the USSR. But even as the American Cold Warriors abandoned millions of Afghans living in squalid refugee camps in Pakistan, the Saudi Wahhabis and Pakistani fundamentalist parties stepped in to fill their place. Thousands of madrassas (religious seminaries) were built in the Pashtun tribal lands of Pakistan at this time. These became orphanages for young exiled Afghan boys who faced the prospect of starvation. As the young orphans grew up on a regime of strict Islam and Quranic rote memorization, they came to be called Talibs ("seekers of knowledge," plural Taliban). Thus were born the messianic fundamentalists known as the Taliban who were to take control of the FATA in the 2000s. Many Pakistani Taliban also fought alongside the Afghan Taliban in the 1990s.

Had the Communists not tried so hard to force their secular values on the conservative Afghan people, Afghanistan might have gradually modernized and secularized at its own pace. Instead, it was forced back to the Stone Age and turned to rubble by the very Soviet forces that had been so successful in building the modern Soviet republics of Central Asia.

As for the USSR, it was internally weakened by the war, which had opened the Pandora's box of distrust and criticism for the government. Once the malaise crept in, it proved difficult to destroy. When President Gorbachev chose not to use force to kill dissidents and protestors (as the Chinese Communists did in Tiananmen Square), the country's fate was sealed. Afghanistan had, in the ultimate of ironies, helped bring down the empire that tried to transform it, and on December 25, 1991, the USSR ceased to exist.

Although it is tempting to compare the Soviet experience with that of the United States and its Coalition allies in Afghanistan today, it should be noted that there are vast differences between the two wars. The Soviets, for example, did *not* have the support of the Tajiks, Hazaras, and a vast swath of the Pashtuns as the U.S.-led Coalition does today. In the 1980s the Hazara lands were a hostile-neutral zone, and the Tajik and Pashtun lands were up in arms against the Soviets. Today, by contrast, the Panjsher Valley and areas north of Kabul are comparatively safe areas for U.S. and NATO troops. In the 1980s they were a kill zone for Massoud's ambushers.

Furthermore, the Soviets did not have the support of the international community. On the contrary, a massive part of the international community, from the United States and NATO to China and the Muslim world (including neighboring Pakistan), was against it. For this reason, the Soviet conscript army of roughly one hundred thousand was forced to fight in many areas (for example, the Panjsher, Shomali Plain, Taloqan, Jalalabad, Kabul environs, Herat) where the United States and its allies do not have to fight today. And it should be stated that the Soviets were confronted with Stinger ground-to-air missiles, something U.S. fliers do not confront today when supporting ground troops. It should also be noted that the approximately 150,000 Coalition troops in Afghanistan as of 2011 are much more welcome than the Soviet army, which represented an atheist invading force, not a force of reconstruction.

The Rise of the Taliban

There is a long tradition of having children trained in the Pashtun lands to serve as Quran reciters known as Talibs. Winston Churchill wrote of his encounters with these Talibs while reporting on British counter-insurgency efforts among the Swat Valley Pashtuns in the late nineteenth century. During the 1980s most mujahideen groups had Talibs who served in their units. But as tens of thousands of Talibs began to subscribe to the strict Deobandi School of Islam (an Islamic sect that emerged in India in the nineteenth century as a response to the empowerment of Hindus at the expense of Muslims), the meaning of "Talib," and thus "Taliban," began to change.

By the 1990s "Taliban" came to mean young Pashtun men who had grown up in madrassas disconnected from their tribal roots and Afghan culture. These students were brainwashed and taught to distrust women and enforce strict shariah law. Many Talibs grew up in Pakistan as exiles without any ties to their country's tribal traditions. In particular, the Talibs had no respect for the mujahideen warlords who were tearing their former homeland apart (although many Taliban commanders were themselves ex-mujahideen, including Mullah Omar, Nek Muhammad, Haqqani, and Dadullah).

In 1994 a group of these Talibs, led by an ex-mujahideen named Mullah Omar who had lost an eye fighting in the anti-Communist jihad, decided to rid their province of predatory mujahideen warlords. These mujahideen plunderers and thugs had taken the once-prestigious name of "mujahideen" and made it synonymous with *jang salars* (warlords) or *topakayan* (gunmen). In the Kandahar district of Sangesar in which Mullah Omar lived, the former mujahideen-turned-bandits had also set up roadblocks where they "taxed" the local people.

Mullah Omar and his band of vigilantes were determined to end the crimes of a local Pashtun mujahideen commander who had recently kidnapped and raped two local teenage girls. Omar and thirty of his followers captured the offending warlord and hung him from the barrel of a tank in the village of Sangesar. His body was left as a warning to other warlords, and thus the legend of Mullah Omar was born. As his followers began to carry out similar acts of vigilante justice, the local villagers came to see the Taliban as Robin Hood–style heroes. One by one the Taliban cleared the district of Sangesar, and then all of Kandahar, of the mujahideen robbers. They soon took the city of Kandahar when the powerful mujahideen leader Mullah Naqibullah joined them.

This style of tough frontier justice has been the key to the Taliban's success to this day. Their justice was and is seen as swift, uncorrupted, and based on the conservative religious values the villagers share. For example, if you commit murder, the murder victim's family gets to kill you in public. If you commit adultery or elope, you are stoned to death in public. In American terms, the Taliban are not "soft on crime," and they defend traditional "family values." While Karzai government judges and police officials are seen as corrupt and bribable, the Taliban shadow courts that have been set up in the southern countryside since 2003 are feared and respected. Thieves have their hands amputated, rapists are killed, land disputes are swiftly decided, and God's order is enforced without the meddling of the corrupt "infidel" government.

The Pashtuns of the Afghan south were not the only ones who began to see the strange Taliban movement as a solution to the depredations of the mujahideen warlords when they first emerged in the mid-1990s. Pakistan hoped the Taliban would end the chaos in neighboring Afghanistan that stemmed from the Afghan civil war. They also hoped that this unifying force would establish trade routes with Central Asia. In particular, they wanted to open oil pipelines to Kazakhstan, natural gas lines to Turkmenistan, and trucking roads to all of the ex-Soviet republics.

For this reason the Pakistani ISI got into the act and began to support the Taliban with fuel, weapons, vehicles, volunteers, and training, hoping they could bring stability to Afghanistan. The Taliban were seen by the ISI as proxies (although the Taliban resented this and by 2001 had broken with their Pakistani masters on many levels). To this day the Taliban's enemies in the Northern Alliance see them as a tool of Pakistan. In truth, the Taliban benefited tremendously from Pakistani training and assistance but were not always beholden to their distrusted Pakistani friends. And it should be stated once again that the United States *in no way* sponsored the rise of the Taliban, as many have erroneously suggested.

With Pakistani logistic support, the Taliban swept through the Pashtun south in 1994 and 1995. While they fought mujahideen warlords on some occasions, on others they simply bribed their opponents into joining them or relied on the Afghan culture of defection to assist them. Momentum appeared to be on their side, and local mujahideen thought it prudent to join them rather than fight them. Oftentimes mujahideen commanders became Taliban by simply donning black turbans, growing their beards longer, and strictly enforcing shariah law. The Taliban were a new movement that gained widespread legitimacy as a cleansing force that fought crime.

Peace was thus brought to the land—but at a price. Although the Pashtuns had a love of wrestling, dog fighting, kite flying, singing, Sufi *zikirs* (chants), and festivals, these were all banned by the grim Taliban puritans who were more intent on enforcing the moral aspects of the faith. It soon became obvious that the Taliban were bent on forcing strict Islamic fundamentalism on the whole country. By 1995 the Taliban expanded to the northwest and captured Ismail Khan's domain in the Iranian-facing town of Herat. They then began to move from their base at Kandahar into the Ghilzai tribal lands of the northeast. In 1996 they defeated Hekmtayar and the mujahideen government of President Burhanuddin Rabbani and forced him and his defense minister, Massoud, to retreat to the Tajik northeast. In 1998 the Taliban forced out Dostum for the last time and conquered Mazar i Sharif and the rest of the northern plains. The Hazara capital of Bamiyan fell to them soon thereafter, and in 2000 Massoud's capital at Taloqan was captured.

By this time the Taliban controlled over 90 percent of Afghanistan. Massoud's Northern Alliance opposition was forced back into the mountains of Badakshan and Panjsher in the far northeast. In addition to this free government enclave, small resistance pockets were found high in the Hindu Kush Mountains north of Bamiyan, where Uzbek, Tajik, and Hazara rebels led by Dostum, Atta, and Khalili operated.

But for all of the Taliban's success, the outside world refused to recognize the Taliban as the official government of Afghanistan. Rabbani was still acknowledged as the Afghan president, and he held the country's seat at the UN. Only three countries recognized the Taliban: Saudi Arabia, Pakistan, and the United Arab Emirates.

Interestingly, the country that appeared to be most at war with the Taliban was not the United States, which actually sought to make oil deals with the Taliban, but the Islamic Republic of Iran. When the Taliban killed several Iranian diplomats following their capture of Mazar i Sharif in 1998, Iran mobilized its armies and prepared to invade. War was eventually averted, but Shiite Iran continued to support Massoud, Dostum, Khalili, Ismail Khan, and other Northern Alliance opposition rebels in the struggle against the Sunni Taliban.

The West's reluctance to recognize the Taliban was partially due to the Taliban's social policies. Although the Clinton administration initially overlooked the Taliban's fundamentalist policies in the interest of realpolitik pragmatism and oil (the U.S. oil company UNOCAL sought to build oil and natural gas pipelines across Taliban territory to Central Asia), this ended by the late 1990s. U.S. Secretary of State Madeleine Albright directly criticized the Taliban for their brutal policies toward women, which soon became a major concern for the U.S. government. Although the Pashtun tribes of the south had always been conservative, the Taliban took their fundamentalism to new levels, and women began to suffer.

Most important, the Taliban took their misogynistic fundamentalism to other regions where women were freer (namely Kabul, Mazar i Sharif, and the Hazara highlands). When the Taliban came to town, women doctors and teachers were forced out of their jobs and told to stay at home. This left many schools without teachers and female patients without gynecologists and female doctors. Many of the women who were driven out of their jobs in cosmopolitan places such as Kabul were widows who were the sole breadwinners of their families. Unable to work, they and their children faced the real prospect of starvation and were forced to beg on the streets to stay alive. There the Taliban took great joy in beating them with iron rods to let them know how much contempt they had for them.

Such practices were only the tip of the iceberg. Women who showed too much ankle beneath their burqas were beaten in public with iron rods. Women caught wearing fingernail polish ran the risk of having their fingers cut off. If a woman was caught in relationship with a man who was not her husband, she was executed in public as an "adulteress." Brave women who continued to teach girls also faced the threat of execution for their activities.

As darkness descended on the land, 50 percent of the country's population (the women) were turned into voiceless chattel. The modernizing dream of the Communists was replaced by a warped medieval version of Islam that surpassed that of Saudi Arabia in its backwardness and barbarity. In the process, Afghanistan became the most repressive Muslim country in the world. Strict adherence to Taliban laws was enforced by a police force called the Committee for the Promotion of Virtue and Prevention of Vice, which was based on a Saudi model. This force's vigilantes used spy networks to hunt out those who had television sets or radios, or those engaged in such sinful activities as dancing, having "Western hairstyles," singing, kite flying, or making snowmen. Men who did not close their stalls during daily prayers at mosque were physically beaten, and scores of Afghans were executed for a range of "un-Islamic activities."

The Taliban's grim fundamentalist prison camp became further isolated when Mullah Omar ordered the destruction of the country's greatest historical treasure, the magnificent stone Buddhas of Bamiyan. These stone giants had guarded the Hazara mountain valley of Bamiyan since the sixth century A.D. But under the influence of his Arab guest Osama bin Laden, Mullah Omar ordered them bombed in April 2001 as "heathen idols." The world looked on in disgust at the spectacle of bearded Taliban extremists screaming "Allah u Akbar!" as they shelled the historic Buddhas to bits and planted bombs at their feet. By this time

Afghanistan was a pariah state and under sanctions for offering sanctuary to Osama bin Laden and his Al Qaeda terrorists.

Although Mullah Omar tried to muzzle bin Laden in order to end his regime's isolation, he could not prevent his Saudi guest from launching terrorist strikes against the United States (the August 1998 bombings of the U.S. embassies in Tanzania and Kenya and the 2000 bombing of the USS *Cole* in Yemen). In 1998 President Bill Clinton responded by trying to kill bin Laden with a cruise missile strike on his camps at Zawhar Kili (mountains near Khost) and Al Badr (near Jalalabad). But bin Laden had left the camp at Zawhar Kili hours before the missiles hit and avoided the fate of dozens of fighter-terrorists who were killed in the fusillade of seventy-five cruise missiles. Many of those who were killed in the camps were Afghans or Pakistanis training for jihad in Kashmir.

The attack on the Islamic Emirate of Afghanistan infuriated Mullah Omar and drove him closer to bin Laden. But many moderate Taliban leaders began to fight bin Laden's undue influence over Mullah Omar. They feared that the "world's first true Islamic state" was needlessly confronting the West by protecting bin Laden and his Arab terrorists. Taliban hawks also turned against bin Laden and disliked the way their local movement was being hijacked by his global jihad.

In response, bin Laden tried to smooth things over with his hosts by contributing money and fighters to the Taliban's spring offensives against Massoud and the Northern Alliance. These fighters of course formed the dreaded 055 jihadi foreign legion. But bin Laden's efforts were only partially successful. Members of the Taliban movement actually warned the United States that bin Laden was plotting to attack them prior to 9/11.

In the end, bin Laden paid back the Taliban for their hospitality by launching the infamous attack on the United States on September 11, 2001. When President Bush demanded that the Taliban arrest bin Laden and turn over his Arab terrorist network, Mullah Omar stood by his Saudi friend. Omar adamantly refused to turn over a "good Muslim" to an infidel. He also rejected the U.S. accusation that bin Laden had carried out the attacks (although bin Laden once again undermined Omar by taking credit for the attacks in a video released to the Al Jazeera network).

As the Taliban drew a line in the sand, Al Qaeda predicted "another Mogadishu" if the Americans were to invade (here Al Qaeda was referencing the "Black Hawk Down" incident in Somalia in which downed U.S. airmen were dragged through the streets of Mogadishu, Somalia, by insurgents). Bin Laden responded to the impending invasion by dispersing his fighters to the north in anticipation of a U.S. military attack. He seemed to have eagerly anticipated a full-scale Soviet-style invasion. Bin Laden predicted that tens of thousands of Pakistanis and Arab volunteers would come to the killing mountains of Afghanistan to transform it into a military, political, and economic quagmire for the "last remaining infidel super power." It would be like the Soviet invasion all over again.

But far from falling into bin Laden's trap, the United States opted for a different approach that would see his Al Qaeda forces virtually annihilated and his Taliban hosts toppled in just three months. This is the untold story of the U.S. "invasion" of Afghanistan.

Chapter 5

The Longest War: America in Afghanistan

In my previous trips to Afghanistan I had seen American and ISAF Coalition troops from afar. Driving the dusty roads of Afghanistan from Herat in the west to Mazar i Sharif in the north to Paktia and Jalalabad in the east (usually in a dirty Corolla that would not attract attention), I have seen them in the form of platoons walking on the side of the road or on distant hills; Apaches, Black Hawks, and Chinooks flying in the hazy sky; convoys nervously pushing through Afghan streets; and guards standing behind Hesco blast barriers and concertina wiring, looking out from their bases at passing Afghans, in search of potential suicide bombers.

In 2007 I once left my Afghan world for a few hours to meet with an Information Operations team at Bagram Airfield (just about an hour north of Kabul). It was an unreal experience. After eating rice pilaf, naan, soup, and kabobs for over a month, I was served a real cheeseburger by U.S. soldiers who rarely left the safety of their massive forward operating base. Although many Coalition troops, especially those in small combat outposts in places such as Restrepo in Kunar Province, were coming into contact with the enemy on an almost daily basis, the greatest contact threats the soldiers at Bagram faced came from brushing shoulders with other soldiers in line for food at the base's Burger King, Popeyes, or Orange Julius.

When I left Bagram, my curious Afghan hosts asked what it was like to enter this base that they felt was not part of their country. I could tell that they were slightly intimidated by the base (they had not been allowed inside when they dropped me off, and they were glad to drive away from the U.S. soldiers at the gate with weapons drawn on them as standard protocol).

Their curiosity and healthy respect of the Americans was typical of their countrymen. For most Afghans, the U.S. military is defined as both a distant source of comfort and an intimidating foreign presence. On a previous trip to Afghanistan in 2003, I approached the Hindu Kush with a truckload of Uzbek friends and had an experience that best defines this dichotomy. When my Uzbek-filled SUV made its way through Charikar, a town near Bagram Air Base, we encountered a snarled American convoy. As the convoy attempted to turn around in a small area, U.S. soldiers in armored Humvees waved their .50 caliber guns at the surging crowds of Afghans, trying in vain to prevent them from swarming too close.

Seeing the legitimate fear on the soldiers' faces at their inability to control the typical Afghan chaos, my heart went out to my countrymen serving in this strange land. But at the same time, I felt the discomfort of my Uzbek hosts. They were grateful to the Americans for freeing them from the Taliban, but they feared these cursing foreign soldiers waving guns in their direction. The Americans were liberators and were there to build schools for girls, fix bombed-out bridges, pave roads, and of course defeat the Taliban insurgents who were a looming presence in the south and east. But they were still foreigners armed with guns, and this made them frightening.

Like my Afghan friends, I was curious to learn more about the U.S. and other foreign troops who had, for all their intimidating appearance, come to this land to protect it from the Taliban. Ever since my brief visit to Bagram, I have sought to live in one of the Coalition's mysterious FOBs (forward operating bases) to see what goes on behind their massive walls and blast barriers. In the summer of 2009, I was finally given the chance when I was hired by the military to work for an Information Operations (IO) team operating at a base known only as ISAF HQ K (International Security Assistance Force Headquarters Kabul). Having roughed it on my previous trips to Afghanistan, I was eager to see the country from the comfort of this new perspective.

Upon arrival in Afghanistan that summer of 2009, I found a brand new airport that had replaced the chaotic shambles of an airport that greeted me on my previous trips, but my U.S. Army hosts were nowhere to be seen. So I waved down a taxi which took me to the outer entrance of ISAF HQ. From there I walked several blocks through a maze of concrete blast barriers to the inner entrance to the base. The Macedonian NATO guards at the base entrance (several of whom would later be killed or injured in a massive suicide bombing blast a few weeks later) carefully checked my military ID and let me in. From there I made my way to the IO's basement headquarters and introduced myself to the team I was to work with.

I was then given a bunk in a small metal barrack room that could barely hold the four beds in it, and I was given a tour of the base. On my tour I was shown the base's Italian pizzeria (which was usually filled with Italian troops); the base's bar, which was open from 5 to 10 p.m. and was usually filled with contract workers (according to General Order 1B,

U.S. troops in Afghanistan are not allowed to drink); the base's barbershop/hairdresser, which was run by garrulous Kazakh women who gave me free haircuts when they learned I spoke Russian; a coffee shop that served up a mean cappuccino; and the crown jewel of the base, a German beer garden that served everything from Kolsch beers to mouthwatering Dunkel Weisses (only the German NATO troops could drink). Sadly, soon after my departure the head of all Coalition troops, General Stanley McChrystal, closed the German bar—I have no doubt that German morale plummeted precipitously soon thereafter.

The whole experience was surreal, and it felt as if I was in an alternative Afghanistan to the country I knew. I wondered how many of the people on the base could have done their jobs from the United States or their own homelands. What struck me as odd was the fact that everyone on this FOB went around armed in case of a Taliban attack. But as far as I could tell, apart from the occasional mortar attack and the one suicide bombing at the gate, there was no way the Taliban could ever break through the massive barriers surrounding this base (which, incidentally, was located right in the heart of the comparatively safe Afghan capital). When I tried telling my Dutch Army roommate—who slept with his gun by his bed in case of an attack—he told me I had no experience in war and should leave the fighting to professionals.

So I kept my thoughts to myself and tried to blend in with the troops, most of whom would never meet an average Afghan or travel through the country they were there to defend. On the rare occasion I did leave base with U.S. troops, I must say I felt uneasy. I was used to keeping a low profile when traveling through Afghanistan in my dirty Corolla, and I felt like an IED magnet barreling through the Afghan streets in a convoy of Humvees. As I stared out the windows of the Humvees that were protected with ECMs (electronic countermeasures) designed to set off IEDs (although they seemed more effective at disrupting the nearby Afghans' cell phone reception) and watched the Afghanistan I knew pass by outside, I began to feel like a prisoner. I was itching to get off base and visit the Babur Gardens, hike through the hills along the medieval walls surrounding Kabul, or enjoy a mouthwatering aush soup, manti (raviolis), and a kabob with fresh naan bread.

Finally I could take it no more and, despite my promises to my wife Feyza that I would not leave the safety of the base to wander around Afghanistan, I decided to leave. One night I made the decision to "break out" of the base, even though I had been warned that this was not permitted. To my utmost surprise, the friendly Macedonians at the gate simply waved me through the gate, and I was free to enter the real Afghanistan. Had I been an average American GI, this would have gotten me

The Longest War: America in Afghanistan

court-martialed, but as it was I would probably just get fired and lose my thousand-dollar-a-day "combat pay."

It was now time to wander around the Afghanistan I had always loved. But first things first, I needed a pint. My first stop was the Gandamack, a well-stocked British pub just fifteen minutes away. The Gandamack was a classic—a safe house that had once been used by bin Laden himself but had recently been taken over by a legendary British journalist named Peter Jouvenal and turned into a pub. Although it did not serve Guinness, the Gandamack had an amazing variety of food and drinks and was a much-beloved watering hole for thirsty expats.

The next day I showed my digital camera photos of my night out to my IO team, and they were green with envy and more than a little concerned for my safety. But after a week of showing them photos from my evening jaunts around Kabul, they came to see that it was not really that frightening beyond the walls of their base.

And so things went for the following weeks as I left base more and more to wander the city, hike in the hills, see old friends, and visit Kabul's Afghan, Lebanese, American, Chinese, and Indian restaurants. But when one of my base commanders learned of my "dangerous" activities in the "red zone," he warned me not to put my life at risk and I began to keep my escapades to myself. I didn't have the heart to tell the commander that I thought Afghanistan was safe enough to have traveled across it on my last two visits with my wife.

My run-in with my commander, however, got me thinking about the lives of those people who are confined to massive FOBs (also known as fobbits, a derisive name given to them by U.S. troops out who actually fight with the enemy and live in dangerously exposed command posts). Only a small percentage of fobbits actually interact with average Afghans due to hyper-protective SOP (standard operating procedures) meant to decrease risks from interaction with Afghans. The only Afghan most soldiers at ISAF HQ met was the base carpet-seller, a Hazara named Mustafa. I felt that this was a tremendous injustice. The members of my IO team were literally chomping at the bit to see the real Afghanistan, but their superiors were afraid to let them out into the world beyond their concrete blast barriers.

This was in many ways a microcosm representing the mistakes of the Afghan war in its early years. It was precisely this siege mentality that had also led the United States to come dangerously close to losing the war in Iraq in 2005 and 2006. U.S. forces in Iraq had been more concerned with force protection than protecting the center of gravity in Iraq, the Iraqi people. It was only when Generals Petraeus and Odierno pushed their troops out of their FOBs and onto the streets of Iraq that they began to make headway in the counterinsurgency. After the nightmares of the notorious U.S. prison at Abu Ghraib and the U.S. massacre of Iraqis at Haditha, Americans began protecting Iraqis and interacting with them in smaller and more exposed command posts. This meant more meetings with Iraqi people, who began to feel that the Americans were protecting them. The Anbar Awakening (a tribal movement wherein Sunni Iraqi tribes turned on Al Qaeda and essentially turned the war in Iraq in America's favor) began when a disgruntled Iraqi sheikh walked across the street to his neighborhood command post and offered the support of his tribe in fighting Al Qaeda.

Prior to President Obama's 2010 surge of thirty thousand troops to Afghanistan, similar siege mentality mistakes were made in the war in that country. With a few exceptions, the Coalition ceded the Afghan countryside of the south and parts of the east to the enemy. Vast swaths of Afghanistan were lost to the Taliban from 2003 to 2008 as U.S. Central Command shifted its attention from the unfinished war in Afghanistan to the war in Iraq. The Bush White House's fear of engaging in nation building allowed the Taliban to fill the void. Pro-government khans and mullahs were executed, villagers were cowed into submission, and "vanguard" groups were sent on to the next province to lay mines and kill "infidel collaborators." With little visible coalition presence outside of the provincial capitals or massive FOBS, the Taliban swarmed the countryside. The scenario was similar to Afghanistan in the 1980s under the Soviets, who controlled the major roads and cities and remained safe in their bases for fear of sustaining casualties.

The U.S. Marines' February 2010 efforts to clear and hold territory in Helmand Province and the ongoing efforts to retake Kandahar represent a welcome break from this barracked mentality. Only by establishing a reliable coalition presence in contested places such as Helmand can the Coalition show the Afghans that they are there to stay and protect them. This means leaving the safety of FOBs and spreading out into the villages that the Taliban have taken control of. With more fobbits out of their bases and working on protecting the Afghans instead of themselves, the United States can avoid the fate of the Soviets. In the end it is only by putting more boots in the countryside that the United States and its ISAF allies can maintain the spectacular gains they made in one of the greatest military successes of modern history, 2001's Operation Enduring Freedom.

Operation Enduring Freedom

U.S. troops in Afghanistan were not originally found in massive FOBs in places such as Kabul and Kandahar. They originally came in after

9/11 in small groups and lived in caves with anti-Taliban troops or in the front-line trenches defending the Panjsher Valley. These small groups of special operators (no more than 350 were involved in 2001's Operation Enduring Freedom) helped bring down an entrenched enemy regime in just over a month. The dynamics behind the U.S.-led victory in 2001's Operation Enduring Freedom are still not fully understood to this day, and this has led some to ex post facto underestimate the very real problems that the U.S. military faced at the time. But the speed with which America's response to 9/11 achieved its goals should not lead to a retroactive discounting of the real obstacles that it faced in the fall of 2001. The task given to CENTCOM—that is, destroy an entrenched and determined foe dispersed across a Texas-size tribal land located in the heart of Central Asia's mountains—was considered impossible by many skeptics who predicted a Vietnam-style quagmire. Even the optimists figured on a long winter campaign that could not be won without the deployment of at least fifty thousand troops from the U.S. Marines, the 101st Airborne, and the 10th Mountain Division.

As CENTCOM began to assess the difficulties involved in projecting U.S. forces into the wintry mountains of Afghanistan, its generals desperately sought the means to crack the Taliban "nut" while avoiding the pitfalls of a full-scale Soviet-style invasion. It was at this stage that the CIA came to the forefront of the war planning. Although CIA director George Tenet was later criticized for his role in the "group think" effort of trying to produce evidence of Iraqi "weapons of mass destruction," on Afghanistan his advice proved to be right on target. He and Cofer Black, head of the CIA's Counterterrorist Center, understood all too clearly that this new war would be driven by intelligence, and they had a plan that would follow this principle.

As it happened, one farsighted U.S. official had already drawn up an outline for an intelligence-driven war against the Taliban. Eight months prior to 9/11, Counter-Terrorism Chief Richard Clarke had provided the CIA with a blueprint known as the Blue Sky Memo, which called for arming the Northern Alliance and using it to attack Al Qaeda. This memo, which was written in January 2001 and shelved until 9/11, called for "Massive support to anti-Taliban groups such as the Northern Alliance led by Ahmad Shah Massoud," as well as winning over Pakistani support and the targeted killings of Al Qaeda leaders using Predator UAVs (robot aerial drones).

Considering the urgency of the task at hand and the glacial speed with which U.S. ground forces were typically deployed, Secretary of Defense Donald Rumsfeld overcame his distrust of the CIA and signed on to Clarke's plan. The final green light was given by Chairman of the Joint Chiefs of Staff Richard Myers to launch a "light footprint" invasion.

This decision to invade came as thousands of Pakistani Pashtuns were led across the border to defend Islam against the American "infidels" in October 2001. This jihadi riffraff was led by Sufi Muhammad, an eighty-year-old mullah from the Pakistani province of Swat (a Pashtun province in the "settled lands" of the North West Frontier Province). But these Pakistani volunteers were used as cannon fodder by the Taliban, who often retreated and left them behind to be killed or captured. One group of eight hundred Pakistanis who were stranded in Mazar i Sharif refused to surrender and were killed in U.S. aerial bombardments.

Sufi Muhammad was later arrested for sending thousands of Pakistani citizens across the border to their death. But his son-in-law, Mullah Fazlullah (a fundamentalist firebrand linked to the Taliban), later stirred up the province of Swat in 2007. For almost two years this scenic mountain province was overrun by Fazlullah's followers who called him Mullah Radio (stemming from his use of the radio to disseminate his sermons). However, in the winter of 2008–2009, Pakistani forces invaded the Swat Valley and defeated Mullah Fazlullah's followers.

As interesting as this Pakistani volunteer episode was, Central Command realized that the real fight was not with the thousands of Pakistani jihadists, but with the Afghan Taliban and Al Qaeda field armies. In October 2001 the United States introduced Special Forces A-Teams to fight alongside such Northern Alliance commanders as Fahim Khan, Daoud Khan, and Bismullah Khan (Tajiks in the Panjsher and Takhar areas), Ustad Atta (Tajik in Dar y Suf Valley of central Hindu Kush), Ismail Khan (Tajik, in western Hindu Kush), Dostum (Uzbek, in Dar y Suf), and Karim Khalili (Hazara, Dar y Suf).

Armed with laser pointers and laptop computers that could communicate coordinates to bombers, Air Force Special Forces operators called in devastating air strikes on the Taliban. Taliban positions that had previously seemed invincible to the Northern Alliance opposition suddenly went up in flames as U.S. JDAMs (satellite-guided bombs) destroyed them. The Northern Alliance fought back in the aftermath of the devastating attacks and began to seize territory.

Although the United States was reluctant to deputize the Northern Alliance as its proxy allies due to their reputation as warlords and American fears of antagonizing the pro-Taliban Pakistanis, the decision to do so nonetheless solved many of their problems. The tough Northern Alliance fighters were Muslims, they knew the lay of the land, and they had thousands of armed men already in the theater of operation.

Thus began the U.S. proxy war on the Taliban that saw no more than 350 U.S. soldiers operating with Northern Alliance allies to defeat the Taliban army of the north. Dostum, Khalili, and Atta took Mazar i Sharif on November 9, 2001. Dostum's seizure of the Shrine of Ali in Mazar i

The blue-domed mosque of Ali in the northern city of Mazar i Sharif.

Sharif inspired the other Northern Alliance factions to go on the move and disheartened the Taliban. In particular, this act galvanized the main Northern Alliance army in the Shomali Plain north of Kabul. This force, led by Fahim Khan, then broke out of its positions and raced across the Shomali Plain to Kabul on November 12. Although many critics predicted slaughter and plundering, the Northern Alliance conquest of Kabul was, like Dostum's conquest of Mazar i Sharif, a relatively peaceful affair. With Ismail Khan's conquest of Herat, Khalili and Mohaqiq's capture of Bamiyan, and the final surrender of the Taliban/Al Qaeda army in the encircled city of Kunduz, the northern half of the country was liberated by mid-November. Wherever they went, the Northern Alliance forces were greeted as liberators.

As these events unfolded, a shocked bin Laden led his followers to his mountain hideout at Tora Bora (Black Dust) in the Spin Ghar Mountains on the Pakistani border. CIA operatives who were tracking him at the time called in dozens of bomb strikes on his positions (including one strike using a Daisy Cutter, the world's largest nonnuclear bomb at the time) and called for U.S. troops to be inserted to cut off his retreat. Reluctant to insert U.S. Special Forces into this mountainous terra incognita in the midst of a battle that seemed to be going its way, CENTCOM instead chose to rely on local anti-Taliban warlords to flush out bin Laden. Their reluctance to insert a battalion-sized unit into the mountains of Afghanistan to cut off bin Laden's escape cost the United States dearly.

The Afghan warlords Hazrat Ali and Haji Zaman, who had been given the task of killing bin Laden, were bribed by Al Qaeda and allowed bin Laden to retreat over the border into the Pakistani tribal agency of Kurram and down to North Waziristan. Thus bin Laden, the primary target of Operation Enduring Freedom, was allowed to escape in early December 2001. One angry CIA officer claimed, "We realized those guys just opened the door. It wasn't a big secret." Although the United States did manage to kill several Al Qaeda leaders, including Muhammad Atef, the Egyptian head of Al Qaeda's military branch (killed by a Predator drone), many of bin Laden's top lieutenants escaped to Pakistan to fight and terrorize another day.

As these events were unfolding in the north, Hamid Karzai, the head of the Popalzai (Durrani) Pashtun tribe from the Oruzgan and Kandahar area, launched a rebellion in the south. Karzai and his Special Forces A-Team entered the south and began to rally disaffected Pashtuns to their side. As Karzai's support snowballed, the Taliban tried to destroy him with a fleet of pickup trucks carrying hundreds of fighters near the town of Tarin Kowt. But as had been the case in the north, the Taliban proved no match for air strikes called in by Karzai's Green Beret A-Team. The Taliban attack was annihilated, and Karzai was able to create what some have called the "Southern Alliance."

At this time, Karzai, an English-speaking moderate with a long history of involvement in mujahideen and anti-Taliban activities, came to be seen as an ideal candidate to rule the country. Most important, Karzai was a member of the dominant Pashtun tribe and did not have blood on his hands like the Northern Alliance warlords. Karzai, of all the Afghan leaders, seemed to have a democratic vision for his homeland that dovetailed with that of the Coalition governments. Some critics pointed out that Karzai had initially supported the Taliban when they first emerged as a relatively unknown factor. But he became an active opponent when they killed his father. He subsequently worked with Massoud and Abdul Haq and other opposition leaders to try to create an anti-Taliban coalition in the south.

As Karzai gathered momentum, another southern leader named Gul Agha "Sherzai" (the Son of the Lion), head of the powerful Barakzai (Durrani) tribe, marched on Kandahar City. But he was beaten there by Mullah Naqibullah, a former mujahideen leader who had fought the Soviets from the "green zone" north of Kandahar. Although Mullah Naqibullah was most responsible for defeating the local Taliban forces in Kandahar, the Karzai government sidelined him and gave the governorship of Kandahar to his rival, Gul Agha Sherzai. Sherzai then depicted Naqibullah as a Taliban sympathizer, and his powerful tribe was marginalized by Sherzai's Barakzai tribe. The story of Mullah Naqibullah is important as a lesson on how the United States made mistakes in the crucial months and years surrounding the defeat of the Taliban.

Mullah Naqibullah, Anti-Taliban Bastion

Mullah Naqibullah was a mujahideen corps commander in Burhanuddin Rabbani's Jamiat i Islam Party in the area north of Kandahar City (Arghandab District) in the 1980s. He was also a tribal leader of the Alokozai (Alikzai) Pashtun tribe, which is powerful in northern Kandahar Province. During the Soviet occupation he earned a reputation as a skilled tactician and once held off a Soviet assault for over a month in the easily defended "green agricultural zone" north of Kandahar.

He became a key Pashtun warlord in the early 1990s, with tanks and artillery at his disposal. He later broke with mujahideen who were plundering the countryside and joined the newly emerging Taliban movement. He was the most powerful mujahideen commander in the Kandahar vicinity, and his decision to join the new Taliban movement was crucial. However, by 2001 he had grown dissatisfied with the Taliban and led his tribe to join Karzai when he arrived to fight the Taliban during Operation Enduring Freedom.

It was Mullah Naqibullah and his men who seized Kandahar City from the Taliban and disarmed them during Operation Enduring Freedom. But the city's governorship was given to his rival Gul Agha Sherzai after a tense standoff. Naqibullah chose not to fight for fear of causing divisions within the anti-Taliban alliance. This led the way for Gul Agha Sherzai to seize authority. With the backing of the U.S. Special Forces, Gul Agha Sherzai became the corrupt and brutal governor of Kandahar while Naqibullah was sidelined (although Karzai chose Naqibullah to be the province's corps commander).

In the years that followed, Gul Agha Sherzai worked to sow the seeds of distrust toward Mullah Naqibullah, who was actually quite moderate. Sherzai, for example, claimed that Mullah Naqibullah was hiding Mullah Omar and that he was "Taliban in all but name." For this reason Mullah Naqibullah's role in safeguarding Kandahar's northern approaches from the insurgency-ridden provinces of Uruzgan and Zabol was underestimated by the Americans and the Karzai government.

Despite this lack of appreciation, Naqiibullah and his Alokozai militia became a bulwark against Taliban encroachment on Kandahar from the north. Naqiibullah was described as the "finger in the dyke" by one analyst who noted that his control of the easily defended "green zone" of Arghandab prevented the Taliban from making it their own.

The Taliban understood just how important Naqibullah was and tried on many instances to coerce him into joining them. They also tried assassinating him on several occasions. He was wounded in a bombing on his SUV in March 2007, which damaged his health, killed one of his sons, and crippled another. When he died of a heart attack (or of a "broken heart" in the words of one observer) in October 2007, thousands of his grieving tribesmen came to his funeral. As the Alokozais tried to regroup from the loss of their charismatic leader, the Taliban overran their province and reportedly celebrated in Naqibullah's home in Chahar Gulhba, Arghandab District.

It was only after he was dead (and the Coalition was faced with the prospect of the Taliban moving to within fifteen miles of Kandahar City directly from the north) that his contribution to the war was finally appreciated. Coalition troops were subsequently forced to launch an operation in Mullah Naqibullah's province of Arghandab in late October 2007 to expel the Taliban insurgents from this strategic area.

Abdul Rahim Jan, a commander of Naqibullah's tribe, rallied the Alokozais after the death of Mullah Naqibullah and expelled the Taliban from Arghandab District. He was, however, killed in one of Afghanistan's deadliest suicide bombings, which killed close to one hundred people, including many Alokozai militiamen attending a dogfighting match near Kandahar in January 2008. Mullah Naqibullah's son Kalimullah Naqib currently has the reins of the Alokozai tribe. It remains to be seen whether Kalimullah (who was a building contractor in Pakistan before becoming chief of the Alokozai tribe) has his father's leadership talents. The lessons from this story are important, for they highlight some of the missteps the Karzai administration made in trying to establish its influence in the provinces after the rout of the Taliban.

The Window of Opportunity: 2001–2003

It soon became obvious that major mistakes were made in the first years after the overthrow of the Taliban. The decision to appoint Gul Agha Sherzai, who had been a predatory mujahideen warlord in the 1990s, to rule Kandahar proved to be among the worst. Sherzai returned to his old ways in no time and antagonized many locals. It should be recalled that it was precisely this sort of pillaging and robbing at checkpoints that gave rise to the Taliban in the first place in 1994. Sherzai's rapacity drove many Pashtuns who were "on the fence" into the arms of the Taliban before he was finally removed from his governorship in 2004.

Today Gul Agha Sherzai is governor of Nangarhar Province, but the damage he has done in recruiting POAs ("pissed-off Afghans") for the Taliban has already been done. Critics of the United States have found an Achilles' heel in CENTCOM's reliance on warlords such as the thuggish Sherzai to run much of Afghanistan after the fall of the Taliban.

But such criticism does not take into consideration the fact that the United States "conquered" a country the size of Texas with no more than a few hundred soldiers in November and December 2001. As the United States rushed further troops into the country in 2002 to push the Taliban and Al Qaeda holdouts out of the Shah i Kot Valley in eastern Afghanistan, Central Command remained focused on counterinsurgency operations. U.S. generals did not have sufficient troops on the ground to guard the provinces and create stability, in part due to the Bush administration's reluctance to have NATO forces spread out beyond the capital. The Bush administration was also reluctant to engage in a massive "nation-building" process and tried to keep the number of U.S. troops in Afghanistan to a minimum. Their aim was to limit U.S. troops to military missions in the east and let the Afghans themselves rebuild their country so that U.S. troops could be used to invade Saddam Hussein's Iraq. But this proved unfeasible and simply gave the Taliban the chance to refill the void and many warlords the opportunity to reestablish their rule.

Local leaders such as Gul Agha Sherzai, Ismail Khan, Ustad Atta, Dostum, Hazrat Ali, and Fahim Khan filled the vacuum created by the Bush administration's shortsighted policy. Many of these *jang salaars* of the Northern Alliance have strong support from their followers. The United States and the Karzai government must therefore walk a fine line in dealing with them. To do as many critics suggest and simply remove all of these powerful figures without proper local support could incite further rebellions among their followers. Sherzai, who as an unpopular Pashtun from the south was easily removed due to limited local support.

To make up for the deficit in troops that caused the United States to rely on local strongmen in the first place, the United States finally asked its NATO allies for reinforcements. These troops formed the International Security Assistance Force (ISAF) and were initially based in Kabul. Their job was to do exactly what the critics had argued for all along: bring stability to the provinces. Having secured Kabul, the ISAF troops then moved out from the capital in stages to the relatively secure north (stage 1), the west (stage 2), and the south (stage 3). ISAF troops included major contingents from Britain, Canada, Germany, Spain, Turkey, Italy, Macedonia, Norway, France, New Zealand, the Netherlands, Sweden, Lithuania, and Hungary. However, only the French, Dutch, Australian, British, and Canadian troops had mandates from their home countries to fight. The rest were restricted from fighting by casualty-phobic home parliaments that feared being sucked into a bloody quagmire, and their troops were thus limited to peacekeeping missions.

But for all of America's mistakes in relying on warlords and avoiding a commitment of troops from 2001 to 2005, there was a brief window when hope prevailed in Afghanistan and many observers believed the Taliban had been beaten. As the U.S. forces in Afghanistan increased in 2002 and 2003 in response to increasing "neo-Taliban" raids from Pakistan, many believed the long era of darkness was over. Women began to unveil in Kabul, and barbershops, DVD stores, and hairdressers began to appear everywhere as Afghans began to rebuild their lives after years of misery under the Taliban. Soon Dostum launched a television station known as Aina (Mirror), which was followed by Ariana (Pashtun) and Tolo (Tajik). Afghans who had not had television for years began to watch local news and video clips, Indian soap operas, and Western movies. A vibrant print media appeared as well. Thousands of NGO workers appeared in Kabul at this time to encourage this process, and the United Nations' mission in the country expanded to most provinces. Many Afghans were heartened by the sight of foreign relief workers zipping about the capital in trucks doing humanitarian work. They also took advantage of new roads that were being built throughout the country.

Soon Kabul had its first "Afghan Fried Chicken" and Chinese restaurants, girls on the streets began to discard their burqas (at first only in Kabul and the Hazara areas) and wear stylish headscarves, and thousands of Afghans rushed out to get cell phones, radios, and television sets. In the countryside NATO Provincial Reconstruction Teams began to work on everything from building schools to bridges and wells. The UN also became involved in de-mining this country that was perhaps the world's most heavily mined war zone. In response, as many as three million Afghan refugees returned to the country to take advantage of new opportunities. Far from being a people unified in their hatred of all foreign invaders (as many non-experts naively described the Afghans), most Afghans wanted a U.S. and NATO presence in their country to help them rebuild their lives. Although there were bound to be bumps in the road, Afghanistan appeared to be traveling down the path of recovery. Many felt that the senseless terrorist acts of a few disgruntled "neo-Taliban diehards" in the south or the clashes between Dostum and Atta in the north could not stop the overall trend toward progress. Momentum was clearly on the side of the Karzai administration and its welcome foreign benefactors.

But many aid workers in Afghanistan sensed hubris and were not sure how long Karzai could maintain his momentum. Although the Karzai government made some excellent choices for governor (most notably Governor Hakim Taniwal of Paktia Province, who was killed by a Haqqani suicide bomber in 2006), not all of its choices were so wise. For example, with U.S. support, Karzai decided to create a centralized state (of the sort forcefully carved by Abdur Rahman) instead of creating a looser federal state that reflected the country's true ethnic diversity. The Afghan government was also failing to support pro-government mullahs and khans in the south and was not moving quickly enough to create an army. Instead, it relied on the Americans in Regional Command East and Regional Command South to fight.

There was also the perennial issue of corruption. President Karzai did not support his anti-corruption squads when they attempted to arrest corrupt ministers, and he was unwilling to remove corrupt governors who were friends. Out of 180 countries rated by Transparency International on their rates of corruption, Afghanistan ranked 179th, with only Somalia ranking lower. Not surprisingly, Karzai began to appear weak and corrupt to many Afghans, and his luster began to diminish in the West as well. One editorial in the *New York Times* described Afghanistan as "Corruptistan."

In addition, the underpaid Afghan National Police earned a reputation for demanding bribes, which infuriated those they shook down and played into the hands of the Taliban. Many average Afghans grew to despise the corrupt politicians, judges, and police who represented the local face of the Afghan government. Then there was the issue of opium eradication. Farmers complained that those who had sufficient money paid off the local police to protect their crops, while the poorer farmers who could not afford to do so had their crops destroyed. The only ones who could protect their crops from the police were the Taliban.

And the money for aid projects was not coming in fast enough. Those on the ground realized that the international community had a small window of opportunity to rebuild the country. This window appeared to be closing as the Taliban regrouped and began to take advantage of the lack of U.S. and NATO troops in the country. It soon became obvious that for all of its assurances that it would provide millions of dollars in aid money, the international community was not fulfilling its promises. The average aid going to Afghanistan per person was $80, while postwar Bosnians, a far more advanced European people, received $275. Yet Afghanistan was the poorest country in Eurasia, with a life expectancy in the low 40s and one of the world's highest infant mortality rates.

As the international donor money failed to come in and corrupt officials became the provincial face of the Karzai government, the United States began to shift its focus toward Operation Iraqi Freedom. Elite special forces units that had established remarkable rapport with Afghans were sent to Iraq. U.S. Predator aerial drone aircraft, which had made their debut in the Afghan conflict, were also deployed to Iraq as were look-down satellites that aided troops on the ground. As CENTCOM focused on the destruction of Saddam Hussein's Baathist-Socialist regime in the spring of 2003, the war in Afghanistan came to be seen in America as the "Forgotten War" or the "Other War." U.S. troops serving in this zone felt neglected as the U.S. president, media, and CENTCOM shifted their attention from Afghanistan to the new war against Saddam Hussein. But it soon became obvious that neither the Taliban nor Al Qaeda had forgotten the war in Afghanistan.

The Taliban Insurgency

By 2003 it became clear that predictions that the Taliban had been destroyed and that "major military operations were over" in Afghanistan were premature. Mullah Omar, who had last been seen riding off on the back of a moped as his state collapsed around him in December 2001, appeared to have retained his authority as the "Commander of the Faithful." His forces regrouped in the Pashtun sanctuaries in Pakistan's tribal zones and prepared to wage a guerrilla jihad against the Coalition "infidels." Various fronts were created, and these were run by Taliban *shuras* (councils) based in Quetta (Baluchistan Province of Pakistan) and Wana (the capital of South Waziristan). Although the Pakistanis officially claimed to be "with" the United States in the war against the Taliban, they were reluctant to move against their former Taliban clients and blatantly allowed them to regroup on their territory. The Pakistanis were both "with" and "against" the United States in the war on terror. They managed to acquire some ten billion U.S. dollars in aid for their efforts, which were initially directed against foreign Al Qaeda, not against local Pakistani and Afghan Taliban.

The Taliban re-infiltration into Afghanistan from their Pakistani sanctuaries typically began when small groups of Taliban "vanguard" units entered a district in Zabul, Kandahar, Oruzgan, and Helmand in conjunction with local supporters who had hidden weapons caches. They then threatened and intimidated pro-government mullahs, women's activists, teachers, or elders and killed them if they resisted. Their next step was to set up Islamic courts that administered the sort of swift, uncorrupted justice the Pashtuns favored. While the government courts were known for their corruption, the Taliban "shadow courts" were known for their refusal to accept *baksheesh* (bribes). The Taliban also played to those tribes that had been disenfranchised in the new power structures dominated by Karzai-supported tribes such as the Popalzai, Achakzai, Barakzai, and Alokozai. There were also those who were willing to join the Taliban because they had lost loved ones in Coalition air strikes or because their sense of *nang* (honor) was offended by U.S.-NATO-Coalition checkpoints, house searches, and other indignities. And there was always the issue of Afghan National Police corruption to drive offended citizens into the hands of the Taliban. As word of the Karzai administration's own corruption at the top filtered down, many Pashtuns began to recall the Taliban puritans with nostalgia. For the conservatives of the population, the stories of burqa-less women, debauchery of Western NGO workers, and alcohol that was said to have been flowing in the comparatively liberal capital of Kabul were enough to make Kabul seem like a veritable Sodom and Gomorrah under the foreigners.

The Taliban began to take advantage of these issues by recruiting local men to join their *andiwali* (networks). They then set up *mahazes* (fighting fronts) that engaged in planting land mines, frontal assaults on police checkpoints, assassinating government officials, sniping, and other insurgent activities. From 2003 to 2005, Taliban units secretly infiltrated a swath of provinces ranging from Nuristan and Kunar in the north to Helmand and Kandahar in the south. By 2007 as much as a third of Afghanistan had fallen to the Taliban who, like the mujahideen, controlled the countryside while the government controlled the towns. At this time the U.S. presence in such provinces as Zabul or Kunar was almost nonexistent due the White House's reluctance to engage in major "nation-building" activities in Afghanistan. NATO's ISAF forces were initially limited to Kabul, and there was only a small U.S. presence of some ten thousand troops in this country that was larger than France. The Bush White House was determined not to use its troops to fill the void of the Taliban collapse, in part because it was planning to use U.S. troops to invade Baathist Iraq. It was only much later that the number of U.S. troops in these northern and central provinces would soar in belated response to the rise of the insurgency. But by then it was too late—the Taliban had already seized the territory and become entrenched.

In the south the Taliban made their greatest efforts to recapture lands and people lost in 2001. The southern front was given to a Taliban commander named Mullah Dadullah, who soon became one of the most feared terrorists in Afghanistan. His story is the story of the Taliban resurrection in Helmand, Zabul, and Kandahar.

Mullah Dadullah, the "Afghan Zarqawi"

Mullah Dadullah was a Pashtun mujahideen fighter in the 1980s. He lost a leg in the 1990s civil war while fighting Ismail Khan in Herat. For this reason he was sometimes known as Dadullah i Leng (the Cripple). Others have called him the "Afghan Zarqawi" for his penchant for beheading his victims in the fashion of the infamous Iraqi terrorist, Abu Musab al Zarqawi. But Dadullah's loss of a leg did not stop him from waging jihad. After losing his limb, Dadullah was made a member of the Taliban's ruling Shura. He served in the Taliban campaigns in the north and was involved in the conquests of the Uzbeks, Tajiks, and Hazaras of the Hindu Kush and Afghan Turkistan. He was known to be a fierce fighter and was said to have killed Taliban who retreated in combat.

Dadullah was feared in the north for his brutality, in particular his treatment of Shiite Hazara "heretics." His forces were involved in the massacre of Hazaras in the Bamiyan region in 2000, for which he was given the nickname "the Black Mullah." As his reputation began to hurt the Taliban movement, Mullah Omar took the unprecedented step of removing him from his position for fear of inciting a backlash among the Hazaras.

But when the United States invaded in 2001, Dadullah was precisely the sort of fierce commander the Taliban needed, and he was reappointed to a command in the north. Dadullah's army based in Balkh Province was, however, overrun by Dostum's Uzbeks in November 2001. Thousands of his men were captured and sent to Sheberghan Prison by Dostum. Fearing retaliation for his oppression, Mullah Dadullah escaped from the besieged enclave of Kunduz in November 2001, despite Dostum's efforts to capture him. He then managed to make his way across the Pakistani border into Waziristan, where he took sanctuary with his fellow tribesmen from the Kakar clan.

As the Taliban leadership regrouped in 2002, Dadullah was given control of Taliban forces in the south. He took advantage of the small number of U.S. forces in Kandahar and Helmand Provinces (no more than three thousand U.S. troops were stationed at Kandahar airport and at a few bases) to reestablish fighting units throughout the south. These forces began to launch swarm attacks on Coalition forces in 2005, but they sustained heavy losses in this sort of frontal combat and re-verted back to mujahideen-style guerrilla warfare.

But it was not Dadullah's guerrilla tactics that gained him fame so much as his bloodthirsty acts of terrorism. He seemed to have been impressed by the terror tactics of Iraqi insurgent commander Abu Musab Zarqawi, who made decapitations his calling card. Inspired by Zarqawi's DVDs (which made their way to Afghanistan via "Al Qaeda in Iraq" emissaries), Dadullah had himself filmed using a small knife to hack off the heads of suspected "CIA spies." These videos and others of Dadullah training with his troops and preparing suicide bombers were soon selling like hotcakes in the Pashtun lands on either side of the border. Many Taliban recruits were drawn to his macabre Iraqi-style executions and cult of martyrdom. In one unbearably gruesome video, Mullah Dadullah even guided a twelve-year-old boy in hacking the head of a man described as a spy.

However, it was Dadullah's use of suicide bombings that gained him his greatest notoriety. It was Dadullah who transformed Kandahar into the number-one target for suicide bombings from 2006 to the present. He recruited hundreds of suicide bombers and threatened to release hundreds more on his targets. Although suicide bombing was once taboo among the Taliban, Dadullah made it his weapon of choice. One cannot underestimate the impact this fierce commander had on destabilizing Zabul, Uruzgan, Helmand, and Kandahar Provinces. His name became a byword for terror, and his penchant for flaunting his power by giving interviews to reporters made him the Taliban's most famous field commander.

But it was this weakness that may have gotten him killed when his movements were reported by a spy. Dadullah's reign of terror came to an end in May 2007 when he was tracked by British Special Forces as he crossed into Afghanistan from Pakistan. He was subsequently killed in an assault on his compound, and his body was taken to Kandahar. There the jubilant governor showed his one-legged corpse to reporters to prove that the dreaded Dadullah was finally dead. His younger brother Mansur Dadullah took over his operations but was later captured by the Pakistanis.

"Mullah Omar's Missiles"

Afghanistan's first suicide bombing was the attack on Massoud the Lion of Panjsher on September 9, 2001. This attack seems to have caught Massoud's intelligence people by surprise, because suicide bombing was alien to their culture. The mujahideen rebels never resorted to suicide bombings against the Soviets in the 1980s, nor did the Taliban in the 1990s. There were a few suicide attacks during the takedown of the Taliban during Operation Enduring Freedom (most notably an attempt on General Dostum's life at Qala i Jengi), but these were, like the killing of Massoud, carried out by Arab foreigners, not local Afghans.

Al Qaeda operatives carried out two to three bombings per year on Afghan government and NATO troops from 2002 to 2004 that were meant to demonstrate the effectiveness of this alien tactic to the local Taliban. These demonstrative acts and videos of successful suicide bombings in Iraq seem to have convinced the Taliban to condone the previously taboo tactic of suicide bombing. By 2005 the Taliban had launched a tentative suicide bombing campaign that saw as many as twenty-three attacks on Afghan targets, including one powerful bomb in Kandahar that killed the Kabul police chief and twenty others. In the following year the campaign escalated to over 130 suicide bombings. The destabilizing impact these attacks had can perhaps best be imagined by those who remember the panic that swept the United States when a domestic terrorist known as the Beltway Sniper stalked Americans in 2002. In the aftermath of bombings, Coalition troops on "hearts-and-minds" campaigns came to fear crowds. In one case, shocked U.S. Marines near Jalalabad who had just survived a suicide attack gunned down innocent civilians. Foreigners and government officials now move more cautiously knowing that suicide bombers are potentially waiting for them.

Despite the seeming randomness of the attacks, patterns nonetheless began to emerge. It soon became obvious that although the Afghan *fedayeen* (suicide bombers) had been inspired by their Iraqi counterparts, they had developed their own targeting characteristics. For example, while Iraqi bombers aimed for high civilian body counts with the aim of shredding the fabric of society, Afghan suicide bombers were more inclined to go after "hard" (government, police, and military) targets rather than "soft" (civilian) targets.

This trend seems to fit the Pashtun warrior code (the Afghan bombers are exclusively Pashtuns, with only a few foreigners) with its emphasis on acts of martial valor. While Arab suicide bombers in Iraq seem to have no compunction about killing unarmed women and children, Afghan-Taliban bombers were clearly reluctant to do so. Instead, the Taliban bombers tended to go after NATO convoys, government buildings, checkpoints, military bases, policemen, and government installations.

This helped explain another bizarre characteristic of Taliban suicide bombers: their low kill ratio. In most cases the Afghan-Taliban bombers killed only themselves and one or two others, usually civilian bystanders.

My own fieldwork on this issue for the CIA's Counterterrorist Center revealed a strange trend wherein Taliban suicide bombers in dozens of cases per year set off their bombs and killed only themselves. In some months the majority of bombers blew up only themselves, which led me to question whether they were committing suicide bombings—or simply suicide.

Part of the reason for this trend became clear to me when I examined military vehicles that had been hit by suicide bombers. Many of these "thick-skinned" armored vehicles were able to withstand direct hits by suicide bombers. Killing innocent civilians in a bread line (as Iraqi bombers are prone to do) leads to higher death tolls than trying to hit fast-moving armored convoys, sandbagged military checkpoints, or heavily guarded and protected government installations.

Then there is the issue of the quality of the bombers themselves. Most Taliban suicide bombers are illiterate young village men who have been brainwashed in the madrassas in Pakistan, trained to drive a car (the Toyota Corolla seems to be the bombers' vehicle of choice), and sent to Afghanistan to strike at difficult targets. Even in the best of circumstances, suicide bombing is not a precise science and, in their final moments of life, many of these immature bombers explode their bombs at the wrong time. There have been some cases of incompetent Afghan suicide bombers running out of gas while driving their VBIEDs (vehicle-borne improvised explosive devices) to their targets, of bombers tripping and setting off their bombs prematurely, and of Afghan security officials finding abandoned suicide bomber vests, indicating a last-minute change of heart.

Yet despite their ineptitude, many bombers succeed, and in 2007 the country experienced 160 bombings. The primary provinces that were targeted were Kandahar, Khost, and Kabul, with most bombs going off in the Pashtun belt. Surprisingly, there have been no bombings in the Hazara-Shiite lands, a trend that differentiates the Afghan bombers from their counterparts in Pakistan and Iraq. There have been three large-scale and deadly suicide bombing attacks in Afghanistan. These have included the November 2007 bombing of a sugar factory in Baghlan Province which killed seventy-five to one hundred people, the February 2008 bombing at a dogfight in Kandahar which killed eighty, and the July 2008 bombing of the Indian Embassy in Kabul which killed fifty-eight (this attack may have been carried out with Pakistani ISI assistance).

Clearly the Taliban have embraced this once-taboo asymmetric tactic and see suicide bombers—who are referred to as "Mullah Omar's missiles"—as an equalizer, much as the Stinger ground-to-air missile was in the 1980s. It remains to be seen whether this bloody tactic, which has (despite its "best" hard-targeting intentions) taken a deadly toll on civilians, leads to bad public relations fallout for the Taliban.

Nek Muhammad

Nek Muhammad represented the face of the new generation of Taliban commanders who took the lead in transforming their movement from a bona fide government and frontal fighting force into a guerrilla/terrorist movement. Unlike the vast majority of Taliban commanders, who came from Kandahar or Uruzgan, Nek Muhammad was a Pakistani Pashtun from the Wana region of South Waziristan. The son of an impoverished tribal *malik* (local ruler) from the Ahmedzai tribe, Nek Muhammad decided to join a madrassa and then fight jihad in Afghanistan on behalf of the Taliban.

There he seems to have earned a reputation as a skilled fighter, and he was given command of the Wazirstani unit, which fought in various fronts against Massoud's Northern Alliance. It was at this time that Nek Muhammad began to interact with Arabs, Uzbekistanis, Uighurs, and other foreigners who had come to Afghanistan to train for jihad. When the Taliban front on the Shomali Plain collapsed under U.S. pressure in November 2001, Nek Muhammad fled back to his native province of South Waziristan, Pakistan. There he appears to have played a key role in assisting fleeing Taliban and the foreign fighters whom he had met back in Kabul.

When the Pakistani Army reluctantly invaded Waziristan under U.S. pressure after 2002, Nek Muhammad put his skills as a military commander to good use in fighting President Musharraf's unskilled troops. He firmly stood by the Uzbeks and other foreign fighters who took sanctuary in his lands. For example, when the Pakistani military surrounded Tahir Yoldoshev, the leader of the Islamic Movement of Uzbekistan terrorist group, Nek Muhammad broke Yoldoshev out of the encirclement by driving a pickup truck through a hail of gunfire. Of the foreign fighters he later proclaimed, "They have fought a jihad against the Russians and before them the British. Now that the Americans are here we will wage jihad against them."

However, Nek Muhammad's main front was not in Afghanistan but in Pakistan. There his fighters fought Pakistani troops to a standstill and, when they agreed to a truce that would involve Muhammad turning over foreign fighters, he quickly broke the truce. Such actions earned him the nickname Bodogay (the Stubborn One) from his friends and enemies. But Nek Muhammad was too brazen in his movements, and the United States finally tracked him down. In June 2004 he was killed along with several of his followers in a Predator drone missile strike on their compound. He was horribly burned and maimed in this first CIA drone attack in Pakistan and died soon thereafter. Ironically, his death may have been a setback, for it opened the way for the rise of a much more dangerous terrorist, Baitullah Mehsud.

Baitullah Mehsud, Pakistan's Enemy Number One

No figure was more notorious in Pakistan than the young Taliban commander Baitullah Mehsud. Mehsud was actually named one of *Time* magazine's one hundred most influential people as a result of his terrorist activities, and *Newsweek* described him as being more dangerous than bin Laden. Such assertions were not mere hyperbole and were based on Mehsud's declaration of an unprecedented terrorist insurgency against the Pakistani government. The Pakistanis blame him and his followers for beheading Pakistani soldiers, killing former prime minister Benazir Bhutto, capturing hundreds of soldiers, overrunning key forts, launching a wave of suicide bombings, and creating a harsh shariah law–based state-within-a-state in South Waziristan. For this reason he was perhaps the greatest threat to nuclear-armed Pakistan.

But for all of his infamy, Mehsud had rather humble origins. He was born in the early 1970s in the Bannu region of Pakistan's North West Frontier Province and belonged to the Shabikhel sub-clan of the powerful Mehsud tribe. The Mehsud tribe gained great fame in the 1920s by killing thousands of British troops in a tribal uprising in Waziristan and are known to be among the fiercest tribes in Pakistan's tribal zone. Baitullah Mehsud seems to have grown up on the stories of jihad, and it was this harsher aspect of the faith that appealed to him.

When he was young Mehsud volunteered to join the Taliban in neighboring Afghanistan and was said to have spent time in a madrassa. This madrassa training and his experience as a Taliban fighter in the 1990s under Jalaluddin Haqqani were his only education. Despite his low level of education, Mehsud was said to be a bright tribal politician, a cunning strategist, and a fanatic fighter.

Like many new-generation Taliban leaders, the media-shy Mehsud rose through the Taliban ranks following the overthrow of the Taliban regime in 2001. As mid-level Taliban leaders rose to fill the depleted ranks of the Taliban in Pakistan, Baitullah Mehsud began to serve under a one-legged Taliban commander from his own tribe known as Abdullah

Mehsud. Abdullah Mehsud gained wide notoriety for kidnapping two Chinese workers working for the Pakistani government in 2004. Mullah Omar, the Taliban's overall leader, saw this as a needlessly antagonistic act at a time when the Taliban did not yet want to fight with its former Pakistani government sponsors. Mullah Omar consequently demoted Abdullah Mehsud and raised Baitullah Mehsud to his position. A despondent Abdullah Mehsud subsequently blew himself up with a hand grenade after he was surrounded by Pakistani soldiers.

Baitullah Mehsud was further propelled to the forefront by the killing of the infamous Pakistani Taliban leader Nek Muhammad in 2004. With the removal of both Abdullah Mehsud and Nek Muhammad, the way was clear for Baitullah Mehsud's rise. After Nek Muhammad's death, Mullah Omar declared Baitullah Mehsud the Taliban commander of the Mehsud tribe. This gave him control over much of the Mehsud tribe's territory in South Wazirstan. The Pakistani government acknowledged Baitullah Mehsud's control when it signed a peace treaty with his fighters on February 7, 2005. The treaty offered peace between Baitullah Mehsud's followers and the Pakistani army if the former agreed to stop attacking Pakistani and Coalition troops and stop working with Al Qaeda. The government even agreed to pay Baitullah Mehsud over half a million dollars to help his Taliban faction pay off money it claimed had been given to it by Al Qaeda to wage jihad.

As the Pakistani troops returned to their barracks, they had high hopes that this policy of appeasement would bring peace to the troubled province of South Waziristan. But Baitullah Mehsud never fulfilled his end of the bargain. He saw it as a total Pakistani surrender and a sign of weakness. He used the reprieve from Pakistani attacks to terrorize local khans and *maliks* into granting him total power. Any tribal chieftain who resisted him was assassinated, and dozens of pro-government or moderate local leaders were murdered in cold blood.

As Mehsud's draconian laws banned the shaving of beards, listening to music, women without burqas, etc., the province of South Waziristan came to resemble Afghanistan under the Taliban. The Pakistanis' policy of appeasement had obviously backfired, and the area was lost to the Pakistani state. To compound matters, Baitullah Mehsud never broke with the Arab and Uzbekistani Al Qaeda fighters as had been promised. On the contrary, he continued to protect them even as he used the cover of the peace treaty to carve out an independent Taliban mini-state in South Waziristan. When the Pakistani army responded to these flagrant breaches of the treaty by launching an offensive, Baitullah Mehsud's fighters fought the Pakistani army to a standstill. This necessitated further humiliating treaties, resulting in a yet another peace deal that simply allowed Baitullah Mehsud to regroup and further extend his power.

Baitullah Mehsud finally ended his on-again, off-again war policy and declared total war on the Pakistani government in July 2007. The declaration came after Pakistani troops stormed the Lal Masjid (Red Mosque), a hotbed of fundamentalist activity in the capital of Islamabad. Baitullah Mehsud was livid that Taliban-style extremists were killed in the siege and vowed to launch a retaliatory wave of terrorism against Pakistan.

Making use of his Al Qaeda contacts, Baitullah Mehsud subsequently declared the creation of a new Taliban alliance known as the Tehrik e Taliban e Pakistan (the Pakistani Taliban) in December 2007. This new Pakistani Taliban group launched dozens of suicide bombing attacks against a wide range of Pakistani civilian and military targets. Thousands died in this terror campaign as the suicide bombing scourge of Afghanistan came to Pakistan. By this stage the Pakistanis' policy of turning a blind eye to Taliban militancy had fully backfired as its own creation turned on it.

Tensions came to a head when Baitullah Mehsud's men humiliated the Pakistani army by capturing roughly 250 Pakistani soldiers in South Waziristan. Baitullah Mehsud demanded the release of thirty of his captured followers, including suicide bombers, in return for the safe release of the captured soldiers. When the Pakistani government did not move fast enough to release them, Baitullah Mehsud had three of the Pakistani troops beheaded. The rest of the troops were released unharmed when Baitullah Mehsud's terrorists were turned over to him.

In January 2008 Baitullah Mehsud's troops also swarmed the Pakistani outpost of Sararogha Fort and overran it, killing its defenders. But Baitullah Mehsud's most infamous act is one that not all observers agree he carried out—namely the December 2007 killing of the former Pakistani prime minister Benazir Bhutto. Bhutto, an exiled moderate leader whose father had once been prime minister before Muhammad Zia, returned to Pakistan in October 2007, vowing to move against the Taliban and other extremists. At the time, Baitullah Mehsud threatened to kill her if she returned to the country. For this reason, when a suicide bomber attacked her convoy in October 2007, killing over a hundred (but missing Bhutto), most observers blamed Mehsud. When Bhutto was subsequently killed in a shooting and suicide blast in December 2007, the Pakistani government released a tape it claimed was of Mehsud congratulating a terrorist for the attack. However, Mehsud changed his tune after the killing and claimed that he would never kill a woman. Pakistanis, many of whom have a tendency to believe conspiracy theories, blamed everyone from Israelis, to Bhutto's husband, to Musharraf for her death.

Critics have claimed that Musharraf's Pakistani government was scapegoating Mehsud for an attack that might have been carried out by Al Qaeda or a Pakistani jihad group known as Laskhar e Jangvi. Such criticisms overlook the fact that Baitullah Mehsud has been the Pakistani Taliban commander who has most extensively used suicide bombings against his own countrymen. Mehsud's *fedayeen* (suicide bombers) have struck throughout Pakistan, and the bombing tends to fit his modus operandi.

In October 2008 a rumor spread that Baitullah Mehsud, who was a diabetic, had died from his disease. But he soon gave an interview to Pakistani journalists, proving that he was alive. His fighters were subsequently engaged in attacking U.S. supply columns traveling to Afghanistan through the Pashtun tribal regions. As his bombers wreaked havoc in Pakistan, the Pakistanis called on the United States to use their unmanned aerial drones known as Predators to hunt him down. The drones almost killed Mehsud when he incautiously attended a funeral for a slain Taliban member in June 2009. While as many as eighty people, most of them Taliban, were killed in the strike, Mehsud escaped. In August 2009, however, one of these drones finally found Baitullah Mehsud on the roof of his father-in-law's house and killed him and his wife with a Hellfire missile. Thus Pakistan's greatest terrorist was killed with the aid of the Americans and for once Pakistanis celebrated a drone strike.

His place was taken by Hakeemullah Mehsud, who promised vengeance on the Americans and Pakistanis for their role in killing his predecessor. This seemed like an empty threat when the Pakistanis invaded the Mehsud territory in October 2009. Against all expectations, the Pakistani force of roughly twenty-five thousand men overran the Mehsud territory in less than a month. Hakeemullah Mehsud responded by launching a wave of suicide bombings that killed hundreds in Peshawar and other cities. He was also involved in sending a Jordanian double agent, who was pretending to be a spy for the Americans, to carry out a suicide bombing on a CIA team based at Camp Chapman in Afghanistan in December 2009. This suicide attack killed the CIA station chief and several other CIA agents involved in collecting data for drone strikes. Despite Hakeemullah Mehsud's victory, the Pakistani army currently controls most of South Waziristan, which nonetheless has led to the displacement of thousands of innocent Pashtun refugees.

Although the Pakistani ground campaign was successful in defeating a major threat to Pakistan, it will probably not have a major impact on the war in neighboring Afghanistan. This is largely due to the fact that the Waziri tribesmen, led by Gul Bahadur Hafez and Mullah Nazir, who continue to attack Coalition troops from South Waziristan, were not targeted in Pakistani operations. The Pakistanis have also avoided attacking the notorious Haqqani network that operates from North Waziristan attacking U.S. and Coalition forces in Afghanistan.

Nonetheless, the CIA's assassination of Baitullah Mehsud and his predecessor Nek Muhammad have seriously disrupted the Pakistani Taliban's leadership.

Pakistan's Role in the War on Terror

Although many non-specialists mistakenly think that the United States created the Taliban, the Pakistanis are the foreign players most responsible for midwifing and nurturing the Taliban in the mid- to late 1990s. As early as the 1980s, the Pakistani government encouraged the expansion of hundreds of madrassas in the North West Frontier Province and in the FATA. These took in the poor, orphans, or impoverished young Afghan refugee boys who went on to become Taliban in both Pakistan and Afghanistan.

When the Taliban emerged in 1994, the Pakistani ISI played a key role in assisting them in their conquests of Afghanistan. This was to further Pakistan's agenda of placing a friendly Islamist (as opposed to a hostile Pashtun nationalist) government in Kabul. Ultimately, the Pakistanis also hoped to use a pro-Pakistani Taliban government as an ally against India, a country they felt was always meddling in Afghan affairs and supporting Baluchi insurgents in their southern lands.

Thus Pakistan was, along with Saudi Arabia and the United Arab Emirates, one of only three countries to recognize the Taliban. The Pakistanis were not pleased with the Taliban's policy of giving sanctuary to Al Qaeda when it was attacking U.S. targets from 1998 to 2000. However, Al Qaeda did not attack Pakistan itself (although Egyptian radicals who would later join Al Qaeda had attacked the Egyptian embassy in Pakistan years earlier), so Pakistan overlooked its faults.

For its part, Al Qaeda did not want to offend the Pakistanis who were supporting both the jihad in Kashmir against India and the Taliban. Both the Pakistanis and Al Qaeda were sponsors of Kashmiri and Pakistani jihadi terrorist groups that operated against India from Pakistan, including Lashkar e Toiba (the Army of the Pure), Lashkar e Janghvi (the Army of Janghvi), Jaish e Muhammad (the Army of Muhammad), and Harakat ul Mujahideen (the Holy War Supporters). There were also powerful fundamentalist religious parties in Pakistan that donated considerable funds to the Taliban when they were fighting U.S. troops, such as the Jamiat Ulema e Islam (the Assembly of Islamic Clergy).

When the United States was attacked by Al Qaeda on 9/11, President Bush famously gave the world an ultimatum to either be "with" the United States or "against" it in the war on terror. Prior to 9/11 the Pakistanis, far from being allies with the United States, had earned America's wrath for building nuclear weapons. After 9/11 U.S. Deputy Secretary of State Richard Armitage warned President Musharraf that if his country did not join the United States in destroying the Taliban regime, it would become a rogue nation. The Pakistanis joined the Americans and in return received ten billion dollars for allowing the United States to base troops in Pakistan during Operation Enduring Freedom.

However, the Pakistanis ultimately found a way to be both with and against the United States. They maintained their ties with their Taliban and Kashmiri proxies (who were officially banned but still tolerated after 2002), while they arrested Al Qaeda operatives who fled from Afghanistan to the tribal areas. In an example of Pakistan's balancing act, members of the Pakistani government actually met with the Taliban after 9/11 and expressed their continued support for them, even as they offered Americans the use of bases in Pakistan to attack the Taliban.

But for all these ambiguities, Pakistani leader Pervez Musharraf was clearly "with" President Bush, and he had the support of the White House. Musharraf, a secular general who had seized power in a military coup in 1999 after launching a failed invasion of the Kargil region in Indian Kashmir, took the U.S. offer he could not refuse and joined the U.S.-led Coalition. With Musharraf's blessing, U.S. troops were subsequently based in Jacobabad and other spots in Pakistan (despite widespread protests and the movement of Pakistani citizens into Afghanistan to fight alongside the Taliban). Pakistani-based U.S. helicopters subsequently launched Marines and search-and-rescue missions from Pakistani soil, which infuriated Al Qaeda and many Pakistanis.

As the Taliban were crushed in Afghanistan in the winter of 2001, the United States hoped that Pakistan would be an anvil to the U.S. hammer. Although hundreds of fleeing Al Qaeda operatives (most notably the planners of 9/11, Ramzi bin al Shibh and Khaled Sheikh Muhammad) were indeed arrested by Pakistani forces, Pakistan acted more as a sponge than an anvil when it came to the Taliban. In some cases Pakistani Frontier Constabulary troops gave in to their religious and ethnic sympathies and gave cover fire to Taliban troops retreating from the United States into Pakistan. The Taliban subsequently regrouped in the Pashtun tribal agencies in Pakistan, especially North and South Waziristan where the frontier had been deliberately left open by the Pakistanis. From there, the Taliban continued to protect Arab and Uzbek terrorists who had fled with them. The United States found it intolerable that bin Laden could be hiding in Pakistan's tribal territories and pushed the Pakistanis to invade the tribal area for the first time ever to destroy Al Qaeda's new sanctuary.

As U.S. money flowed in to sweeten the deal, the Pakistani army entered the tribal areas in July 2002 and began to attack compounds suspected of offering shelter to Al Qaeda in the Khyber and North and South Waziristan Agencies. These attacks succeeded in killing Taliban militants, and the army initially seemed to have the upper hand. However, as Pakistani troops moved into Pashtun tribal lands that had not been intruded on since the foundation of Pakistan in 1947, the local tribes rose up against them. By 2004 the Pakistani army was faced with a full-blown tribal insurgency of the very sort that had cost thousands of British troops their lives in the mountains in the 1920s. This somewhat eased the pressure on the American side of the border in Afghanistan, since the Waziri Taliban were fighting the Pakistani army. The Waziris, who had been the toughest of all the Pashtun tribes confronted by the British, proved to be particularly inclined to resist. They fought back against the government in the South Waziristan capital of Wana in March 2004. In the ensuing government assault on Taliban compounds, dozens of Pakistani troops were killed, and a high-ranking Arab target that many speculate was Ayman al Zawahiri escaped via an underground tunnel complex.

However, by the following month the Pakistani government had made the first of several peace deals with the Taliban that would ultimately give the militants free reign in the tribal areas. As the government withdrew to its military bases, the Taliban began to execute local *maliks* and tribal leaders who were known to be pro-government. They also began to enforce harsh shariah law and to relaunch attacks across the border into Afghanistan. For the most part, however, the Taliban appeared to be loath to take on the Pakistani army, and a tentative peace was reached. Although there were low-level attacks on army checkpoints and military responses, there were no full-scale operations on either the Pakistani or Taliban side.

This tentative peace began to unravel when the United States launched a Predator aerial drone missile strike on a suspected Al Qaeda compound in the town of Damadollah, Bajaur Agency, in January 2006. The attack was in response to stepped-up cross-border Taliban and Al Qaeda terrorism. Eighteen people were killed in the missile barrage, infuriating thousands of local tribesmen who vowed revenge. Across Pakistan protestors chanted "Death to America!" and public opinion surveys showed that Pakistanis feared the United States more than Al Qaeda or their country's traditional foe, India.

By this time Baitullah Mehsud had emerged as the dominant Pakistani Taliban leader, and he appeared much more eager than Nek Muhammad to use terrorism against the Pakistani state. This was in keeping with Al Qaeda's calls for the overthrow of the "shameful" President Musharraf, who survived several suicide bomb strikes carried out by Al Qaeda.

It was in this climate that the United States launched another drone attack on a madrassa located in Chenegai in the Bajaur Agency on October 30, 2006. As many as eighty people may have died in this attack on a madrassa known for sheltering Taliban and Al Qaeda. As in the Damadollah strike, it appears that Al Qaeda (specifically Ayman al Zawahiri) was the target of the attack. Most of those killed in the strike were, however, young Taliban militants.

In response to this attack, Taliban/Al Qaeda militants launched a suicide attack on Pakistani troops serving in Bajaur that killed forty-two of them. But as tensions heated up, a truce was once again called between the militants and the Pakistani army in March 2007. That spring there was cause for optimism as a Taliban commander in South Waziristan named Mullah Nazir turned on the Uzbek IMU terrorists who had taken refuge in that province. This internal conflict began when the Uzbeks killed some tribal leaders belonging to Nazir's tribe. As many as 250 Uzbek jihadi militants were killed in the violence that took place in March and April 2007.

But in the end, a peace treaty was signed between Mullah Nazir and the Uzbeks who came under the protection of Jalaluddin Haqqani and Baitullah Mehsud. For his part, Mullah Nazir continued to proclaim his desire to defend bin Laden and launched a series of attacks on Coalition troops in Afghanistan. The United States subsequently tried to kill him in several Predator drone air strikes.

The next stage in Pakistan's war with the Taliban took place not in the tribal zones but in downtown Islamabad, the capital of Pakistan. Although the inhabitants of the Pakistani capital had been able to distance themselves from the war in the Pashtun tribal areas (which they saw as driven solely by U.S. interests), by the summer of 2007 the militants had come to the capital. They came in bands of fundamentalist vigilantes who began to terrorize the neighborhoods around their mosque, known as the Lal Masjid (the Red Mosque). These militants, including scores of women clad in head-to-toe black veils and armed with assault rifles, were essentially trying to impose Taliban-style fundamentalism in the comparatively secular capital. Although the Pakistani government had always tolerated Islamic militancy as part of its foreign policy vis-à-vis Kashmir and Afghanistan, the secular elite were alarmed by this behavior so close to home. Members of the Lal Masjid were openly calling for the assassination of President Musharraf and the implementation of strict shariah law.

Tensions came to a head when the Lal Masjid militants attacked a nearby government building and fought an armed battle with Pakistani Rangers in which several were killed. Although the Pakistani government had tried to avoid confrontation with the extremists, the attack forced its hand. President Musharraf decided to attack the mosque and clear out the militants. From July 3 to 11, the Pakistani Special Services besieged the mosque and finally stormed it. The militants, who had turned the tunnels beneath the mosque into a defensive warren, fought back ferociously, killing the Pakistani commander. But in the end they were overwhelmed, and dozens of them were killed. More than 154 people were killed in the resulting carnage. One of the two leaders of the mosque was captured trying to sneak out of the mosque in a burqa, while the other was shot and killed.

Many of those who attended the Lal Masjid Mosque had been Pashtun fundamentalists from the tribal areas. Their deaths infuriated militants such as Baitullah Mehsud, who then declared all-out war on the Pakistani government. "President Bush's war" became Pakistan's war as its years of cozying up to militants and protecting the Taliban came back to haunt it. Within days of the siege, Taliban suicide bombers began to strike military targets in the tribal zones. These suicide attacks then spread beyond the tribal zones and soon included attacks on pro-government *jirgas* (tribal meetings), restaurants, barracks, checkpoints, government officials, an ammunition factory, political rallies, arms plants, Sufi shrines, a Marriott hotel, a visiting cricket team from Sri Lanka, hospitals, funerals, ISI bases, mosques, military bases, and a host of other targets. By year's end hundreds of Pakistanis had been killed in the approximately fifty suicide bombings, and the campaign has racked up thousands of deaths since then.

Baitullah Mehsud's fighters operating in the mountains of Waziristan also began to attack Pakistani troops and overrun checkpoints. Coalition convoys bringing supplies and equipment to U.S. troops in Afghanistan from Pakistani ports were also attacked and burned by tribesmen operating in the Khyber Agency. By the summer of 2008, the militants had grown so bold that they threatened the major frontier town of Peshawar. The Pakistani army was forced to push them back into the mountains, and in so doing sustained significant casualties. By this time the Pakistanis had lost more than one thousand troops in fighting the Taliban, compared to the roughly five hundred U.S. troops lost in Afghanistan. It appeared as if Pakistan was engaged in a full-scale counterinsurgency in the tribal zones along the Afghan border, and by 2011 the Pakistanis had more than two thousand losses in their war with the Pakistani Taliban.

It was not only in the tribal agencies that the Pakistani military, which had been trained to fight a frontal war with India, found itself bogged down in a guerrilla quagmire. In one of their first moves out of the tribal areas, militants led by Mullah Fazlullah (also known as Mullah Radio) seized the scenic mountain resort valley of Swat, located just to the northwest of the capital Islamabad. He and his followers tried to implement strict shariah law in this Pashtun area. This was seen as direct threat to the capital, and the Pakistani military launched several large-scale campaigns to re-seize the resort valley. By December 2007 the militants had been temporarily forced out after fighting a tenacious struggle that left hundreds of them dead. In 2009 the Swat was again invaded by the Pakistani army and reconquered after the militants shocked the nation by filming themselves beheading Pakistani police and whipping local women. The video of a girl being brutally whipped was posted online in Pakistan and upset many Pakistanis who had previously been tolerant of the Taliban.

As all of these battles were taking place, General Musharraf found himself unexpectedly assaulted by the country's lawyers, who might have seemed aligned with him in light of his battles against militants. The cause of the friction with the lawyers was Musharraf's decision to remove Chief Justice Iftikhar Chaudry from office in November 2007. This move was taken after Chaudry chose to challenge Musharraf for launching a state of emergency that gave Musharraf more power and led to the arbitrary arrest of Pakistanis. Chaudry was subsequently arrested, and thousands of Pakistani lawyers took to the streets to protest the arrest of this champion of democracy. As the protests spread to the general population, Musharraf's popularity, which had already been hurt by his support for the United States in the war, began to plummet. Many Pakistanis saw him as a dictator who was a threat to Pakistani democracy and a puppet of the Americans.

The United States, which had come to depend on Musharraf as an ally in the war with the Taliban and Al Qaeda, chose to stand by him, further heightening anti-American sentiment in the country. As the Pakistanis pointed out the irony of U.S. efforts to build democracy in Afghanistan and Iraq while supporting a military dictator in their own country, many began to criticize the Americans for putting all their eggs in one basket. Why not allow former prime ministers Benazir Bhutto and Nawaz Sharif to return to the country and contest Musharraf's rule in an election, they asked.

In an effort to bolster their ally's democratic credentials, the United States finally encouraged Musharraf to let Bhutto and Sharif return in the fall of 2007. The United States saw a Bhutto-Musharraf combined political ticket as a dream team and felt that the popular Bhutto, head of the Pakistani People's Party, would work well with Musharraf in fighting terrorism. Bhutto was, however, killed in a suicide bombing in December of that year. After her death, her husband, Asif Ali Zardari, went on to win the election and become president. Musharraf, who had resigned from his military post, stepped down, and Zardari, who is generally seen as being pro-American, currently rules in a coalition with his rival, Nawaz Sharif. He has been weakened by his pro-American stance and charges of corruption from an earlier period.

Zardari has been confronted with the task of trying to suppress an increasingly vicious Taliban insurgency without appearing to be a puppet of the United States. There are many anti-U.S. elements in the Pakistani military and intelligence community, including troops operating on the border that have shot at U.S. helicopters, fired across the border into Afghanistan in support of the Taliban, and turned a blind eye to Taliban infiltration into Afghanistan. These forces must be controlled or placated. The same holds true for Pakistan's notorious ISI, which, incidentally, has been hit by Taliban suicide bombers. Although Zardari made an effort to seize control of the powerful ISI, his bid failed and he has had to use a more gradualist approach to extend his power.

Since Zardari came to power, his task has been complicated somewhat by American actions, including the increasing use of UAV (unmanned aerial vehicle) Predator drones to kill Taliban and Al Qaeda targets in the tribal agencies (as well as one in Bannu in the North West Frontier Province). Although these attacks appear to be based on solid intelligence and usually kill Taliban and Al Qaeda targets, they are highly unpopular in Pakistan. While Zardari and many in the army may have secretly condoned the attacks, which have taken out top Al Qaeda leaders and denied its operatives freedom of movement, they are a public relations liability and must be publicly criticized by the government and military.

If the dozens of Predator and Reaper (a new, more advanced aerial drone) strikes are causing ripples of anti-Americanism, then the September 3, 2008, military incursion into South Waziristan by U.S. troops caused a tidal wave. This attack on a Taliban/Al Qaeda sanctuary by U.S. heliborne troops, which killed fifteen people, caused Pakistani military leader Pervez Kayani to draw a line in the sand in defense of his country's sovereignty. He warned that if the United States reinvaded his country, Pakistan would drop out of the anti-Taliban Coalition. The United States clearly could not launch any more ground incursions into sovereign Pakistan. In the fall of 2010, U.S. helicopters rocketed two Pakistani checkpoints, killing Pakistani border troops after sustaining fire from them. In response, the Pakistanis closed down the Khyber Pass to U.S. supply convoys (90 percent of U.S.-NATO supplies in Afghanistan come from Pakistan) for several days before reopening it.

In an effort to head off further attacks and appease their American allies, who are always demanding more, the Pakistani military launched a full-scale invasion of the rebellious Bajaur Agency in the fall of 2008. After several months of tough fighting that saw hundreds of thousands of local tribesmen displaced and scores of Pakistani soldiers killed, the

Taliban militants were defeated. This was the first time the Pakistani army had taken a tribal agency from the Taliban. As previously mentioned, this campaign was followed up in the fall of 2009 by an invasion of the tribal agency of South Waziristan. The Pakistani force of twenty-five thousand bombed the Taliban in their bases for several days before moving into the region and encountering surprisingly light resistance. This campaign, which was focused on the Mehsud tribe, was assisted by the fact that other local Pashtun tribes, including the Waziris, remained neutral. It remains to be seen whether the Pakistani military, which has been far more successful in its efforts to defeat ethnic Baluchi militants operating in the south, can carry such operations to other tribal agencies, including North Waziristan.

As the war on terror has spread from Afghanistan to the tribal zones of Pakistan and into its cities, the Pakistani leadership must clearly walk a fine line in its struggle against Muslim militants that come from its own country. Pakistan is essentially involved in a civil war. This war increasingly pits the moderate Sufi majority, who belong to the Barelvi Sufi brotherhood, against the increasingly militant Deobandis. Most alarmingly, there has been a rise in what has been called the Punjabi Taliban in Pakistan's most heavily populated province. In the course of this war in the summer of 2010, the Taliban launched a deadly suicide bombing in Lahore's (Punjab's capital) most important Sufi holy spot, the Data Kanj Baksh shrine. Dozens were killed in this slaughter, which appeared to have awoken many average Pakistanis, who traditionally saw Israel, India, and the United States as their greatest enemies. This Pakistani-on-Pakistani violence (with its related issues of cross-border sanctuaries), combined with Islamabad's control of nuclear weapons and dangerous relations with India, make Pakistan perhaps the hottest zone in the global war on terror.

Death from the Skies: The CIA's Predator Drone War in Afghanistan

In the spring of 2004 the CIA began its most extensive targeted assassination campaign since the Vietnam War. It launched dozens of unmanned aerial drones into the inaccessible tribal regions of Pakistan to hunt and kill Taliban and Al Qaeda militants. Since then, there have been over 150 CIA drone strikes in Pakistan, killing more than 1,500 people. The drones have killed HVTs (high-value terrorist targets), average Taliban, and innocent civilians. Al Qaeda and the Pakistani Taliban leadership have been reeling from the deaths of their operatives even as the Pakistani public has commenced an outcry against this violation of their sovereignty and the deaths of civilian bystanders.

The primary weapon used in the aerial assassination campaign, the MQ-1 Predator UAV, had its debut as an unmanned spy plane in 1995 and was used in the campaigns against the Serbs in Bosnia and Kosovo. Although the original version of the Predator had the ability to loiter over the enemy, sending live video links back to its pilots operating from trailers at Creech Air Force Base in Nevada or CIA headquarters in Langley, Virginia, it had no weapons systems at the time. However, as the CIA's Counterterrorist Center picked up increasing "chatter" from Al Qaeda in early 2001, it began to explore the possibility of arming the Predator to hunt bin Laden. In February 2001 the Air Force succeeded in mounting a laser designator to the Predator's nose and adapting its wings to fire AGM-114 Hellfire missiles. The Predator's deadly laser-guided anti-tank missiles were reconfigured to penetrate mud-walled compounds and SUVs and destroy them.

The armed version of the Predator saw considerable action during 2001–2002's Operation Enduring Freedom. It was used to fire on Taliban who were surrounding Northern Alliance commander Abdul Haq, and it was used again to kill Al Qaeda's number-three leader, Muhammad Atef, as well as to assist U.S. troops in Operation Anaconda. It was also used in an unsuccessful attempt to kill the pro-Taliban Hezb i Islam warlord Gulbuddin Hekmatyar.

As the Taliban subsequently retreated and regrouped in Pakistan's FATA, U.S. commanders in Afghanistan became increasingly frustrated by the enemy's ability to launch cross-border raids from these untamed tribal regions. It also became obvious that Al Qaeda had found a sanctuary in FATA with such Pakistani-based Taliban commanders as Maulana Nazir, Jalaluddin Haqqani, and Nek Muhammad. In FATA, Al Qaeda operatives plotted further terrorist attacks, including the 2005 London bombing and the 2006 plot to blow up planes flying from Heathrow Airport with liquid explosives. By 2004 the CIA was using Predator drones to monitor more than 150 Al Qaeda training facilities and Taliban bases in Pakistan's FATA. At the time, the press reported that the spy drones operating in Afghanistan were flying from a Pakistani base in Jacobabad in western Pakistan.

On June 18, 2004, Taliban leader Nek Muhammad, who just two months earlier had vowed to continue his support of Al Qaeda and jihad against the United States, was killed in a mysterious explosion. At the time, Pakistan's *Dawn* newspaper reported that witnesses had seen a spy drone flying overhead minutes before the missile attack. But in the same article a Pakistani general rejected the claim and insisted that

Pakistani forces had carried out the attack. The Pakistanis clearly did not want negative public relations fallout from publicly acknowledging that a distrusted foreign power was acting in its own interests to kill Pakistani citizens on Pakistani soil.

There were no further strikes in 2004, but in May 2005 the CIA launched two aerial drone strikes, this time against Al Qaeda targets. The first killed a high-ranking Yemeni explosives expert named Haitham al Yemeni; the second killed Al Qaeda's new number-three leader, Abu Hamza Rabia. Both were killed in the tribal agency of North Waziristan. The Pakistani government once again denied that the attacks were carried out by the Americans, but local villagers found pieces of Hellfire missiles at the sites of the attacks. A local villager who photographed the pieces of the U.S. missiles and sent them to the Western press was subsequently kidnapped and killed by embarrassed Pakistani security forces.

Thus far the drone strikes were relatively "clean" in regard to unintentional civilian deaths, but the next strike was not. On January 13, 2006, several drones firing up to ten missiles destroyed three homes thought to be housing Ayman al Zawahiri (Al Qaeda's number two) in the village of Damadola in the tribal agency of Bajaur. Eighteen people were killed in the strike (four of them Al Qaeda), but al Zawahari was not there. This bungled attack caused thousands to protest across Pakistan and led to official condemnation of the attack by furious Pakistani officials.

Perhaps as a result of the disastrous public relations fallout, it was not until October 30, 2006, that a Predator again launched a strike. This time it was on a madrassa just north of Damadola in the village of Chenagai. This massive strike killed Mullah Liaquat, an extremist commander who had given sanctuary to al Zawahiri, along with as many as eighty of his followers. Thousands of local tribesmen protested the strike, and the Taliban responded by targeting a Pakistani military training facility in Punjab with a suicide bomb that killed forty-five soldiers. The CIA followed up this attack with five strikes on Taliban and Al Qaeda targets in 2007, predominantly in North Waziristan. At the time, leaflets began to appear in the tribal agencies warning local tribesmen in Pashto that they would be bombed if they harbored Al Qaeda or the Taliban.

In 2008 the aerial campaign intensified considerably, and between thirty-three and thirty-six attacks were recorded. The pace of the attacks picked up notably in August 2008 after the Bush administration made a unilateral decision to carry out attacks without seeking Pakistani permission first. This diminished the risk of the Taliban or Al Qaeda being tipped off by sympathizers in the Pakistani military, as had happened on several occasions in the past. In 2009 under the new Obama administration, the CIA launched more than fifty drone attacks. In 2010 the CIA launched more than 110 drone strikes in the FATA, mainly in North Waziristan. Despite the public relations fallout, the Obama administration has clearly come to see these drone strikes as a vital component of its war against terrorism in Pakistan and Afghanistan.

The vast majority of the CIA's UAV strikes have been directed at North and South Waziristan, but there have also been a few strikes in the agencies of Bajaur, Khyber, Kurram, and Orakzai, as well as three strikes in Bannu. The strikes in Bannu are important in that this province is located in the North West Frontier Province (NWFP), not FATA, and thus represents an escalation of the drone campaign. In the spring of 2009 there was talk of President Obama extending the campaign to Taliban hideouts in the Pakistani province of Baluchistan (where Mullah Omar is said to be hiding), but so far this has not happened due to fears of a Pakistani public outcry.

In 2007 the CIA's ability to hit targets in Pakistan increased with the introduction of a much-improved drone known as the MQ-9 Reaper. The Reaper has a much larger engine, allowing it to travel three times the speed of the Predator and carry fifteen times as much armament. This ordnance includes GBU-12 Paveway II laser-guided bombs and Sidewinder missiles.

In late May 2009 it was reported that the Predators and Reapers were being aided by secret electronic transmitter chips known as *pathrais* that were placed near targets by tribesmen working for bounties. South Waziristan Taliban leader Mullah Nazir, a frequent target of drone strikes, claimed that the "SIM-card transmitters" were actually planted by agents of the Pakistani ISI. This might account for the drones' success in taking out dozens of high-value Al Qaeda and Taliban targets. Increasingly the drones seem to be targeting moving Taliban and Al Qaeda targets in cars, SUVs, or even on motorcycles. It is the undoubted tactical success of the drones that has made them America's greatest asset in killing those who are deemed terrorists.

It is clear from its success rate in killing high-value targets that the CIA has excellent intelligence resources in the tribal areas. These locals have tracked the Taliban and Al Qaeda leadership, often for money or out of distaste for the extremists who have beheaded many moderate *maliks* (Pashtun tribal heads). In addition to killing more than a dozen mid-level Taliban leaders, the strikes have taken out ten of Al Qaeda's top twenty leaders.

The list of high-value Al Qaeda targets assassinated in Pakistan is impressive and includes:

• Sa'ad bin Laden, Osama bin Laden's third son, who was involved in Al Qaeda attacks in North Africa.

- Abu Laith al-Libi, the latest Al Qaeda number three who was responsible for a suicide bombing at Bagram Air Base targeting Vice President Dick Cheney.
- Osama al-Kini, a Kenyan national and Al Qaeda's external operations chief, who was wanted for the 1998 bombings of the U.S. embassies in Nairobi and Dar es Salaam.
- Khalid Habib, the commander of the Lashkar al-Zil (the Shadow Army), Al Qaeda's fighting force.
- Abu Khabab al-Masri, the chief of Al Qaeda's weapons of mass destruction program.
- Rashid Rauf, the suspected mastermind of the 2006 Heathrow airliner plot who had escaped from a Pakistani jail the previous year.
- Baitullah Mehsud, the former head of the Tehrik e Taliban e Pakistan (TTP) and Pakistan's most wanted man, along with his predecessor Nek Muhammad. The killing of these two leaders in August 2009 was the drones' greatest success.

This list represents some of America's greatest successes in the war on terror. The unpredictable Predator attacks on convoys, *hujras* (guest houses), compounds, convoys, training camps, and madrassas have wreaked havoc in the Taliban and Al Qaeda ranks. As a result, Al Qaeda members have been forced to dismantle their training camps in favor of hidden classrooms; they no longer communicate using cell phones for fear of being tracked; they have been forced to replace trusted veterans who have been killed with less experienced operatives; and they have launched what has been described as a "witch hunt," killing real or perceived spies and traitors.

U.S. officials are of course thrilled by the success. According to a senior U.S. counterterrorism official, "These attacks have produced the broadest, deepest and most rapid reduction in al-Qaeda senior leadership that we've seen in several years." Regardless, such successes clearly come at a high political price in the form of civilian bystanders who have been killed in the strikes. The strikes may have turned many Pakistanis outside of the tribal zone into enemies and might thus represent a strategic defeat in the greatest battle in this front-line country—the battle for the hearts and minds of the Pakistani people.

According to polls, 82 percent of Pakistanis consider drone missile strikes unjustified, despite their popularity among counterterrorism officials in the United States. In April 2009 the Pakistani newspaper *The News* published figures from Pakistani officials which showed that 687 civilians and 14 Al Qaeda leaders have been killed in drone strikes since January 2008. This meant that more than fifty civilians have been killed for every Al Qaeda target. However, this suspiciously high number has been questioned, and even a cursory glance at *The News*'s own reporting shows a much higher rate of militant deaths than civilians. Most sources, including the widely respected *Long War Journal*, claim that far more Pakistani militants have been killed than civilians. A recent study I carried out with two colleagues at the University of Massachusetts Dartmouth also found a much higher militant death toll to civilians in the Pakistani media In a case by case study of drone strikes we found that a mere 5 percent of strike victims were described in the press as civilians. A similar study by Peter Bergen and Katherine Tiedemann at the New America Foundation found that in 2010 approximately 6 percent of those killed in drone strikes were listed as "civilians." In March 2010 the Pakistani commander in charge of forces in North Waziristan, Major General Ghayur Mehmood, backed up these findings when he told reporters that "a majority of those eliminated (in the drone strikes) are terrorists, including foreign terrorist elements."

Regardless, there can be no doubt that the killings, especially of innocent Pakistani women and children in their own homeland, have caused tremendous outrage among average Pakistanis who are already predisposed to anti-Americanism. And the discontent has spread from the Pashtun tribal belt to such provinces as Punjab and Sindh, the heartlands of Pakistan. This has undermined the Pakistani military's own campaign against the Taliban by painting it as driven by U.S. interests.

Fully aware of the unpopularity of the strikes, the Pakistani government has sought to outwardly distance itself from them. This has taken the form of a flow of public statements criticizing the attacks, as well as two dressing-downs of the U.S. ambassador Anne Paterson. In the Pakistani newspaper, *Dawn*, Pakistani prime minister Yousuf Raza Gilani described the strikes as "disastrous" and said that "such actions are proving counter-productive to [the government's] efforts to isolate the extremists and militants from the tribal population" (although in Bob Woodward's 2010 book *Obama's War*, Gilani is also reported as saying that he secretly supports the strikes). Pakistani general Athar Abbas claimed that the missile strikes "hurt the campaign rather than help." Abdul Basit, a Pakistan foreign office spokesman, expressed his opposition to the strikes in *Dawn*, saying, "As we have been saying all along, we believe such attacks are counter-productive. They involve collateral damage and they are not helpful in our efforts to win hearts and minds."

It is the last concern that is most important to the Pakistanis. The fear is that the collateral damage in the form of dead civilians could lead to a public relations windfall for the Taliban and Al Qaeda. This could drive Pashtun tribes that are on the fence to declare *badal* (revenge) against the U.S. or Pakistani governments. The resulting alienation from the deaths of a few Taliban and Al Qaeda leaders could drive tens of thousands of armed tribesmen into militancy. Although these fears seem to be exaggerated, there have been several protest marches against the strikes and several retaliatory suicide bombings by the Taliban or enraged Pashtun tribesmen. One typical account reads, "My neighbor was so furious when a drone killed his mother, two sisters and his 7-year-old brother last September that he filled his car with explosives and rammed it into a Pakistani army convoy. He had to avenge the death of his loved ones." On another occasion a Waziri Pashtun tribesman who lost his legs decided to sue the CIA over the loss of his legs and family members who were killed in a strike. His lawyer also released the name of the CIA station chief in Islamabad, forcing him to flee the country for his safety. In April 2011 the head of the Pakistani Army, General Pervez Afshaq Kayani, also warned the Americans not to carry out any more drone attacks after a Predator killed forty people, including some Taliban but mostly Pashtun elders, gathered at a tribal meeting.

Whole Pakistani Taliban factions that had previously agreed to peace treaties with the Pakistani government, most notably those of Mullah Nazir and Hafiz Gul Bahadur (both of whom have nonetheless been involved in attacks on the United States in Afghanistan), have broken their truces and attacked Pakistani troops as a result of the U.S. strikes. Bahadur's belief that the Pakistani government was, for all its public statements of outrage, somehow complicit in the strikes was not uncommon in the country. One Pakistani summed up this belief, arguing, "The people know that there is a tacit understanding between the government and the U.S. regarding the drone attacks."

Pakistani officials dismissed such charges as "absurd" until Senator Dianne Feinstein, Chair of the Senate Intelligence Committee, dropped a bombshell in a February 12, 2009, conference when she claimed, "As I understand it, these [drones] are flown out of a Pakistani base." Feinstein's comments were widely reported in Pakistan and caused considerable uproar. Five days later, the *Times* of London published an article featuring satellite images obtained from Google Earth that depicted Predator drones on a runway in Shamsi, an airbase in the Pakistani province of Baluchistan.

Taken together, the *Times* article and Feinstein's statements exposed the Pakistani government's double game of officially rejecting the strikes while quietly providing logistic support to the CIA. Some elements in the Musharraf and Zardari governments—the military and perhaps even the ISI—were clearly supporting the drone strikes.

They were not the only ones. In a strange twist that seemed to fly in the face of the common belief that the Pashtun tribes in the FATA were being driven into the hands of the Taliban by the strikes, a Pakistani think tank carried out an opinion poll in the region that seemed to prove just the opposite. In the spring of 2009, the Aryana Institute for Regional Research and Advocacy interviewed hundreds of Pashtuns in FATA and found that 52 percent of them considered the air strikes to be accurate, 58 percent of them did *not* believe that the strikes caused anti-Americanism, 60 percent of them felt that the strikes damaged the militants, and 70 percent of them felt that the Pakistani army should also target the militants (although it should be stated that these findings were contradicted by another poll carried out by the New America Foundation, which found that Pashtuns in the FATA dislike the drone strikes).

The results of the poll, the first of its kind carried out in this region that has born the brunt of the UAV strikes, would seem to indicate that many Pashtun tribesmen welcomed the strikes even if the rest of their countrymen did not. One Pashtun even wrote in the Pakistani newspaper *The News*:

> Hatred against the Taliban in the Pakhtun [Pashtun] areas is at an all-time high and so is disappointment, even resentment, about the Pakistani army for its failure to stop the Taliban. Many people in the Taliban-occupied territories of the NWFP and FATA told me they constantly pray for the US drones to bomb the Taliban headquarters in their areas since the Pakistani army is unwilling to do so. Many people of Waziristan told me they are satisfied with the US drone attacks on militants in Waziristan and they want the Americans to keep it up till all the militants, local Pakhtun, the Punjabis and the foreigners, are eliminated.

In addition, a Pashtun policeman could not contain his admiration when he described the drone strikes as "very precise, very effective, and the Taliban and al-Qaida dread them."

It is perhaps this sort of Pashtun sentiment, and a growing realization among all Pakistanis that the creeping Taliban movement represents a threat to their state (especially since the Taliban's bold seizure of Swat Province, which lies close the capital), that drove the Pakistani government to openly acknowledge in May 2009 that the planes were being launched from Pakistan. They also seem to be flown from a U.S. air base near Jalalabad on the Afghan side of the border.

The Pakistani government's tacit support seems to have increased since President Zardari came to power. The United States has, for example, been sharing its images from its Predators and using them as spy platforms to help the Pakistani military arrest Taliban figures. Although for security reasons the United States has turned down the Pakistani request to fly the planes, the United States has used the drones to take out targets requested by the Pakistanis. The U.S. government has also given

Pakistanis unarmed spy Shadow drones to assist them in their own missions.

As the United States and Pakistan increase their cooperation on the drone attacks, the Pakistani public seems to have grown more used to them, despite their distaste for them. Tellingly, there was no Pakistani outcry when Baitullah Mehsud, the man responsible for suicide bombings that killed thousands of average Pakistanis, was killed in an August 2009 drone strike. The same held true when Tohir Yuldushev, the head of the IMU terrorist organization, was killed in a drone strike. Although the issue was reignited in 2010 when a CIA contractor in the Pakistani town of Lahore killed two Pakistanis who tried to hold him up in January 2011. The drone strikes were discontinued for a while to calm down Pakistani anger over the killings, but as soon as the contractor was released from a Pakistani jail, they picked up again.

Clearly the Obama administration—which has rejected so many of the Bush administration's war-on-terror tactics—has, with Pakistan's reluctant connivance, hit up drone strikes as its best "worst option" in the campaign against Al Qaeda and the Taliban. While the Pakistani officials continue to publicly protest the strikes, most notably after a March 17, 2011 drone strike in the tribal areas that killed as many as forty Pashtun elders, they hold their tongues and secretly tolerate them.

May 1, 2011: The Take Down of bin Laden

In the aftermath of the 9/11 attack, CIA Counterterrorist Center chief Cofer Black told CIA SAD (Special Activities Division) operatives that were deploying to Afghanistan that he wanted them to "capture bin Laden, kill him and bring his head back in a box on dry ice." President Bush also famously pledged to get bin Laden "dead or alive." But as has already been pointed out earlier, bin Laden, the focus of the largest manhunt in modern history, was allowed to escape from Tora Bora in December 2001. From there he made his way into Pakistan's Federally Administered Tribal Agencies and then disappeared into thin air for almost a decade. Every day, week, month, and year bin Laden remained at large served as a victory for Al Qaeda and inspiration for extremists who subscribed to this warrior-prophet's struggle against the American *hubal* (idol of arrogance). His sermons, threats, and mocking words were also a finger in the eye to the grieving post-9/11 Americans and a source of funds for Al Qaeda and its Taliban allies.

While there were reports of Al Qaeda number two, Ayman al Zawaheri, being active in the tribal agency of Bajaur (which resulted in two attempts to kill him in drone strikes), there was no information on bin

Laden's whereabouts in the succeeding years. In one of his numerous videos sent to threaten the West and garner support from followers, bin Laden and Zawaheri were, however, seen walking together on the side of a rocky hill leading some to speculate that they were both still in FATA. There were several FATA-based Pakistani Taliban commanders who were known to protect Arabs in their midst, so most assumed that bin Laden would not venture out from this protected tribal zone.

But the CIA's drone strikes made this sanctuary far from secure forcing many Arabs and Taliban leaders to flee the FATA. Several high-ranking Al Qaeda members who earlier left the tribal zone, including Khaled Sheikh Muhammad, the mastermind of the 9/11 attacks and Ramzi bin al Shibh, the hands-on coordinator of the attacks, were, however, arrested by the Pakistanis and sent to the United States (providing proof that the Pakistanis were with their American allies in the war on terror).

For this reason most analysts felt bin Laden was in the FATA, but this was pure speculation because he proved impossible to trace. It quickly became obvious that bin Laden was incredibly security conscious and was not going to make the same mistake as Pakistani Taliban leader Nek Muhammad, who was killed by a drone after the United States honed in on his cell phone signal. Bin Laden only communicated using couriers. So America's counter-terrorist agencies focused on trying to find the identity of bin Laden's couriers. If they could find bin Laden's messengers, they might be able to find bin Laden himself.

U.S. counter-intelligence officials began to question such high-profile detainees at Guantanamo Bay as Khaled Sheikh Muhammad and former Al Qaeda number three, Abu Faraj al Libi, about the identities of bin Laden's couriers. During this interrogation process Khaled Sheikh Muhammad and Abu Faraj al Libi held out on information concerning one courier whose *kunya* (nickname) had been mentioned by another captive. The interrogators grew suspicious that the courier who Khaled Sheikh Muhammad and Libi were covering up for might be important and might even have direct contact with bin Laden.

In 2007 the real name and identity of the courier was discovered. He was Sheikh Abu Ahmed al Kuwaiti, a Pashtun who had been brought up in Kuwait. However, it proved all but impossible to find the courier in Pakistan, a country of 170 million people.

Then, in August 2010, the Kuwaiti courier finally tripped up when he incautiously answered a call from another Al Qaeda operative who was already being monitored by the Americans. The courier was quickly traced from the location of his phone call in Peshawar to a compound in a town in northeast Pakistan known as Abbottabad. When the American spy satellites began to monitor the compound, the CIA and NSA grew increasingly excited. Ahmed al Kuwaiti was living in a recently built, walled concrete compound surrounded by eighteen-foot walls topped with barbed wire. Satellite images also showed images of a tall man going for walks in the compound garden (bin Laden was said to be over six feet, four inches). The compound, which was built in 2005, seemed to have been constructed to house someone important. Most interestingly, the NSA soon discovered that the compound did not have phone or internet connections that could be tapped and monitored. This seemed bizarre in a mansion worth over $1 million and indicated that its owner(s) had something to hide.

To investigate the matter further, in September 2010 the CIA set up a surveillance safe house near the compound to monitor its inhabitants. The CIA agents quickly began to notice other strange behavior, such as the fact that the compound's inhabitants burnt their trash instead of having it picked up like everyone else in the neighborhood. The inhabitants of the compound also kept to themselves and rarely left it except to go shopping or to attend Friday prayers at the mosque.

There seemed to be three families living in the compound. The family of the courier, Ahmed al Kuwaiti, his brother's family, and a third family that seemed to be roughly the size of the family bin Laden was estimated to have traveling with him. After months of surveillance by spies and satellites the CIA was said to be 60–80 percent sure that bin Laden was hiding there. This was enough certainty to convince the U.S. president to launch an attack on the compound.

By late April 2011 President Obama held several meetings with his national security team to plan a covert attack on the Abbottabad compound. While a strike by a robotic Reaper seemed to be the most obvious path to take in light of Obama's stepped-up use of drones against Al Qaeda, this was quickly ruled out. The Reaper did not carry enough munitions to totally destroy the strongly built compound. In addition, the slow moving Reaper drone would have been easily detectable on Pakistani radars. Since the town of Abbottabad was located in the so-called Air Defense Intercept Zone for the Pakistani capital of Islamabad, the drone would have been quickly shot down.

President Obama then consulted with General Bill McRaven, the head of Joint Special Operations Command, the unit tasked with organizing the mission, about the prospect of using B-2 stealth bombers to bomb the compound. But the heavy payload dropped by the bombers would kill all twenty-two people estimated to be in the compound, including women, children, and neighbors. The bombs would also obliterate bin Laden's body thus preventing the CIA from getting any DNA proof of his death. Al Qaeda could then claim he was still alive and Pakistanis would be infuriated by the deaths of so many innocents.

In the end Obama decided to approve a third approach that was fraught with risks, a helicopter-borne "capture or kill" raid on the house. There were two previous debacles stemming from similar heliborne missions that pointed out the dangers of such a risky decision. The first was President Jimmy Carter's fateful decision in 1980 to send in helicopters to free fifty-two U.S. hostages being held in Tehran, Iran by Iranian militants. Unfortunately, during the operation known as Eagle Claw one of the helicopters carrying elite Delta Forces crashed into a fuel transport plane killing eight soldiers and destroying both aircraft. The mission was subsequently aborted and Iranian news proudly broadcast images of the blackened remains of the aircraft in the Iranian desert. As the man who took the risky decision to order the raid, Carter took the blame for the debacle and the incident contributed heavily to his defeat by Ronald Reagan in the presidential elections held that year.

The second incident that set a dire precedent for Obama was the September 3, 2008 raid by three to five Black Hawk helicopters carrying U.S. Navy SEAL Special Forces on a Taliban-controlled town in the Pakistani tribal agency of South Waziristan. In the ensuing raid as many as twenty people were killed, including women and children. U.S. sources claimed the women who were killed were actively helping the militants. Several suspected Taliban militants were also killed or captured by the U.S. soldiers in the helicopters, who then disappeared into the night. After the raid a local reported, "The situation there is very terrible. People are trying to take out the dead bodies."

As word of the SEAL raid in Waziristan spread in Pakistan, including news that innocent Pakistani women and children had been killed, there were howls of outrage from Pakistani leaders across the board. One senior Pakistani official called the night raid a "cowboy action" and criticized it for not targeting anyone "big." The Pakistani Foreign Ministry condemned the attack, and called it "unacceptable" and "a grave provocation . . . which has resulted in immense loss of civilian life." But it was the Pakistani military that drew the firmest line in the sand. Using bellicose terms more suited for an enemy than an ally the new head of Pakistan's army, General Pervez Ashfaq Kayani, stated that Pakistan's territorial integrity would be "defended at all cost." Lest there be any ambiguity, Kayani also stated, "There is no question of any agreement or understanding with the coalition forces whereby they are allowed to conduct operations on our side of the border . . . No external force is allowed to conduct operations inside Pakistan."

By deploying U.S. "boots on the ground" in a bold helicopter raid on a town that was just seventy-five miles from the Pakistani capital and home to its most prestigious military academy, *without notifying the Pakistanis*, Obama was taking a huge risk. He would be risking his presidency, the lives of the special forces, and the already shaky alliance with America's most important strategic partner in the war on Al Qaeda and the Taliban, Pakistan.

But the chance to kill bin Laden, a man who had been hunted by three American presidents, proved to be worth the risks. The word to launch the raid was given and President Obama went off to put on a public face and attend an annual correspondent's dinner with the media. The mission was kept secret even from America's closest allies. As previously stated, the Pakistanis were not notified since CIA head Leon Panetta worried that "any effort to work with the Pakistanis could jeopardize the mission. They might alert the targets."

After waiting two days for cloudy skies and low moon visibility, four U.S. helicopters, two Black Hawks and two larger Chinook transport helicopters, carrying an elite Navy SEAL unit known as Team Six, flew from a U.S. base in eastern Afghanistan at Jalalabad into Pakistani airspace. The helicopters were flown by the 160th Special Operations Aviation Regiment (SOAR), the air unit that had earlier flown the A-Teams into Afghanistan to liaise with Dostum and other Northern Alliance warlords in October 2001. The UH-60 Black Hawks the SOAR "Night Stalkers" flew were a new stealth variant that few knew existed before the raid. These Black Hawks had been modified to evade radar and emit less noise. The larger Chinooks carried extra reinforcements in case one of the Black Hawks that was tasked with landing in the compound and carrying out the raid crashed. The reinforcements were also prepared to fight with Pakistani forces should they encounter resistance from nearby troops. It spoke volumes to the importance of the mission that the Americans were willing to fight their way out of Pakistan and further jeopardize relations with the Pakistanis to pull it off.

American special forces had now penetrated Pakistani airspace to engage in the first raid since the September 3, 2008 fiasco in South Waziristan. The helicopters arrived at bin Laden's compound in Abbottabad at 1 a.m. Sunday morning (May 1) Pakistan time and one of the Black Hawks promptly crashed and rolled over onto its side, possibly after clipping a compound wall. Its twelve occupants were, however, unhurt and together with the twelve soldiers from the other helicopter breached the compound's walls using explosives.

At this time the courier, Al Kuwaiti, fired on the Americans and was killed. His brother was also killed as was a woman (probably the courier's wife) who was caught in the crossfire. One of bin Laden's sons, a twenty-year-old named Khaled, was also killed as the twenty-four SEALs swept the compound, room to room, wearing night vision goggles.

But their chief prey, bin Laden, was not found until the SEALs burst onto the third floor of the compound. There they found bin Laden and his youngest wife, a 29-year-old Yemeni named Amal al Sadah. When his wife rushed at the SEALs, she was shot in the leg and an unarmed bin Laden was shot in the chest and head. A SEAL then radioed that "Geronimo was EKIA" (Geronimo being bin Laden's code name and EKIA signifying Enemy Killed in Action). Cheers swept the White House situation room where President Obama, Secretary of Defense Robert Gates, and Secretary of State Hillary Clinton were watching the operation unfold in real time (most likely from satellites, drones and helmet-mounted cameras). The SEALs then transported bin Laden's body to the helicopter after his wife identified it.

But the mission was not complete. The SEALs then located and removed what has been described as the "single largest collection of senior terrorist material ever," i.e. computer hard drives, thumb drives, and disks from the compound. These would later reveal plans by Al Qaeda to attack U.S. rail systems on the tenth anniversary of 9/11. After a harrowing forty minutes on the ground the SEALs then returned to the one functioning Black Hawk and a backup Chinook, which had just landed. On their way out the SEALs blew up the top-secret stealth Black Hawk that had crashed upon landing to prevent its secrets from being revealed. As the helicopters flew away, frightened neighbors peered out their windows at the burning wreckage and Pakistani jets scrambled to intercept the intruders but were either too late to shoot them down or decided not to attack.

From Abbottabad the helicopters safely flew back over the Himalayan foothills and Pashtun tribal lands to their base in Jalalabad. Incredibly not one SEAL had been killed or wounded in the stealth attack. Despite the considerable risks, it had been a complete success. Considering the distance involved, uncertainty as to who was in the compound, and shaky relations with the Pakistanis, it was the most successful raid in modern U.S. military history and put to rest the demons of the failed 1980 Iranian operation under Jimmy Carter.

Bin Laden's DNA was subsequently confirmed and his body was then flown to the aircraft carrier the *USS Carl Vinson* and buried at sea after performing proper Islamic rituals in Arabic. While photos of bin Laden's gun-shattered face were taken after his death, President Obama decided not to release them for fear that they would appear on jihadi Web sites and placards at rallies, etc. to incite hatred and revenge among extremists for years to come. In essence, the United States made bin Laden, the founder of Al Qaeda and icon for jihadis and militants across the globe, disappear without a trace.

While there were of course conspiracy theorists and doubters who did not believe he was dead (the Taliban and Pakistani Islamist groups initially rejected the claims of his death), Al Qaeda subsequently did confirm his death. After seeing the broadcast images of thousands of jubilant Americans spontaneously celebrating the death of bin Laden in Times Square, the White House, and the site of the World Trade Centers, Al Qaeda announced on its Web site "Soon, God willing, their happiness will turn to sadness. Their blood will be mingled with their tears." One jihadist Web site known as Islamic Awakening captured the sentiment of many Al Qaeda supporters when it declared "God damn you Obama!"

The American public was more supportive of the raid and Obama's 11:30 p.m. address to the American people was the most watched presidential address in a decade (57 million Americans watched it). Not surprisingly Obama's poll numbers went up and he received a 9 percent bump in approval ratings in a poll carried out by Pew Research Center and the Washington Post. Support for his handling of the war in Afghanistan went up 17 percent and his handling of terrorism went up 21 points. Similar spikes were recorded by George H. W. Bush following the successful completion of Operation Desert Storm in 1991 and the destruction of the Taliban during George W. Bush's presidency in 2001 (at that time he recorded an unprecedented 90 percent approval rating).

With recognition of bin Laden's death by Al Qaeda there were limited protests in Karachi and other Pakistani cities organized by the country's Islamist parties and the Taliban threatened revenge. But most importantly, there were no widespread protests in the Arab world. By the time of his death the world that had produced bin Laden and his Egyptian number two, Ayman al Zawaheri, had been radically transformed by the so-called Arab Spring. This was a popular secularist revolt that began in Tunisia in the winter of 2011 leading to the overthrow of its dictator, President Ben Ali. This was followed by the overthrow of the secular Egyptian dictator Hosni Mubarek, a leader who Zawaheri and his Egyptian Al Qaeda followers had long dreamed of toppling in a jihadist revolution. But Al Qaeda's dream of establishing a shariah-law, jihadist caliphate in Egypt, home to 80 million Arabs, was preempted by the overthrow of the regime by young, largely secular Arab youth. These young Arabs who rallied on Facebook and Twitter demanded democracy, not shariah law. They resoundingly rejected bin Laden and his increasingly shrill calls for jihad. He was seen by many as an embarrassment to Arabs and Islam, especially after the Arab on Arab bloodshed and mayhem caused by Al Qaeda in Iraq after 2005. In essence, bin Laden's death marked the passing of an era that had begun with his attacks on the U.S. embassies in Africa in 1998. While there are bound to be additional attacks by Al Qaeda, the odds are that these will be led by lone wolf "self starters" like Faisal Shahzad, the Pakistani who attempted to set off a car bomb in Time Square in May 2010.

Bin Laden's death of course had more important implications for the war in what had increasingly became known as the Af/Pak theater. Many U.S. congressmen felt that bin Laden could not have been living so close to Pakistan's most prestigious military school, the Kakul Pakistani Military Academy in Abbottabad, had he not been protected by elements of the Pakistani military, ISI or government. While the Pakistanis were angered by this accusation and pointed out the difficulties the United States had in finding criminals on the FBI's Most Wanted List, one poll showed that 84 percent of Americans believed that high level Pakistanis knew where bin Laden was hiding. Congressmen on both sides of the aisle called for a cutting off of the billions of dollars of U.S. aid that has been given to the Pakistanis to help them in the war on terror. Many pundits called on the United States to begin treating Pakistan not as an ally, but as an enemy.

In defense of the Pakistanis it should however be noted that Al Qaeda and its Taliban allies had killed thousands of Pakistani soldiers, made several attempts on the lives of Presidents Musharraf and Zardari, and that the Pakistanis had arrested the number three in Al Qaeda, Khaled Sheikh Muhammad, and over six hundred other Arab fighters or terrorists fleeing Afghanistan after Operation Enduring Freedom. It should also be noted that President Zardari's wife, Benazir Bhutto, had been killed by these terrorists as had thousands of average Pakistanis. It seems highly unlikely that bin Laden would have trusted his security to the Pakistanis in this environment of distrust, nor that the Pakistanis, who received more than 20 billion U.S. dollars since 2001 to fight the common enemy, would have risked angering America and the West by harboring the world's most wanted man. Most importantly, President Musharraf secretly gave President Bush the permission to launch a raid on bin Laden should he ever be found on Pakistani soil.

While the Pakistanis were certainly humiliated by the unexpected raid deep into their country that captured bin Laden (and threatened that a repeat of the incursion would be seen as an attack on their sovereignty), they had initially approved it back in 2001. After the raid they continued to cooperate with the Americans and allowed them to interrogate bin Laden's wives who were arrested by the Pakistanis at the compound. It should also be noted that NATO convoys continue to supply troops in Afghanistan via Pakistan's strategically important Khyber Pass. For all its obvious flaws and deep levels of distrust, the partnership with the Pakistanis is America's most important alliance in the war against Al Qaeda and the Taliban . . . with perhaps the exception of the American alliance with the Karzai government in Afghanistan.

Which brings us to the impact of bin Laden's death on the war in Afghanistan. The death of bin Laden was celebrated by many Afghans, especially those belonging to the Northern Alliance opposition who had been fighting his forces and warning the West of his terrorism since the late 1990s. In the Pashtun south opinions were more mixed. While the Taliban threatened revenge for bin Laden's death (which is ironic considering it was his terrorist attack on the United States that led to the destruction of their regime when the Taliban refused to turn him over) it may have removed one of the primary reasons for their alliance with Al Qaeda. Namely, Mullah Omar's promise to offer bin Laden *melmastiia* (the Pashtun honor obligation to offer sanctuary to a guest). Some argued that bin Laden's death would essentially allow the Taliban to divorce from Al Qaeda. It was also speculated that the Taliban would resent fighting against the Americans who were killing them in the thousands while bin Laden, the catalyst for the invasion, lived in relative security in a mansion far from the battlefront.

Bin Laden's death it was theorized would also dishearten Arab jihad volunteers fighting in the region and send a cautionary message to arm-chair jihadis in the Middle East who were contemplating traveling to Afghanistan to fight. With the removal of the most famous financial source for the jihad it was also bound to decrease financial contributions to the Taliban and Al Qaeda in the Arab Gulf states.

Others felt that the Taliban might take heart from bin Laden's death. With his departure, the rationale for the Americans being in Afghanistan was removed. The Taliban could now start counting the days for the Americans' withdrawal. The mood was said to be calm at the Taliban shuras in Pakistan where a message from Zawahiri was read that stated, "killing bin Laden is just like taking a single grape from a bunch of grapes." A local Taliban commander defiantly stated the opinion of many rank and file in Afghanistan when he proclaimed, "he was a leader and a man, but there are hundreds of other Osama bin Ladens left behind."

For their part, many average Afghans who had benefited from the NATO occupation feared that with bin Laden's death, the Americans and their allies would argue that the rationale for U.S. troops being in Afghanistan had been removed. In this assumption they were not wrong Both Democrats and Republicans began to argue that bin Laden's death and the dismantlement of Al Qaeda's sanctuary in Afghanistan meant that America had achieved the original goals of Operation Enduring Freedom. Democrat Senator John Kerry allied with Republican Senator Richard Lugar to a call for an end to the war. Kerry stated "We should be working toward the smallest footprint necessary, a presence that puts Afghans in charge and presses them to step up to the task. Make no mistake, it is fundamentally unsustainable to continue spending $10 billion a month on a massive military operation with no end in sight." These calls of course overlooked the fact that a precipitous decrease of U.S. troops would embolden the Taliban, who have not renounced their ties with Al Qaeda nor their goal to reconquer Afghanistan and expand into Pakistan.

To allay Afghan fears of such an outcome that came from such calls for a speedy withdrawal of NATO troops, U.S. Ambassador to Afghanistan, Karl Eikenberry, promised that "this victory will not mark the end of our effort against terrorism" and pledged that "America's strong support for the people of Afghanistan will continue as before." For the Afghan government and millions of Afghans who have moved back to Afghanistan since 2001 with the aim of rebuilding their lives his comments were cause for hope. The world that the United States and its NATO allies created in Afghanistan that includes a tremendously increased GNP, schools for millions of newly enrolled children (including girls), a bustling capital swelled by over a million newcomers, cell phones, numerous television channels, beauty shops, DVD stores, jobs, democracy, skyscrapers, new roads, and de-mined fields, was inadvertently made possible by bin Laden. In a roundabout way, many average Afghans, especially those Uzbeks, Hazaras, and Tajiks (the majority of the country) who live in the comparatively calm north and fought to be free from Al Qaeda's Taliban allies, owe bin Laden a debt of gratitude. Had he not attacked the United States, these improvements in their lives would not be possible. For better or worse, perhaps bin Laden's most lasting legacy will be the emergence of a post-Taliban generation of Afghans who grew up in this new environment instead of suffering under the rule of the most oppressive regime in Eurasia.

Afghanistan: Now Obama's War

During his 2008 election campaign, Barack Obama repeatedly promised that if he were elected president, he would take troops out of Iraq and transfer them to Afghanistan. He referred to Afghanistan as a "war of necessity" against Al Qaeda, while the war against Saddam Hussein in Iraq was painted as a "war of choice." Since becoming president, Obama has done as he promised and begun a gradual drawdown of troops in Iraq and a buildup of troops in Afghanistan. The drawdown of 130,000 U.S. troops in Iraq and the transfer to Afghanistan, where there were roughly 68,000 U.S. troops in 2009, was facilitated by successes in the Iraqi war, which has calmed down considerably since 2008. The objective was to leave 50,000 troops in Iraq and to bolster the war effort in

Afghanistan, the original theater of action for the war on terror. All U.S. troops are in theory supposed to be withdrawn from Iraq by the end of 2011.

In August 2009 word leaked that the top U.S. general in Afghanistan, Stanley McChrystal, wanted an additional forty thousand troops to help fight the Taliban in the south and east. Vice President Joe Biden wanted to focus on tracking Al Qaeda instead of the local Taliban, thus presenting some resistance to this proposal, but he was overruled by Obama. Obama clearly believed that there was no difference between waging a counterinsurgency against the Taliban and a counterterrorism campaign against Al Qaeda when the two groups had morphed into one. The Obama administration saw victory in Afghanistan as a chance to roll back a dangerous manifestation of Islamic fundamentalism in a strategic country, and in so doing stop it from becoming a hotbed for future terrorism.

After much agonizing, on December 1, 2009, Obama made a speech to the American people in which he promised to send an additional 30,000 troops to McChrystal to help protect population centers and defeat the Taliban insurgency. This brought the number of U.S. troops in Afghanistan up to 98,000 (with an additional ISAF-NATO Coalition contingent of more than 40,000). With the later addition of 2,000 Marines, the number reached 100,000.

General McChrystal, the former head of Special Operations Command and head of all Coalition forces in Afghanistan, had the full support of the U.S. president in using these troops. He also took the advice of counterterrorism analyst David Kilcullen and called for an emphasis on protecting the Afghan people, the real center of gravity in Afghanistan, during the COIN (counterinsurgency) campaign. In fulfilling this "population-centric" mission, McChrystal ordered his troops to be very cautious about using close air military strikes, since these often killed Afghan civilians and were said to drive the surviving Afghans into the hands of the Taliban. This cautious policy caused some resentment among U.S. troops who felt that their hands were tied in combat with the Taliban, but it did lead to a decline in civilian deaths. By contrast, the Taliban continued to kill large numbers of civilians, often with suicide bombings and IEDs.

McChrystal used the additional troops given to him by Obama to bolster U.S. forces in contested frontier provinces in the south and east and to help the U.S. Marines fighting the Taliban in Helmand Province. Most important, in February 2010 McChrystal launched the largest military campaign of the entire war, Operation Moshtarak ("Together"). The goal of this operation was to seize the town of Marjah in Helmand Province. The town had been captured by the Taliban and had become their de facto capital in Afghanistan. It had also become a center for their opium trade.

In following his new policy of protecting civilians, McChrystal decided to warn the Taliban that Coalition troops would be invading the town of Marjah. He hoped that this would encourage the Taliban to retreat from the city and thus prevent a large-scale battle in a "civilian rich" environment. Forewarned that the United States and its allies, including a large Afghan contingent, would be coming, the Taliban withdrew many of their forces but left some scattered around the town to harass the invading allies. On February 13, 2010, a wave of ninety Chinook, Super Stallion, and Cobra helicopters ferrying thousands of Coalition troops descended on the town of Marjah. The Taliban fought back sporadically with sniper fire and land mines, but the allies nonetheless succeeded in seizing the town in a short time. Although there was a sizable Afghan contingent in the invading force of fifteen thousand, reporters from the *New York Times* reported that most of the fighting was done by U.S. and NATO troops.

Having taken the town with minimal losses, the Coalition then flew in what became known as a "government in a box." This consisted of a governor, administrative officials, and policemen. There were high hopes that the incentives offered by this government and the protection offered by the Coalition troops would wean the people of Marjah away from the opium trade and the Taliban. Unfortunately, all did not go as planned in Marjah. Taliban insurgents remained scattered among the people and killed those who cooperated with the Coalition troops and government. As of 2011, this showcase operation appears to have stalled and is a stalemate at best.

In essence the Marja campaign was an act of micro-nation building, one province at a time. It was also a microcosm of the larger Counter Insurgency strategy which posited that if you "cleared, held and built" you would protect the local population who would then support you vis-à-vis the Taliban. Unfortunately there have been mixed results, at best, from this new military creed that has stressed winning hearts and minds over killing. There does not seem to be a tremendous amount of correlation between regular or Provisional Reconstruction Team "good will" projects—like building roads, schools and wells—and winning over the local Afghan population. Time and again U.S. and Coalition troops have engaged in a goodwill "hearts and minds" project and then been attacked by local insurgents who hide among the people. Despite the goodwill projects by U.S. troops, the local population often remains on the fence or continues to assist the Taliban insurgents out of fear or sympathy with their cause.

Another large U.S. operation was carried out in Kandahar in the summer and fall of 2010. This operation took advantage of twelve thousand reinforcements sent to the province as part of Obama's troop surge. The operation began with an August sweep through the Mehlajat region on the southern fringe of Kandahar, then proceeded to the Arghandab region to the north. From there, U.S. troops moved into the Zhare District on the western side of Kandahar City. In late October U.S. forces then moved to an area known as the Horn of Panjwai and commenced an airborne assault on the Taliban-controlled villages of Mushan and Zangabad. U.S. troops were able to make considerable gains in these operations, in part due to the use of a new mobile rocket system known as the Himars (High Mobility Artillery Rocket System), which has been described as a "small cruise missile." The Taliban sustained considerable losses in this campaign, which also relied on stepped-up airstrikes.

Throughout the summer and fall of 2010, the United States stepped up a massive bombing campaign against the Taliban that began to show results. This aerial campaign was combined with a three-thousand-man CPT unit (CIA-Afghan Counterterrorism Pursuit Team) and Joint Special Operations Command teams. These hunter-killer teams were responsible for killing hundreds of Taliban commanders in the south and forcing much of the leadership to retreat back across the border into Pakistan by the winter of 2010. The larger strategic objective of this campaign seems to have been to break the Taliban's will to fight a costly war and push them to the negotiating table. In the fall of 2010, NATO troops actually guarded several Taliban commanders who made their way into Afghanistan to begin negotiations (although one of these was later found to be a fraud). The American military command aimed to drive the Taliban to negotiate before a planned initial withdrawal of some U.S. troops by July 2011, a date Obama announced to appease antiwar elements in the Democratic Party. So far there seem to be no signs of a willingness to negotiate by the Taliban despite their heavy losses.

Interestingly, the top U.S. commander in Afghanistan, General McChrystal, was removed from the scene before the aforementioned operations in Kandahar took place. McChrystal was removed from his post following the publication in *Rolling Stone* magazine of a controversial interview with him and his staff. During the course of the interview, McChrystal's aides in particular made disparaging remarks about Vice President Joe Biden and the U.S. civilian leadership in Afghanistan led by Richard Holbrooke. Obama had no choice but to remove the general, who had become too controversial following the publication of the article.

In a brilliant masterstroke, Obama chose General David Petraeus, the tremendously popular head of CENTCOM, as McChrystal's replacement. Petraeus was famous for his success in Iraq during the 2007 "surge" of U.S. troops. Petraeus helped arm local Sunni tribes in Iraq's Anbar Province to stand up to Al Qaeda in Iraq and used the additional twenty thousand troops given to him by the Bush surge to help secure Baghdad. These two events helped turn the tide in the war in Iraq, and Petraeus was subsequently promoted and made head of CENTCOM. Petraeus, who was McChrystal's strongest supporter, has followed in his predecessor's footsteps and has continued a policy based on the mantra "You can't kill your way out of an insurgency"—rather, you have to win over the hearts and minds of the Afghan people who support the insurgents. He has, however, doubled the number of Kill/Capture night raids by Joint Special Operation Command forces ordered by his predecessor. As of April 2011, Petraeus has been offered the position as head of the CIA and his days leading U.S. troops in Afghanistan appear to be numbered.

Both generals' efforts were confounded by the fact that the Afghan regime they were fighting to save was accused of widespread corruption. It will be recalled that Afghanistan was ranked second to last in the world in an annual corruption survey (only Somalia had worse corruption). Perhaps the most notable example of this corruption was the fraudulent loss of as much as $900 million dollars from the Karzai-linked Kabul Bank in the fall of 2010.

The problems clearly stemmed from the top. In the fall of 2010, the Web site known as WikiLeaks leaked several classified cables from the U.S. State Department detailing problems with Afghan president Hamid Karzai. He was described in these candid messages as weak, vacillating, and suffering from mood disorders. Although Karzai, who is a polished English speaker, had originally been courted by Washington as a source of hope for Afghanistan, opinion of him had deteriorated considerably, especially in the U.S. military. On several occasions Karzai condemned General Petraeus for carrying out very effective special forces night raids on suspected Taliban hideouts in the south. Karzai criticized the United States military for inflicting "collateral damage" civilian casualties. While the "Kill/Capture" program run by Joint Special Operations Command (JSOC) is controversial for the fact that its critics say it drives many Afghans subjected to night raids to support the Taliban, it is perhaps America's most effective tool in killing insurgents. In 2010 alone JSOC claimed the Kill/Capture night raids led to the death or capture of as many as twelve thousand militants. Perhaps reflecting the night raids' unpopularity among average Afghans, Karzai nonetheless continues to condemn them even as he tries to reach out to his Taliban "brothers."

Never were the problems with Karzai more apparent than in the August 20, 2009, presidential elections. In the runoff between President Karzai and his chief opponent Abdullah Abdullah, a Tajik leader who had served Massoud, Karzai's supporters were accused of ballot stuffing in many southern Pashtun districts. Hundreds of thousands of votes were illegally cast, particularly in areas of Kandahar controlled by Karzai's brother, Ahmed Wali Karzai. The UN election observers reported on the fraud, and there were calls for a runoff election with Abdullah. In the end, Abdullah chose not to contest the election with Karzai in order to bring peace and consensus. It remains to be seen whether Karzai can end the nepotism and corruption that have defined his regime and finally become a reliable partner for Petraeus' successor.

Under such circumstances, America's longest war shows no signs of ending anytime soon. In recognition of the realities on the ground, President Obama has moved the drawdown date for U.S. troops in Afghanistan from 2011 to 2014, disappointing many antiwar activists while pleasing those who fear the consequences of withdrawing from this strategic country too early. As of spring 2011, the United States had lost approximately 1,550 troops in Afghanistan (roughly 2,300 Coalition troops in total), and thousands of Afghans have died. The war has also spread to neighboring Pakistan, where more than 2,000 troops have died fighting the Pakistani Taliban, and more than 4,000 Pakistani civilians have been killed by Taliban and Al Qaeda terrorism.

The Obama administration is, however, hoping to use the breathing spell that has come from the 2010 troop surge to clear and hold key areas in Helmand and Kandahar. The ultimate goal is to train the Afghan Army and Afghan police so that they can carry on the war once the Americans and their Coalition partners complete their withdrawal, which began in the summer of 2011. Although there are currently 150,000 Afghan Army troops, the plan is to increase this number to 260,000 by 2014. Afghanistan is not Iraq, but it is hoped that these troops, combined with 150,000 foreign troops, can wage a war of attrition that drives the Taliban to the negotiating table. This would allow the United States and its allies to withdraw from Afghanistan without leaving it in the control of the Taliban who have brought so much misery to the long-suffering people of this country in the past.

For their part, the Taliban insurgents hope to defeat the U.S.-led Coalition by simply surviving and spreading their influence further into the countryside. While the Taliban have taken heavy losses since the Obama troop surge, they are resilient and rely on discontent with the corrupt Karzai regime to gain followers. Mullah Omar is adamant that no peace can be signed until all "infidel" troops leave Afghan soil. Omar's followers, like the mujahideen before them, are tough and resourceful fighters. They are fired by their devotion to jihad and aim to duplicate the expulsion of the Soviets and the British before them. The Taliban take heart in the memory of their people's previous defeats of invaders and sum up their resolve by indicating that the Americans might have the watches—but they have the time.

Index

Acknowledgments

I received a tremendous amount of help and support in researching and writing this book. Thanks first of all to my wife, Feyza, who accompanied me on several legs of my expeditions in Afghanistan and surrounding regions. Thanks also to my parents Gareth and Donna, who proofed this work for me and encouraged me to follow my interests in Central Asia in college and graduate school. I would not be who I am today without them. I also owe a tremendous debt of gratitude to Uli Schamilogu, my former advisor and friend who patiently taught me Central Asian Turkic-Mongol tribal history at Indiana University and the University of Wisconsin.

Most important, I would like to send my thanks to Colonel Mark Shankle and his team at the Joint Information Operations Warfare Command at Lackland Air Base, Texas, for inspiring me to write this book as a field manual. It was an honor to work with Colonel Shankle and his dedicated team on this project. I received additional support and hospitality from Colonel Arthur Tulac and his Information Operations team at NATO headquarters in Kabul in the summer of 2009.

Thanks are also due to my colleague at the University of Massachusetts Dartmouth, Avery Plaw, who proofed this work and added his helpful comments. Invaluable assistance was also rendered by Tim Paicopolos in providing proofing and editing.

I also owe a debt of gratitude to the legendary CIA field operative, terrorism analyst, and author, Dr. Marc Sageman, for his eyewitness insights into the anti-Soviet jihad of the 1980s. Sageman's accounts of his role in training and funding the mujahideen during the Cold War proved to be invaluable. And I would like to express my gratitude to Bart Decker from the Air Force's elite 23rd Special Tactics Squadron based at Hurlburt Airfield, Florida. Master Sergeant Decker, who fought alongside the horse-mounted Northern Alliance warlord Abdul Rashid Dostum in 2001's Operation Enduring Freedom, proved to be an unparalleled eyewitness source of information on this remarkable campaign.

This book could not have been completed without the help of numerous people in Afghanistan and Pakistan. I would like to thank Northern

Alliance commander General Abdul Rashid Dostum and his son Batur and brother Abdul Kadir for their hospitality in Mazar i Sharif and Sheberghan. Thanks also to Ahmed Khan, the Uzbek mujahideen leader of Tash Kurgan, for spending endless hours explaining the role of the Uzbeks in the anti-Soviet war. I am also grateful to the Turkmen spiritual leader Serecettin Mahdum, who spent the summer of 2005 patiently guiding me across northern Afghanistan from the Dar y Suf Valley to the Panjsher Valley. And I would like to thank Tugay Tuncer from the Turkish diplomatic service for his introductions to Dostum and other Afghan leaders.

I would have never grasped the nuances of Afghan ethnicity were it not for the patient help of parliament member Faizullah Zeki, so *tashakor* to him as well. In addition, I would like to thank Ahmad Rafay Alam and his wife Aysha for letting me stay with them in Pakistan in 2010. I also owe a great debt to my editor at University of Pennsylvania Press, Bill Finan, for his hard work in transforming my earlier manual for the military into a book. And last, thanks to my father-in-law and mother-in-law, Feruzan and Kemal Altindag, for providing me with a quiet place in their home on the coast of Turkey to write up the civilian version of this book.